Prima's Quake™

Strategy Guide

Unauthorized

NOW AVAILABLE FROM PRIMA

Computer Game Books

1942: The Pacific Air War—The Official Strategy Guide
The 11th Hour: The Official Strategy Guide
The 7th Guest: The Official Strategy Guide
Across the Rhine: The Official Strategy Guide
Alone in the Dark 3: The Official Strategy Guide
Angel Devoid: The Official Strategy Guide
Armored Fist: The Official Strategy Guide
Ascendancy: The Official Strategy Guide
Buried in Time: The Journeyman Project 2—The Official Strategy Guide
CD-ROM Games Secrets, Volume 1
CD-ROM Unauthorized Game Secrets, Volume 2
Caesar II: The Official Strategy Guide
Celtic Tales: Balor of the Evil Eye—The Official Strategy Guide
Civilization II The Official Strategy Guide
Command and Conquer Secrets and Solutions
Cyberia: The Official Strategy Guide
Cyberia2 Resurrection: The Official Strategy Guide
Dark Seed II: The Official Strategy Guide
Descent: The Official Strategy Guide
Descent II: The Official Strategy Guide
DOOM Battlebook
DOOM II: The Official Strategy Guide
Dragon Lore: The Official Strategy Guide
Dungeon Master II: The Legend of Skullkeep—The Official Strategy Guide
Fleet Defender: The Official Strategy Guide
Frankenstein: Through the Eyes of the Monster—The Official Strategy Guide
Front Page Sports Football Pro '95: The Official Playbook
Fury3: The Official Strategy Guide
Hell: A Cyberpunk Thriller—The Official Strategy Guide
Heretic: The Official Strategy Guide
I Have No Mouth and I Must Scream: The Official Strategy Guide
In The 1st Degree: The Official Strategy Guide
Kingdom: The Far Reaches—The Official Strategy Guide
King's Quest VII: The Unauthorized Strategy Guide
The Legend of Kyrandia: The Official Strategy Guide
Lords of Midnight: The Official Strategy Guide
Machiavelli the Prince: Official Secrets & Solutions
Marathon: The Official Strategy Guide
Master of Orion: The Official Strategy Guide
Master of Magic: The Official Strategy Guide
Mech Warrior 2: The Official Strategy Guide
Mech Warrior 2 Expansion Pack Secrets and Solutions
Microsoft Arcade: The Official Strategy Guide
Microsoft Flight Simulator 5.1: The Official Strategy Guide
Microsoft Golf: The Official Strategy Guide
Microsoft Space Simulator: The Official Strategy Guide
Might and Magic Compendium:
The Authorized Strategy Guide for Games I, II, III, and IV
Mission Critical: The Official Strategy Guide
Myst: The Official Strategy Guide, Revised Edition
Online Games: In-Depth Strategies and Secrets
Oregon Trail II: The Official Strategy Guide
Panzer General: The Official Strategy Guide
Perfect General II: The Official Strategy Guide
Power Pete: Official Secrets and Solutions
Prima's Playstation Game Secrets: The Unauthorized Strategy Guide
Prince of Persia: The Official Strategy Guide
Prisoner of Ice: The Official Strategy Guide
The Residents: Bad Day on the Midway—The Official Strategy Guide
Return to Zork Adventurer's Guide
Ripper: The Official Strategy Guide
Romance of the Three Kingdoms IV: Wall of Fire—The Official Strategy Guide
Shannara: The Official Strategy Guide
Sid Meier's Civilization, or Rome on 640K a Day
Sid Meier's Civilization II: The Official Strategy Guide
Sid Meier's Colonization: The Official Strategy Guide
SimCity 2000: Power, Politics, and Planning
SimEarth: The Official Strategy Guide
SimFarm Almanac: The Official Guide to SimFarm
SimIsle: The Official Strategy Guide
SimLife: The Official Strategy Guide
SimTower: The Official Strategy Guide
Stonekeep: The Official Strategy Guide
SubWar 2050: The Official Strategy Guide
Thunderscape: The Official Strategy Guide
TIE Fighter Collector's CD-ROM: The Official Strategy Guide
Under a Killing Moon: The Official Strategy Guide
WarCraft: Orcs & Humans Official Secrets & Solutions
WarCraft II: Tides of Darkness—The Official Strategy Guide
Warlords II Deluxe: The Official Strategy Guide
Werewolf Vs. Commanche: The Official Strategy Guide
Wing Commander I, II, and III: The Ultimate Strategy Guide
X-COM Terror From The Deep: The Official Strategy Guide
X-COM UFO Defense: The Official Strategy Guide
X-Wing Collector's CD-ROM: The Official Strategy Guide

How to Order:

For information on quantity discounts contact the publisher: Prima Publishing, P.O. Box 1260BK, Rocklin, CA 95677-1260; (916) 632-4400. On your letterhead include information concerning the intended use of the books and the number of books you wish to purchase. For individual orders, turn to the back of the book for more information.

Visit us online at http://www.primapublishing.com

Prima's Quake™

Strategy Guide Unauthorized

Kip Ward & Mike van Mantgem

Prima Publishing
Rocklin, California
(916) 632-4400

Project Editors: Chris Balmain & Julie Asbury

ISBN: 0-7615-0532-6
Library of Congress Catalog Card Number: 96-67196
Printed in the United States of America

96 97 98 99 BB 10 9 8 7 6 5 4 3 2 1

Contents

Acknowledgments

Quake has rocked many, many worlds at Prima's California offices. And once again Prima's second-to-none staff laughed off this potential cataclysm and rocked right back.

Thanks especially to Chris and Julie for taking charge, and squarely hitting an impossible deadline. In fact *Quake* shook Chris so hard that he fled to Mexico for a week.

Big thanks go to Sam for sweating the details, and pointing out that sometimes a doggie isn't a Rottweiler—nor a catwalk always a walkway.

Once again we're indebted to Connie, 2nd Street's benevolent map goddess and designer extraodinaire, for a job above and beyond. And speaking of maps, a collective thanks is owed to Rod for generating the mission maps. If there were an international competition for map-making, Rod and Connie would own the world record.

A very special thanks goes to Kari for deciphering our cryptic scrawls and miraculously fusing all the pieces together. We think you'll agree that the fit is seamless. We can't thank Mike and Victor enough for their fabulous cover. You guys rule.

And finally, Mike would like to thank Diane for giving him the energy to make his work shine. And Kip would like to say a special 'hi' to Hillary, who's in his thoughts alot lately.

Kip Ward & Mike van Mantgem
August, 1996

Introduction: The Complete Picture

Thinking back on when we first set to strategizing our way through the *Quake* shareware, eons ago, it would be easy to take a misty-eyed view of our initial glee. Even now, there remains within us a deep and abiding respect for the meticulous craftsmanship and innovative genius that begat the *Quake* experience, and we'd really like to share with you, at length, those touchingly personal revelations.

But, mostly, we'd like to talk about blowing up Zombies. Whammo! Little chunks of Zombie all over the place...

Wherever you choose to rank *Quake* among the all-time great 3D games, or wherever we might choose to rank it, the experience doubtlessly succeeds on a number of levels. And having blasted our way from one end of *Quake* to the other more times than most people would consider reasonable, we're happy to report that it's still enthralling.

Eventually, of course, you start to slip into a surreal danger zone, where the boundaries between *Quake* and reality become extremely fragile. The symptoms include catching glimpses of ammo boxes out of the corner of your eye... at home or in the office... and not being really concerned. In fact, you're not concerned at all, except maybe to wonder; 'Is that a big box of nails, or just a small one?'

That's where we were while writing most of this book. Welcome aboard...

Potential Strategy

We make no pretense of deep insight here. Though the engine that drives the *Quake* world is certainly a leap from the land of *Doom*, your options for interaction aren't expanded nearly as exponentially. If you've ever knocked around the likes of *Doom*, *Hexen*, or *Duke Nukem*, you get the general idea.

The *Quake* bag of tricks features some subtle refinements on the weaponry of its predecessors, but nothing so radical that you'll be groping to understand the tactical implications. So we're taking the easy way out, and assuming that if you've purchased this book, you've probably come far enough in the 3D gaming world that we don't have to tell you what the directional arrows are for.

If you are in desperate need of a primer—your friends roll their eyes when you question them sincerely on matters such as acquiring ammo—check out the game documentation. Consider that basic training.

From our own strategic standpoint, what we've done here is to give you our specific situational insights, as well as pointing out the subtle differences between this game and any other. Most of *Quake*'s features are familiar, but utilizing them in the most effective way—realizing your full potential in terms of manipulating those subtle differences—can be a nuisance if you have to stumble over every nuance yourself. We hope we've streamlined the process.

Oh Yeah: The Maps

Of course, our sterling prose and insights aside, the best thing we have to offer you are the detailed maps that accompany the walkthrough for each mission.

Since *Quake* doesn't include an automap feature, getting oriented can be one of the game's most vexing aspects. These maps probably won't win any major awards—though they might, lovingly hand-rendered as they are—but they can provide invaluable aid as you try to find your way through strange new territory. All the pertinent info is there, even if the relative scale tends to fluctuate. And every Secret Area is clearly marked, along with things like hazardous terrain and sneaky switches. The walkthrough and maps together should get you where you need to go in style.

Making Things Difficult

For the full-version *Quake* strategy guide, we opted to go with the Hard mode of difficulty in terms of the walkthrough section. If you're just starting out with the game, you'll probably want to get oriented at the Normal skill level, but you probably won't want to play at anything less than Hard once you've mastered the basics.

At the Hard level of difficulty, the game takes on another dimension relative to Normal or Easy modes. Not only, of course, are there more and tougher monsters to battle, but the placement of the beasts becomes downright diabolical. Also, in most missions, there are at least a couple of small antechambers that only open in the Hard difficulty mode. It would be a shame to miss out on any of the bad guys waiting inside…

To the Death(match)

Of all *Quake*'s advancements in 3D look and feel, a more concrete leap forward concerns the structure of a game in progress, and how that relates to Deathmatch play.

Be sure you check out the chapter on Deathmatch for specific insights, along with tips for best utilizing all the bells and whistles. *Quake* supports options like team play, where your shots won't harm your buddies, and even allows players to enter a game that's already underway. Cool stuff you should know about.

Note

Before you start a single-player game, check which multiplayer status setting you want. You have two choices—Deathmatch or Cooperative play. Unlike Doom or any if its clones, there is no real single-player game. In other words, Quake thinks of single-player games as multiplayer games with only one player.

What does this mean in terms of actual game play?

When you play against the computer with your multiplayer setting on Deathmatch (the default), the game reloads the mission from scratch when you die (unless you re-load a saved game). The monsters you killed are alive and well, all items are back where they should be. It's a clean slate. However, if your multiplayer setting is Cooperative (again in single-player action), when you die the game re-loads where you left off. This means all the monsters you killed stay dead, and every item you grabbed is gone. However, if you find your cold corpse you can loot it—he didn't need it anymore anyway.

On With the Show

Prior to the walkthrough, give the other chapters a quick look. There won't be a test afterward, but knowing up front the best way to handle the individual monsters, as well as the value and importance of some of the power-ups, can make the trip a little less confusing. Later, if you have a particular problem, you'll be familiar enough with the book to find the answer quickly.

Finally: Enjoy! We sure did. All of a sudden, the future of 3D gaming is now. Do your part.

Getting Started

Prefacing the walkthrough, this section includes everything you should need to make your *Quake* experience complete. There's quick bits on all the monsters and items, as well as some sage observations on the *Quake* world in general. Hit it for the highlights, and refer back if you're having any specific dilemmas during play.

Quake Tactics

Thriving, not simply surviving, in the *Quake* environment is a trick in itself. Fortunately, you'll accomplish it easily with some basic skills and some judiciously applied savvy.

And thriving is the key to enjoying the game completely—there's little glory (and very little fun) in getting hammered from one end of an episode to the other with no respite to pause and sniff the slime, as it were.

This section expands on some basic movement options, and points out strategies that are probably pretty familiar to those who've played a 3D adventure before. The best teacher, of course, is practice. Brief yourself, and cross-reference the Combat Tactics with our specific recommendations for battling each monster in the Essentials section.

General Exploration Tactics

The world of *Quake* (monsters aside) can be hazardous simply by virtue of the traps and blatantly hazardous terrain. A few things to consider, then, even when the monsters aren't nipping at your heels or hacking out your guts:

Saving the Game

Of course, the standard gamer's credo is, "Save Early, Save Often." This becomes an essential part of enjoying the action, especially when playing a game for the first time. In short, saving often prevents you from having to replay large chunks of dungeon upon your untimely demise.

In *Quake*, note that a single Save slot functions as two—when you go through the Game Files menu to save your game, there it sits. But, while you play, you can also Quick Save to the same slot without overwriting the game you saved using the Game Files route.

In effect, you can use the Game Files save when you're feeling pretty good about your accomplishments (when you're in good Health, have plenty of ammo, and are not in a precarious position).

The Quick Save functions as a kind of tether to the main Save slot. It allows you to extend yourself a little further from the comfort zone of the full Save. Think of it as a "see what happens" option. Accessing the different saved games follows logically: The Quick Load cues up the game from the last point you Quick Saved, whereas a Load through the Game Files menu brings up the last game you saved there.

Note

Probably the best thing you can do for yourself, if you've played another 3D game enough to feel comfortable with the controls, is to remap the keyboard to that familiar configuration. The range of movement options in *Quake* isn't any larger than in most other 3D games. You can easily remap the keyboard in *Quake* under the Options menu.

Opening Doors, Throwing Switches

One of the nicest things about *Quake* is that you no longer have to open each door and throw each switch manually. Just walk right up; if there's an action that can be performed, you'll trigger it just by being there. Of course, some switches require that you shoot them from a distance, and likewise some doors must be shot to gain access to the rooms they conceal.

Always Run

Go under your options menu and set the Run option so it's always on. If you need to start off slowly with *Quake*, play the game in Easy mode. The plodding pace when you're not running serves no purpose—other than to make you easy prey for your enemies.

Watch Your Step

Quake often requires you to negotiate hazardous areas where a misstep can cost you more than most monster attacks. When you must leap, or have just completed a difficult one, point your view directly down at your feet, and orient yourself properly. You can't actually see your feet, of course, but you can tell if you're standing in a relatively stable position, or if you're about to slip off the edge of a platform.

If you see that you are, in fact, dangerously off-center, turn and face the direction where you're least stable, and tap the backward arrow to center yourself. If you plan to jump, you can use the same method to make sure that you can take at least a small step before leaping from a perch. As we'll explain, that can be essential.

Master the Art of Jumping

One of the most vexing components of *Quake* gameplay can be the properly executed jump. Unlike games such as *Duke Nukem 3D*, *Quake's* jumping parameters seem a little strict. As a rule, you need some kind of a running start to jump an appreciable distance. Even if you're standing on a relatively small platform, like the top of a switch, it behooves you to back up as far as you can and take that half-step before making the next leap. Otherwise, you tend to hop lamely from your perch and go nowhere. Conversely, if you get a good run at a chasm, you'll be pleasantly surprised at your leaping ability. If you're used to judging jumpable distances in other 3D games, you'll need to recalibrate the upper limits when making those evaluations here.

Diving

Occasionally, you'll want to jump in water (or maybe even slime) to explore. Slime-surfing requires a Biosuit, or your skin peels off in about 20 seconds. In water, you'll hold your breath for a considerable amount of time before you begin to register damage. Usually that's long enough to determine if you've got any good reason to be swimming around, or if you're just wasting time.

If you hop into water (or slime, or even lava) you'll sink slowly. If you do this you're useing half your protective Biosuit just getting properly submerged. Use the directional arrows to center your view on an underwater target—be it a doorway or some power-up—and then use the forward arrow to move rapidly in that direction. Note that you can also designate one key as a 'submerge' button, which is extremely useful for those exploratory dives.

You can surface at any time by pressing Spacebar (or any key you've designated to be your Jump key), so you don't have to worry about being properly oriented before swimming back to the surface. Of course, you want to be ready for whatever awaits you above, but it's usually easier to surface and then straighten out your line of sight relative to your new surroundings.

Combat Tactics

Combat in *Quake*, as with all the best 3D action games, is a combination of brute strength and finesse in varying amounts. Generally, the tougher the opponent, the more of each you must bring to bear.

Beginning with the Ogre, you realize there's more to combat success than simply trading punches. You must study your adversary and figure out what his specific weaknesses might be. As we said before, refer to in the Essentials section for specific monster analyses.

That done, apply appropriate tactics with a combination of brawn and wile to gain the upper hand. For instance…

Strafing

Yes, it's another 3D gaming standard, but *Quake* is damn near impossible to survive at the harder skill settings unless you can avoid some incoming fire. The most effective way to do that, and get in some licks of your own, is the time-honored strafe. Strafing through a doorway—sliding by and firing—is the single most effective way to deal with tougher monsters or crowds of foes when you're low on certain kinds of ammo. In that way, you can chip away at foes with your Shotgun, instead of expending other ammo that might be scarcer than Shotgun Shells. On a relevant tangent, you'll find that some monsters have a hard time navigating through portals, and by strafing you can take better advantage of any confusion or limitation an enemy displays.

An Option menu item in *Quake* allows you to strafe automatically (using the keys you normally use to pivot) while you gaze upward. That comes in handy sometimes, but it can also be a limitation, especially when dealing with Scrags. Get used to strafing in one direction while turning in the other, and you'll find it's easy for you to target objects above you, while those foes will have a much harder time pegging you as you make quick circles below.

Attack Angles

There's probably never been a 3D game that pays as strict attention to attack angle as *Quake* does. To date, most other 3D action games let you get away with pointing in the general direction of a foe, with little regard to the target's elevation relative to your own position. Such is not the case in the land of *Quake*. Sure, you can still hit that Scrag by shooting 10 feet below it, but it'll take three times as many shots to finish it off. Meanwhile, you'll take damage and burn ammo like crazy. Get used to adjusting your angle of attack, not just side to side but also up and down, and you'll notice a remarkable increase in the damage you inflict.

Mix It Up

Most of the monsters you meet share some exploitable tendencies. Probably the most satisfying of these is their homicidal attitude toward each other. You can't always count on it, but when you blast a horde of foes, odds are a few monsters will catch flak from their brethren in the ensuing pandemonium, and take exception. Better they whack on each other than you.

Lie in Wait

The corollary to the preceding tactic concerns what you should do while the monsters sort out any personal conflicts. Hopefully (unless you've been running in a blind panic), there's relatively clear ground behind you in the dungeon—an area you've already blasted through. That being the case, and knowing that any monsters not trading punches will immediately take to hunting you down, look for vantage points as you clear each room in case you have to double back and play sniper. Note the monsters' initial positions in each room: That's usually a good indicator of the prime spots from which to stage an ambush in Deathmath play.

Conserve Your Resources

At higher levels of difficulty—Hard and Nightmare—it's essential to attend to your rate of fire and to be extra mindful of taking on refills. Don't waste ammo over your maximum by picking up crates that only net you a few shells. If you have 98 Shotgun Shells, walk around that big box and come back for it when you can better benefit from a substantial reload. In this way, you can often load up on ammo or even Armor at the end of one mission, and gain a significant advantage in the mission ahead.

Rune Their Day

When you claim one of the rune power-ups, do so with foresight. If you stand around congratulating yourself while half a Quad Damage charge dissipates, you need to get a clue. Assuming the rune has served its intended purpose, in your strategic estimation, go ahead and Quick Save the game. Then sprint into the next room and open fire. What's the worst that can happen?

Telefragging

An interesting aspect of *Quake* is the ability you have to 'telefrag' monsters—and, of course, to get telefragged yourself. By positioning yourself at the exact spot where an enemy teleports into a room, you can disrupt the process with gruesome results, exploding the monster in one tremendous blast just by being in the way. Many times, monsters arrive at a point above the ground, and drop into a room, which effectively deprives you of the chance for a cheap kill. But there are some good opportunities. We'll occasionally point them out in the walkthrough, especially when a well-placed telefrag might help diffuse an otherwise deadly situation.

The Rocket Jump

Late in each Episode—and early in each Deathmatch, if you have even the smallest clue—you'll lay hands on the Rocket Launcher, and thereafter can execute the truly impressive Rocket Jump. Point the Launcher at the ground, near your feet, and jump at the same time you fire the shell. Usually, jumping backwards works much better than trying to go forward. You'll find you can actually leap three or four times as high as would normally be possible with the addition of rocket power. In single-player games, this tactic is seldom worth the damage it inflicts. But in Deathmatch, where there's power-ups aplenty, the Rocket Jump allows you to reach vantage points that are entirely inaccessible otherwise. Sniping from those locations can be especially deadly, since opponents won't automatically consider looking for you way up on the side of a cliff or castle… until it's far too late.

NOTARGET

Easily the coolest Cheat Code in the game, we thought NOTARGET deserved a mention purely as a strategic device. By typing the command into the pull-down console, monsters you have yet to meet won't recognize you as an intruder. Of course, if you walk up and blast them, they figure it out in a hurry, but that's not what we're recommending. Having a hard time judging the initial position of the monsters in a certain area? Want to know exactly where that Scrag teleports in? Reload from your last Quick Save and go NOTARGET, and you can explore without fear of hostile intervention, even getting cool close-up perspectives of foes that you usually only see in the heat of battle.

A Note on Zero-G

The only time you encounter "Gravity-Lite" in *Quake* is in "Secret Mission: Ziggurat Vertigo." Check that mission's walkthrough for specific combat advice and general strategies for surviving and thriving in the moon-like gravity.

The Essentials

A new lexicon of mayhem comes part and parcel with the realm of *Quake*, and the following pages detail the monsters, weapons, and items you'll encounter as you quest for Gold, Silver, and Rune Keys en route to the final showdown with vile Shub-Niggurath.

In addition to simple explanations, we've included our recommendations and observations regarding game-world objects, animate and otherwise. Most of our brilliant insights become achingly apparent with a little experimentation, though a couple of quirks here and there may take some stumbling around before you grasp them. At the very least, then, we hope these pages will save you some time-consuming trial and error.

Guns and Ammo

Quake features an impressive assortment of implements for inflicting pain and death, some with familiar effects, and some rather unique impacts (as it were). Along with each weapon, you'll find an account of the ammo required, and the amount found in a small ammo box. As a rule, a large box holds twice as many refills as the small version.

Axe

The basic Axe is the default weapon of *Quake*. In a pinch, perhaps you could whack someone to death, but hopefully it won't come to that. When playing Deathmatch, try fighting with "Axes Only." It's the next best thing to being a real-live axe murderer.

Shotgun

The simple Shotgun is your starter weapon, a tool with limited range and effect on the con side. But then again, it's a hell of a lot better than swinging that Axe at everyone you meet. A small box of Shotgun Shells holds 20 cartridges.

Double-barreled Shotgun

Generally, this is the first weapon upgrade you lay hands on. We have no doubt the Double-barreled Shotgun will quickly become your weapon of choice for general patrolling purposes. You'll find it strong enough to get the attention of most foes, but unsuitable for fighting major badasses.

Nailgun

The Nailgun is a treat, though it gulps ammo at an alarming pace. Its rapid rate of fire often allows you to keep larger foes in a state of pain and disorientation, thus rendering them incapable of counterattack. Very effective. Refills are technically termed "Flechettes," though the game will report them as "Nails" when acquired. A small box contains 25 Nails.

Supernailgun

The supercharged brother of the Nailgun, this baby packs a serious wallop that'll leave even the deadliest opposition wishing they'd found someone else to hassle. Of course, the rate of ammo dispensation is devastatingly impressive, as well, so reserve the Supernailgun for the times when your need is greatest. As with the Nailgun, refills are technically termed "Flechettes," though the game will report them as "Nails" when acquired. A small box contains 25 Nails.

Grenade Launcher

The Grenade Launcher lobs explosive shells at your enemies, and the key word here is "lobs." Grenades detonate on contact only if you hit an opponent outright, but going right for the kill requires employing a self-preservation tactic. In other words, fire and back quickly away, or you'll suffer some serious blast-radius damage.

Other than that, work on your trajectories, and use this weapon, in essence, to drop time-delay explosives onto platforms above your head or around corners. In fact, the most versatile way to use this weapon is to bounce a Grenade off a wall or doorjamb so that it caroms around a corner, hammering any foes before they have a chance to return the favor. Small boxes of Grenades hold five projectiles, and you'll find that Ogres relinquish them in pairs upon death.

Note

As with the larger weapons in other 3D games, the explosive power of both the Grenade Launcher and Rocket Launcher comes with a warning: Consider your proximity to your foes before pulling the trigger. Also notice that, although *Quake* switches to a new weapon automatically if the one you're firing runs out of ammo, it'll never switch to the Grenade or Rocket Launcher because of the likelihood of self-inflicted damage.

Rocket Launcher

Akin to the Grenade Launcher, this weapon instead tacks a propellant onto the back of the explosive charge, resulting in a straight-shooting instrument of destruction. There's no finesse here—no bouncing of projectiles or trajectory considerations. Just point and deliver a compact blast of destructive force. Once you acquire the Rocket Launcher, late in an Episode, you'll rarely want to use anything else for a distance attack. The Rocket Launcher also uses Grenades as refills. Small boxes of Grenades hold five projectiles, and you'll find that Ogres relinquish them in pairs upon death.

Thunderbolt

Acquired only in the later missions of Episodes 2, 3, and 4, the Thunderbolt is one way to show every monster who's boss. Even the feared Shambler isn't immune to the awesome electrical burst of the Thunderbolt, and most foes immediately go all to pieces when you show it off. Usually, you'll receive either the Thunderbolt or the Rocket Launcher, and not both, until the very end of an episode. The gun burns roughly six charges for each second of use, and you'd have to be an idiot to fire it underwater.

Monsters (and the Weapons That Kill Them)

Battling the *Quake* baddies can be a rugged proposition, especially as the difficulty level of the game increases. If you've got the game cranked up, you need to pay particular attention to weapon selection to get the most out of the firepower at your disposal.

Rottweiler

The rabid pups of *Quake* are target-practice material. The Double-barreled Shotgun is the generally accepted method of keeping them off your leg.

Rotfish

Found only in the azure-blue ponds of *Quake*, a lone Rotfish is more a nuisance than a threat. Schools of these scaly scum-suckers can effectively immobilize you, however, and nibble you to death in a hurry. To clean out a Rotfish-infested pond, jump into the water and use your body for bait. As soon as they bite, hop out of the pool. There should be tiny dorsal fins breaking the surface near where you swam ashore. Ever heard of shooting fish in a barrel?

Grunt

The standard foot soldier in the realm of *Quake*, the aptly named Grunt is just a little bit tougher than his four-legged friend. Of course, the Grunt has at least mastered the use of his Shotgun—and thus a crowd of them can require some measure of evasive capability. Whip out the Double-barreled Shotgun and hammer away, or use a larger shell if you have to deal with a pack of trouble. Spitting Nails at these bozos really isn't the wisest use of ammo.

Enforcer

His body armor makes him only slightly tougher than his Grunt buddies. Put a Double-barreled Shotgun in his face and pull the trigger twice for gruesome results. A laser gun is his weapon of choice, making an Enforcer a potentially deadly foe—especially if he happens to be stationed somewhere above you. From a distance, however, you can easily dodge those laser bolts. When an Enforcer's corpse hits the deck, it graciously yields five energy cells, redeemable only when you get your hands on the awesome Thunderbolt.

Knight

Even though they possess no distance attack, Knights can be a royal pain. They move quickly, and a couple of them standing and hacking on you can do big damage in a hurry. For that reason, you may need more than Shotgun pellets to ensure they never get the chance to slash. If three or four Knights sprint in your direction, especially at close range, don't be afraid to nail the initial wave. For lesser numbers, the Double-barreled Shotgun does the trick quite nicely. If you stir up these fearless protectors of the realm and run away, they'll hunt you down, but they may also take exception to other monsters they meet along the way—unwittingly helping you in your quest. They seem to bear a particular animosity toward Scrags. But then again, who doesn't?

Death Knight

This canned bad guy is the angry, bigger brother of the standard Knight, able to withstand a substantial assault before his knees buckle. His blade whittles Vores, Fiends, and heroes down to size at an alarming rate. But if that was his only attack he'd be nothing more than Shotgun fodder. When he spies you at a distance, he sweeps his sword in front him, unleashing a blazing fan of deadly energy bolts. His armor keeps him slow, so use a Supernailgun to open him up from a distance while dodging the energy bolts. He'll be kneeling before you in no time.

Zombie

Deal harshly with these disgusting denizens of *Quake*. If you use anything less than an explosive shell, these rotting rejects simply rise to fight again—usually clawing at your back after you've run by their flattened form. Load up the Grenade or Rocket Launcher and blast these punks into chunks, or you'll be sorry.

Scrag

The sickly white Scrag is a flying menace that looks something like a huge bloated larva. Because of their flying ability, the Scrags can often get the jump on you, scoring an initial hit while you scan the heights looking for your target. Try not to get all the way into a room before retaliating, or the Scrags will have you for dinner. Strafe like a madman, and dispense Nails with authority. You might deal with one Scrag using just the Double-barreled Shotgun, but otherwise you're going to want something in hand that doesn't require lengthy reloading. If your aim is quick and sharp, you might also consider a little Rocket-launching to take care of business.

Ogre

The most common of the midlevel badasses, the angry Ogre drags his chainsaw through the halls of *Quake* looking for fresh flesh. Of course, if all Ogres had going for them was a chainsaw, they'd be pushovers. Perhaps that's why they also come equipped with a bottomless bag of Grenades, which they deliver with depressing accuracy. These guys generally require the harshest treatment—preferably Grenades or Nails. Occasionally, you'll come across an Ogre with some kind of structural limitation hampering his Grenade-tossing efforts, but most of the time they show up with truly wicked strategic consideration. Sometimes it's actually better to run right up to a lone Ogre: Your proximity makes him switch attack modes from Grenade-tossing to chainsawing. At that point, you can back off just a few feet, out of range of his blade, and blast away. Of course, if you retreat too far, it's Grenade eatin' time again.

Spawn

Surprisingly fast and agile, these blue, self-styled Bouncing Betties pack quite a wallop. Enter rooms with extreme caution if they appear strangely empty. Usually, there's a spawn or three hiding nearby, and you want to spot them before they notice you. Lob Grenades, or fire Rockets, before they get a chance to start bouncing. Spawns not only inflict serious damage hopping, but they detonate upon death—particularly useful if there are other enemies in the vicinity; but exceedingly painful if you kill them at close range.

Fiend

The fierce Fiend possesses blinding quickness and leaping ability—in addition to the razors on the ends of its arms. A Fiend standing in front of you and slashing does tremendous damage, if it doesn't kill you outright. Use Grenades or Nails, and stay mobile. In fact, do anything it takes to kill these guys from a distance. And if you get too close, break off the attack and put back some distance. If you can draw the Fiend into a relatively confined area, you'll greatly hamper his evasive techniques (which amount to bouncing off the walls while he heads in your direction). He may even become effectively immobile behind a relatively small obstruction, due to his excitement at the pending rending of your flesh.

Vore

These squealing, three-legged nightmares of Pan are death incarnate to all but the most battle-savvy *Quake* veterans. A telltale whooshing sound is a dead giveaway that at least one Vore is nearby, warming up his major–league–caliber, spikeball–heaving hand. His spiked spheres doggedly track targets, and thus your only hope when fired upon is to take some tight turns and hope the projectile crashes against a wall or doorway during pursuit.

In close- or medium-range combat, only the Supernailgun's relentless fire prevents a Vore from unleashing upside your head. At long range, however, you can avoid damage with a quick duck and cover. Be prepared for a last-gasp volley as the Vore curls up and dies.

Shambler

Large, white, angry freak of *Quake*, the Shambler is indeed a fearsome foe. Explosive shells seem to have little effect on him, so our recommendation starts with Nails, preferably from the business end of the Supernailgun. In a pinch, it's possible to strafe and do good damage with a Double-barreled Shotgun from some portal the Shambler can't squeeze through. But Nails were made for the Shambler, and you should put them to their intended use. Close-quarters combat, is seldom advisable, unless the Shambler faces some structural limitation to keep it from batting you like a cat toy.

Items of Interest

Of course, in addition to the weapons and monsters, the realm of *Quake* has its own assortment of miscellaneous items to aid you on your journey. This section includes a couple of worthwhile tactical notes, as well as simple definitions.

Health

Health boxes come small (15 points) and large (25 points). Once you start to recognize the subtle differences between the two types, you can pass up the bigger boxes until you really need them.

Megahealth

The large Megahealth box adds 100 points to your Health total, though it soon begins to drain away. All points over the standard 100 total eventually vanish, so it's a good idea to save this item to use prior to a big battle. You'll lose the bonus anyway in a matter of minutes, so you might as well use it to absorb enemy fire.

Armor

Quake features a stoplight selection of Armor: Green, Yellow and Red. Grabbing Green Armor adds 100 points to your total, while Yellow gains you 150 and Red bestows the maximum 200 points. You lose Armor points when you take any damage—not exclusively in lieu of Health points, but nonetheless providing a substantial cushion.

Biosuit

The Biosuit lets you enter damaging areas of slime without feeling the ill effects. Of course, the suit has a limited duration, so you'll usually find it hanging nearby when a specific task requires it. Save the game before you suit up, then explore nearby. Once you've found the suit's obvious intention, and the most expedient path to your goal, reload the game and do it for real.

Quad Damage Rune

Probably the most common of the *Quake* runes, Quad Damage is another of those items you should avoid acquiring until a big battle rears its ugly head. Sometimes, of course, there's just no one nearby who warrants the harsh treatment Quad Damage allows you to inflict. Check the vicinity before powering up, just to be sure. One of these babies and a few Nails make such short work of a Shambler it seems almost unfair. Almost.

Ring of Shadows

The Ring of Shadows rune renders you invisible, for all intents and purposes. Minor monsters seem entirely incapable of targeting you, and even the big boys struggle to find the range. Save it until you need it, and it will bless you a thousand times over.

Pentagram of Protection

The Pentagram of Protection is the granddaddy of all runes, keeping you safe from enemy attack for the duration of the spell or allowing you to despense large shells at close range. This rune can have several tactical implications, allowing you to pound on a stronger monster with no fear of reprisal—perhaps while ignoring other, lesser, monsters until you finish off the major threat. It also allows you to travel in hazardous areas, just as the Biosuit does, but the Pentagram keeps you even safer. In the Secret Mission of Episode 1, you actually use the Pentagram to swim in lava. Smokin'! Note that the Pentagram doesn't afford your Armor any protection; it merely maintains your health for the duration of the spell.

Game Start

To play the episode of your choosing, first you must select the degree of difficulty by passing through one of the three hallways you see as the game begins—thereby choosing among the Easy, Medium, or Hard settings. There is also a Nightmare mode available from this small network of rooms and hallways.

If you feel you're ready for a challenge of Nightmare proportions, traverse any of the initial three hallways, and then pass through the portal leading to Episode 4: The Elder World. Stop at the edge of the pool of water. Slowly step over the edge of the pool, and backpedal as you fall. You should land on a large wooden beam, above floor-level in the area beneath the pool. Follow the beam around to the left. In that hallway, you'll find a molten Teleporter—welcome to Nightmare mode!

Episode 1

Dimension of the Doomed

No doubt you know that Episode 1 is the much-ballyhooed shareware version of *Quake*. *Newsweek* reported that by late July, over 1,000,000 copies of the shareware had been downloaded from various Internet sites worldwide.

If you bought the full version of *Quake* through a retail outlet, or haven't played enough of Episode 1 to master the quirks of *Quake*, we recommend you get familiar with the game by exploring Episode 1 before tackling the other episodes. The tight, easy-to-navigate mission maps, combined with a liberal compliment of firepower (and not-too-deadly bad guys) make this a fine introduction.

Of course you can play any episode in any order, but be forewarned that as the episode number increases, you'll encounter increasingly difficult monsters, puzzles, and mission maps. Until you learn what to look for and how to lay down the law with your Grenade Launcher, *Quake* may frustrate you to the point where the game isn't any fun to play. And make no mistake, *Quake* is a fun game, especially when you're experienced enough to enjoy the final sprawling episode in Nightmare mode. Take your time. Let yourself grow with the game. After all, you want to enjoy your trip, savor the bone-crushing action, and relish the sweet smell of seared Ogre flesh.

In the beginning missions of Episode 1, you're quietly introduced to the joys of battling easy-to-chunkify bad guys while you practice jumping, button pressing, Biosuit swimming, powerup rune killin', and Secret Area searching.

If you survive the missions at the end of this Episode, *Quake* will probably begin to transcend the bounds of mere entertainment, and doom you to a new way of life. At least that's what the team at id Software hopes will happen.

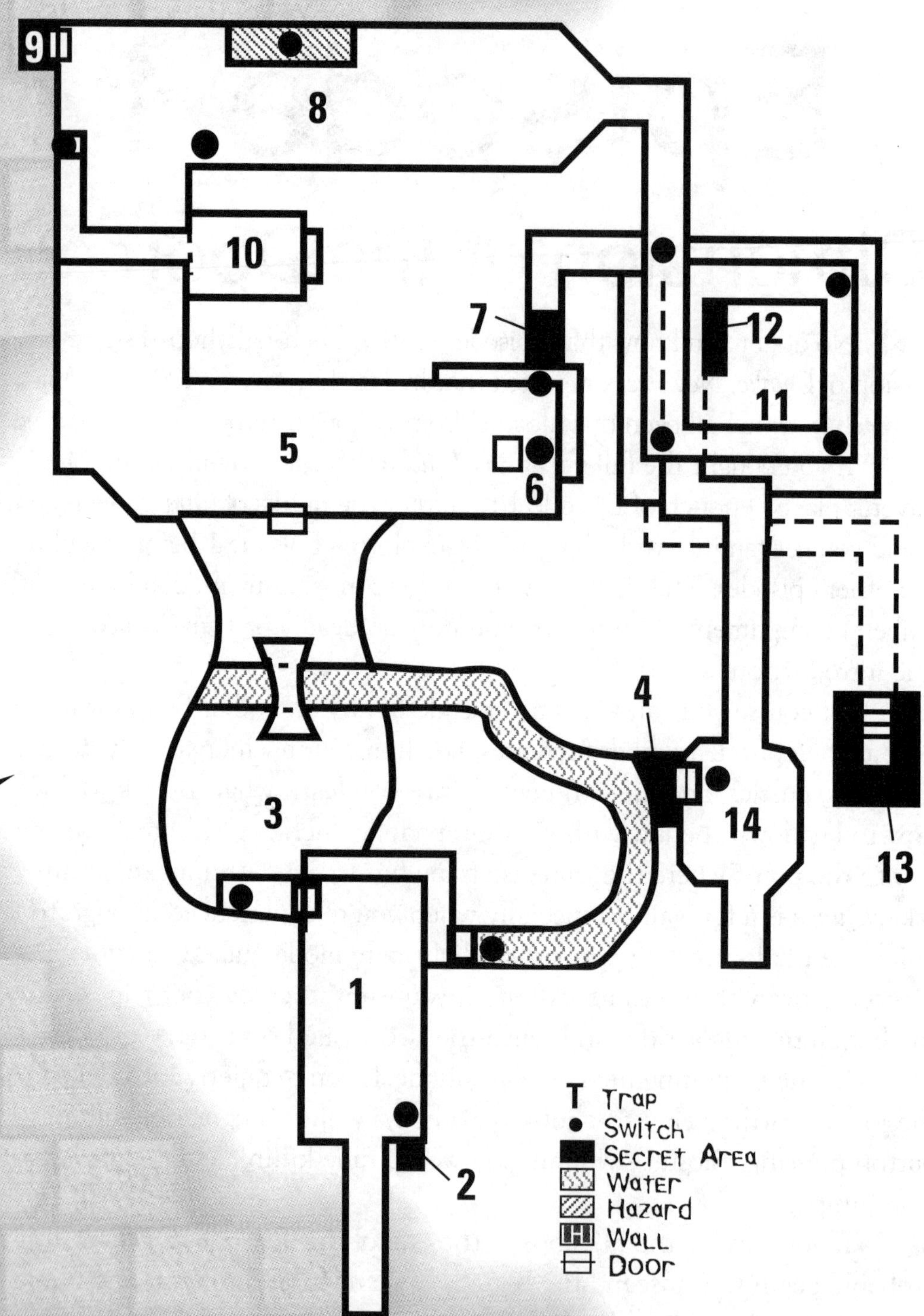

1
2
3
4
5
6
7
8
9
10
11
12
13
14
T Trap
Switch
Secret Area
Water
Hazard
Wall
Door

Mission 1: Slipgate Complex

The Slipgate mission, as you might expect, lets you experience *Quake* with relatively little fear of reprisal. Grunts and their doggies patrol the complex, and there's more than enough supplies on hand to take care of the likes of them.

Get used to the sights and sounds, and get in some target practice. Things heat up considerably in the missions ahead.

Mission 1: Slipgate Complex At-a-Glance (E1M1)

1. Shotgun Shells, Green Armor
2. **Secret Area.** Shotgun Shells
3. Health
4. **Secret Area.** Megahealth
5. Health
6. Shotgun Shells, Health
7. **Secret Area.** Quad Damage
8. Switch
9. **Secret Area.** Double-barreled Shotgun
10. Nailgun, Flechettes
11. Switches, Biosuit
12. **Secret Area.** Megahealth
13. **Secret Area.** Yellow Armor, Health
14. Health, Flechettes

Highlights:

 Six Secret Areas

 Exploding Bad Guys

Into the Great Unknown

1. Enter the Slipgate Complex and explore the large hallway, slaying the Grunt lurking to your right. You can reach the ledge at the far end of the hall with a running leap, defend yourself against another Grunt, and net more ammo for the Shotgun. At the end of the short hallway in that direction you'll find a suit of Green Armor.

2. **Secret Area.** Jump onto the ledge near where you disposed of the first Grunt, and shoot the red panel on the wall. A compartment holds Shotgun Shells, and you should dispense some on the Grunt behind the large doors before riding down to the yard below.

3. Below, hammer the Grunts and the Rottweiler. You'll find two big boxes of Health near where you exit the lift, and another to the left of the door across the bridge. Before venturing inside, drop down into the stream and swim through the tunnel to a Secret Area.

4. **Secret Area.** Inside the tunnel on the left is a landing with a Megahealth dose and a locked door, guarded briefly by a Grunt. If you continue downstream, you'll access a lift back to the complex upstairs. Then you can double back to the door across the bridge.

5. When you open the door, dispose of the Grunts and their doggies. Shooting the large box you see through the doorway proves quite effective. You'll find a small box of Health nearby, as well.

6. In the area to the right of the entrance, you'll find a box of Shotgun ammo. Stand facing the column with your back to the ledge and shoot the picture of the rotating Earth to ride a lift up to the ledge. There you'll find more Health, and another Earth to blast.

7. **Secret Area.** Shooting the picture of Earth on the ledge opens a room to a Quad Damage power-up. It'll only last a few minutes, so sprint down around the corner of the large hallway and clean house while you've got the power.

8. Down the other wing of the large hallway, hammer the Grunts and look to the walkway above for a patrolling pup. Trigger the switch to cross the slime, and perhaps wreak more Quad havoc on the hallway beyond. When things have quieted down, return to the midway point on the bridge, and from there shoot the switch on the wall.

9. **Secret Area.** Shooting the wall switch opens a small room to your left, containing your first weapon upgrade—the Double-barreled Shotgun.

10. Use the lift to access the upper walkway. The room above holds Grunts, as well as the mighty Nailgun, which you acquire shortly before the lights go out and a double-Grunt ambush ensues. Grabbing the Flechettes (like nails, only special…) turns the lights back on again.

11. Once across the bridged slime pit, descend the walkway while blasting Grunts, mindful of the one sniping from the darkened doorway above. At the corners of the descending ramp, push the switches to unseal a portal at the bottom of the walkway. Before continuing to the end of the mission, however, sidetrack to locate two more Secret Areas.

12. **Secret Area.** As you stand near the last switch, near the bottom of the ramp, notice that a series of leaps will gain you access to the Grunt's sniper nest. If you hop onto the light fixture near the switch, then onto the switch itself, you can leap to some stone steps protruding from the small room's wall. It's tricky—look at your feet, back up as far as you can on the switch, then take a short run before jumping. Inside the small room a box of Megahealth awaits you.

> **Note**
>
> **Notice that before you descend the walkway, you can pause at the top and shoot the wall to your right. What appears to be an electrical panel slides to reveal a short passage connecting this area with the secret hall where you picked up the Quad Damage rune earlier.**

13. **Secret Area.** Near the bottom of the ramp, as you descend to the doorway, look behind the pillar on the right and you'll find a Biosuit. Once you have it on, about face and jump over the railing, through the small opening in the corner Below, you should see the opening to an underwater passage. Follow the passage and surface to emerge in a Secret Area with Yellow Armor and boxes of Health. The Teleporter there drops you on the ledge above the door where you first entered the building—kind of a drag right now, but a very cool trick in Deathmatch…

14. Continue down the hallway from where you acquired the Biosuit, battle a few more Grunts, and collect plenty more Health and a box of Flechettes en route to the exit Slipgate. Notice that if you shoot the wall to your right as you enter the small, widened chamber in the hallway, a portal opens. That's the door you saw so long ago from the Secret Area down the stream.

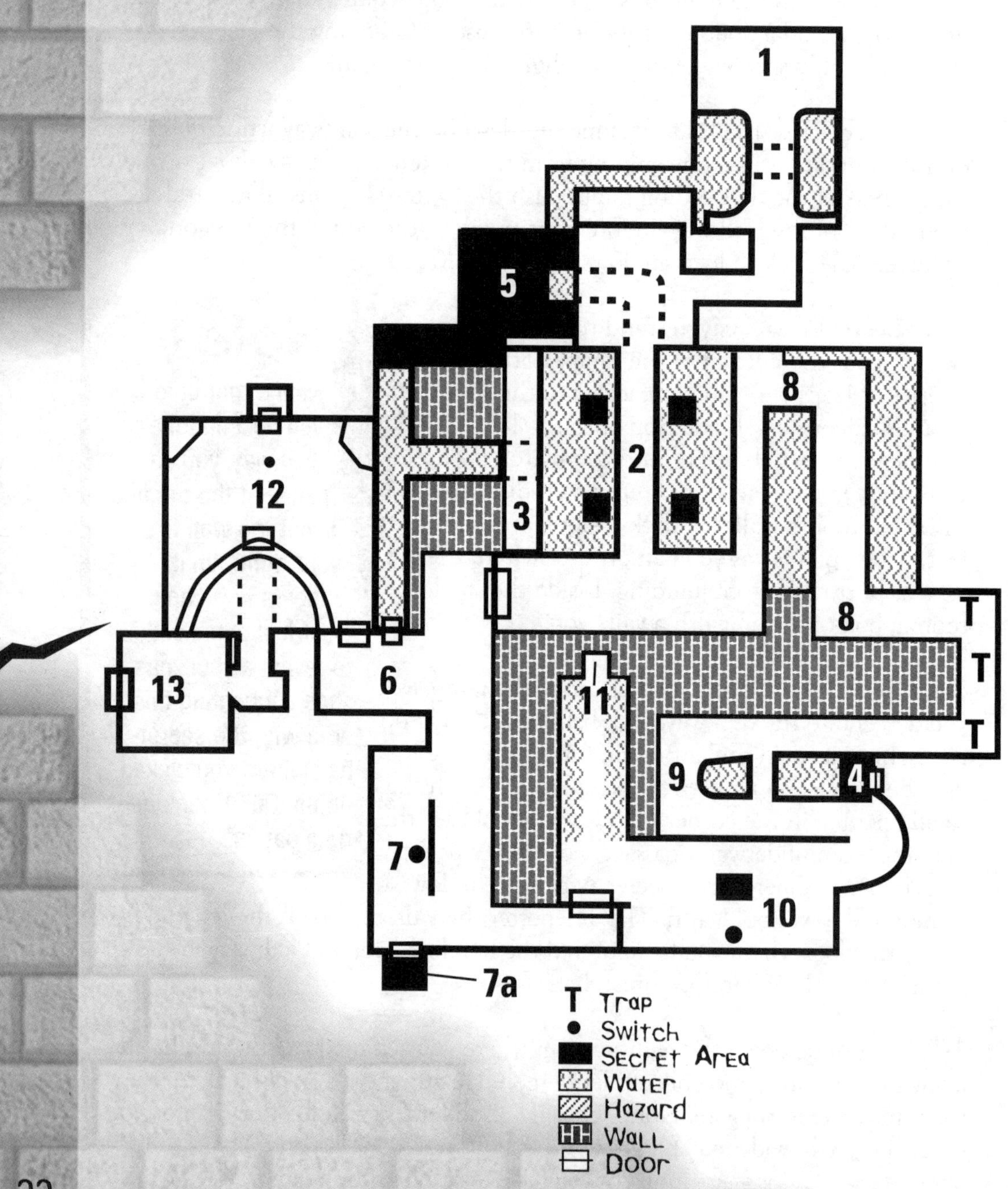
1
5
2
8
12
3
8
T
T
T
6
13
11
9
4
7
10
7a
T Trap
Switch
Secret Area
Water
Hazard
Wall
Door

Mission 2: Castle of the Damned

This is where *Quake* finally gets medieval on your ass. A nasty troop of Ogres, some Grunts, and their canned-ham Knight pals stand between you and the exit. Along the way you'll also swim with the Scrags and (hopefully) survive an encounter or two with a Fiend.

The lighting and underwater effects are truly dazzling. As a bonus, the puzzles aren't too complex and the combat absolutely rocks. If the first *Quake* mission didn't impress you, this one will.

Mission 2: Castle of the Damned At-a-Glance (E1M2)

1. Health, Shotgun Shells, Flechette
2. Health (en route), Shotgun Shells, Double-barreled Shotgun
3. Green Armor, Health
4. **Secret Area.** Health, Flechette, Slipgate to 3
5. **Secret Area.** Shotgun Shells, Health
6. Shotgun Shells, Blue Key door
7. Health, Shotgun Shells, Switch to open 7a

7a. **Secret Area.** Quad Damage rune

8. Shotgun Shells, Nailgun trap
9. Yellow Armor, Shotgun Shells, Health
10. Health, Flechette, Shotgun Shells, Switch to access 11
11. Blue Key. Health, Flechette (under bridge)
12. Health, Shotgun Shells, Fiend trap, Flechette
13. Health (en route), Shotgun Shells. Mission exit.

Highlights:

- Three Secret Areas

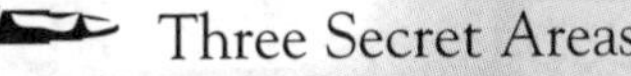

- Teach Yourself to Swim Without Drowning
- Your First Chance to Play with Ogres, Scrags, Knights, and Some Unfriendly Fiends

Medieval Evil Is the Worst Kind

1. At the start, you should see a pair of Grunts and an Ogre. Prepare for your first real test. Before you leave the start room, dive under the wooden bridge for Flechettes. Shoot the off-colored patch of wall (underwater, on the right) for a shortcut to Secret Area 5.

2. Battle your way up the stairs. Watch out for another Ogre and his flying grenades. A Grunt guards the bridge proper, and yet another Ogre stands below the red symbol. Watch that you don't take too much unfriendly fire from the Grunts to your left and right. The right-side Grunt guards area 3.

3. Leap to the right ledge for Green Armor and a Health box. If you miss the ledge and fall into the drink, dog-paddle to the sunken lift to the left of the red symbol; the lift automatically brings you up when you step on it.

4. **Secret Area.** Step off the center bridge, swim past the sunken lift and under the arch. Veer right until you're above the water's surface (you should see a steel catwalk above you). Follow the passage until you find yourself under the Yellow Armor (area 9). Take out any Grunts and an Ogre if you can. Turn left (a portion of wall will drop). Go up and plow into the Slipgate. Welcome back to the Green Armor ledge (3).

5. **Secret Area.** Drop off the Green Armor ledge into the drink, turn left and swim under the arch directly beneath the center bridge—you should be moving away from the red symbol. Slog up the ramp to claim your ammo and Health prizes. The stagnant pool on your right leads back to 1. Climb the stairs to the left. Watch out for a Scrag attack from the left! Jump into the water and churn full steam ahead until you wade up the far ramp.

6. The wall at the top of the ramp opens as you approach it. Congratulations—you've just ambushed a team of Grunts. The staircase in front of you leads to an ambush, a Health box, some ammo and a hidden Quad Damage rune.

7, 7a. **Secret Area.** To get the Quad Damage rune, turn right at the top of the stairs, go under the first arch, then turn to face the center column with the burning torch. Press in the protruding stone and turn right: A section of the far wall slides open to reveal 7a—and the precious rune. (7a counts as the Secret Area.). Leave the rune for now. Trust us, it's not going anywhere. You'll need it when you blast through the Silver Key door, (area 12).

Run down the stairs and turn right in 6. You're back in 2. Hustle down the hallway, turn left at the end and creep up toward the archway.

8. Scrag attack! And as if that's not bad enough, a clutch of angry Ogres launch a catwalk attack. Stand around long enough and they'll come to you. But wait, there's more! As soon as you make your first left, you trigger a trio of wall-mounted Nailguns into action!

A careful jump between nails while hugging the outside walls easily outwits this trap. Don't be surprised if you're penned in by nails as Ogres and/or Scrags come out to play. While it's possible to draw them into the trap, it's better for your health if you carry out their death sentence with your own hand.

9. This is the Yellow Armor you saw at 4—except now you have to battle a couple of Grunts if you didn't already kill them. Once you've chunkified the bad guys, shoot the red button beneath the armor (it's above 4). The columns protecting the armor rise, and all you have to do is jump up the steps to claim your booty. If you haven't learned how to "Quake-jump" yet, now would be a good time. If you fall into the drink (and didn't save your game before you fell), we suggest you go through the Slipgate at 4 and work your way back down the catwalk to try again.

10. Creep up the stairs and get ready for an ambush. As soon as you step onto the main floor, the left walls drop and a gang of four impatient Knights come out swinging. Press the pulsating switch and you trigger an Ogre into action. Down him, go to the end of the hall and turn right. Watch out for another angry Scrag!

11. Hitting the switch in 10 caused a wooden plank to span the water, giving you easy access to the much-needed Silver Key. Grabbing the key opens the door behind you. Remember the Quad Damage rune? You can go through this door to get to 12, but read the sidebar before you go!

12. Even though Quad Damage power is pumping through your veins, jump back as soon as you open the Silver Key door! An Ogre takes a sucker-swing at you. Time's a wastin' so burst in, nails flying, and slay the Ogres to your left en route to stepping on the switch on the floor in the center of the room.

Note

To get an otherwise out-of-reach Flechette and a Health box, stand on the right side of the plank (facing the distant Silver Key alcove), and slowly step off the ledge. Back up as you fall to avoid dropping into the water.

While you wait for the floating cubes to magically insert themselves in the wall, blast the Grunts on the ledge above. As soon as the floating cubes plug into their wall sockets, three things happen: Slipgates appear in the right and left corners on either side of the floor switch; the bars that lock you out of the arched passage to the exit slide away; and a Fiend leaps out to disembowel you. The moment you rip him apart with your Quad-Damage powered Nailgun, two more Fiends teleport in. Escape into either Slipgate if your Quad Damage is gone (or if your health is low) and show them who's king of this castle from the ledge above.

13. Walk through the arches and clank up the stairs. All that stands between you and the next mission is a Scrag, a Knight, and another Ogre (that lurks on the ledge to the right of the stairs). Hint: Knights and Ogres love to fight Scrags. When all's quiet, go through the big wooden door to end your stay in this tragic kingdom.

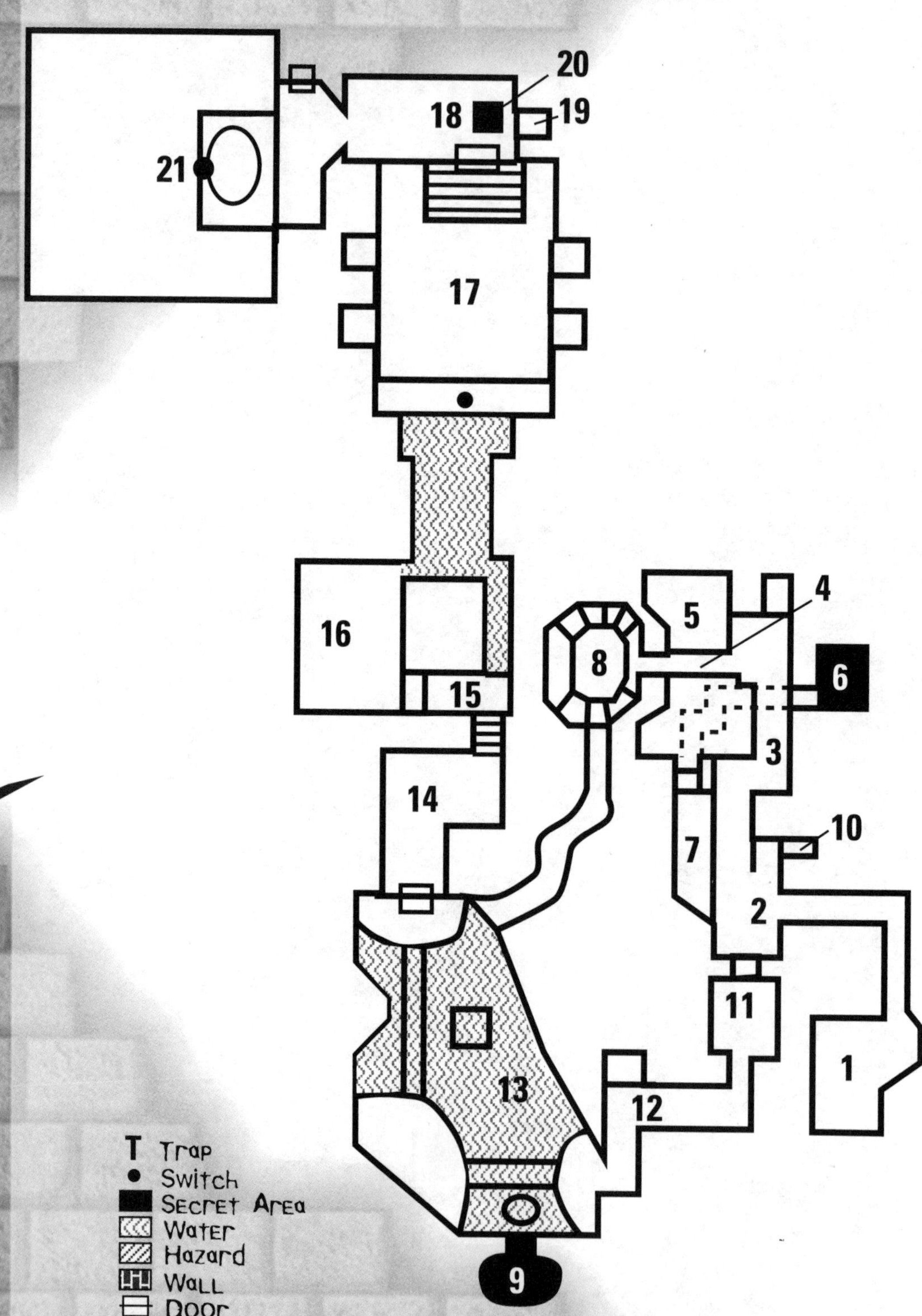
1
2
3
4
5
6
7
8
9
10
11
12
13
14
15
16
17
18
19
20
21
T Trap
Switch
Secret Area
Water
Hazard
Wall
Door

Mission 3: Necropolis

The Necropolis mission definitely turns things up a notch in Quakedom. Four Fiends and a Shambler are waiting for the final showdown at the end of the level; a real test of how far you've come toward mastering the game's controls.

Still, plenty of supplies lie about—even a Ring of Shadows in a particularly sneaky Secret Area. Practice your strafing—and running in a blind panic—then step knee-deep into the dead.

Mission 3: Necropolis At-a-Glance (E1M3)

1. Health, Shotgun Shells
2. Grenade Launcher, Health, Grenades
3. Double-barreled Shotgun
4. Bridge Ambush
5. Shotgun Shells, Health, Flechettes
6. **Secret Area.** Health, Grenades
7. Green Armor
8. Grenades, Health as you traverse the tunnel, Gold Key
9. **Secret Area.** Ring of Shadows
10. Health
11. Nailgun
12. Flechettes, Grenades
13. Health, Grenades, Shotgun Shells, Flechettes
14. Gold Door, Shotgun Shells, Flechettes, Health
15. Ramrod Trap
16. Health, Grenades, Shotgun Shells
17. Health, Grenades, Flechettes, Shotgun Shells
18. Health
19. Yellow Armor, Shotgun Shells
20. **Secret Area.** Grenades
21. Health, Shotgun Shells, Mission Exit

Highlights:

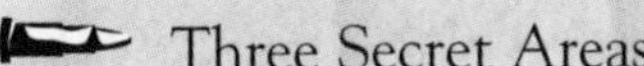

- Three Secret Areas
- The Ring of Shadows
- Fiends and Shamblers Aplenty

Death Comes to Town

1. You arrive in a small room, empty except for Health boxes and some Shotgun Shells. Rest assured that stepping into the outer area breaks off the calm in a big way.

2. Grab the Grenade Launcher and flip a few at the local Zombie populace. If you round the corner, an Ogre—who has an excellent vantage point—besets you. If you approach the Ogre, a pair of Fiends leap from either side of the area, at which point you should back-pedal frantically while dispensing death. With the Fiends foiled, you can run right up to the caged Ogre, and your proximity will motivate him to switch to a woefully ineffective chainsaw attack mode. Pick up more Health and a box of Grenades nearby.

3. When the coast is clear, peak downstairs and provoke the Ogre. He'll chase you, and can be easily slain from the other side of the stair rail. Grab the Double-barreled Shotgun, but be quick. When you venture into that room, an Ogre tosses Grenades at you from an opening in the wall, above and to the left as you claim the weapon. You won't be able to see him in that dark niche, and when you run forward for a better angle, you usually attract the attention of a Scrag in the adjoining room. Usually you have enough time to whack the Scrag before the Ogre above finds the range, though you may want to retreat momentarily to catch your breath if the big brute starts Grenading you mercilessly. When the Ogre above dies, a door opens on a small antechamber below his niche, and another Ogre gets in a few licks.

4. As you approach the small bridge, watch for that Scrag if you haven't dispatched him already, and be mindful of the Ogre in the niche behind you and to your left as you traverse the span. If you need to, run into the round room ahead and stock up before dealing with the Ogre. Sometimes he even aids your cause with his Grenade-tossing efforts. Afterwards, Grenade the Zombies and jump off the bridge to the area below.

5. Beneath the bridge, you'll discover Shotgun Shells, Health, and Flechettes. If you haven't managed to already, shoot the wall behind the nails. It slides to reveal a Secret Area.

6. **Secret Area.** A juicy box of Health and some Grenades await you.

7. If you ride the lift up, you'll access the area behind the bars from which the Ogre attacked earlier. When you step on the switch therein, the cage opens.

8. In the circular room with the two staircases, ride the lift down and dismember the Zombies. You'll find Grenades near the lift, and Health as you traverse the tunnel. When the tunnel empties into the water, you'll spy the Gold Key on a small island nearby. Prepare for a Zombie ambush when you pocket the prize.

9. **Secret Area.** If you exit the tunnel and swim directly up to the Gold Key, after you pick it up you'll stand facing a wall between two huge stone block supports. If you walk near that wall—specifically near the darkened center—you'll drop into a sinkhole leading to a Secret Area. Swim up into the small cavern where you'll find a Ring of Shadows.

10. If you hurry back to the area near the previously caged Ogre, you can use the Ring of Shadows to aid your assault on a newly arrived Ogre thereabouts. You'll also see that a small alcove has opened up near where the Fiends leapt from earlier. Inside you'll find more Health.

11. Once through the door, grab the Nailgun and shoot the switch. The floor drops away before the ceiling can crush you, and you enter another small tunnel.

12. Pick up the Flechettes and watch your back as you near the other end of the tunnel. A wall drops and some Zombies hurl themselves in your direction; inside their small room you'll discover more Grenades.

13. Peek into the large room and get the attention of the Scrags, then back into the tunnel to deal death. When you approach the nearby landing, a Shambler attacks from your left—again, strafing from the tunnel is quite effective. Another Shambler ports in after the first succumbs to your assault, but after that there's only one more pair of sneaky ceiling Scrags between you and Health, Grenades, Shotgun Shells, and Flechettes.

14. Pass through the Gold Door, dispose of the Ogre and the Scrag that rush from around the corner to the right, and gather ammo for the Shotgun and Nailgun, as well as a box of Health.

15. Down the short flight of stairs, stick to the left wall or a large ramrod will hammer you. Once the trap is sprung, leap (or fall) into the water below.

16. Clear the watery passage of Zombies and bear to your left, up the ramp. An Ogre and more Zombies wait in the room above—as well as plenty of Health, Grenades, and Shotgun Shells.

17. The two parallel waterways lead to another, wider ramp, where another Ogre presides. Deal with him. You encounter two more saw-dragging freaks on a ledge behind you as you enter the room from the ramp. Run to the area in front of the door—careful not to go so far that the door opens—and the Ogre' Grenades will fall harmlessly at your feet while you nail them to the wall. You'll find Health boxes next to the stairs, and if you hop up the steps, you can reach the Ogres' overhang. You'll find Grenades there, and a switch that unseals nearby alcoves with Zombies and other more interesting items, like Flechettes, Shotgun Shells, and Health.

18. Ogres begin to pummel you from platforms above as you enter this room, trying to distract you from the Fiend that'll come running to join the battle. Retreat to the previous room to deal with the Fiend, then return to hammer the overhead enemies. Health waits down the hall, and your foes' death opens the nearby barrier.

19. In addition to the Yellow Armor and Shotgun ammo, you can shoot the rear wall of the alcove to reveal a Teleporter to the platforms above.

20. **Secret Area.** Claim the Grenades off the platform and drop back to the ground below.

21. When you push the switch in this room, it seems as if the ceiling will come down and crush you, but never fear. At the last minute, the ceiling parts, and a lift carries you to this mission's final battle zone.

Upstairs, a pair of Fiends await you, and another ports in shortly. Before you get the Fiends attention, walk along the far edge of the platform until it returns to the bottom of the pit. You'll find that the overzealous Fiends are quite prone to critical missteps. If you stand on the very edge of the pit, across from the Fiends, they'll leap at you. Even if they connect, there's nothing beneath them when they land, and down they go. Each time you finish off one of the original Fiends, another arrives to continue the battle. When the four Fiends expire, a Shambler shows up to make matters worse. You can play cat and mouse with him around one of the large pillars, or go for the Telefrag when he jumps in. If you fall into the hole in the floor, you can perhaps restock and use the newly revealed Teleporter to return to the fray. When anyone else takes the plunge, be a pal, and point out to them the tactical disadvantages of fighting from the bottom of a well. When it's all over, claim the Health and Shotgun Shells, back track for any goodies you might have left behind, then exit the mission through the huge doors.

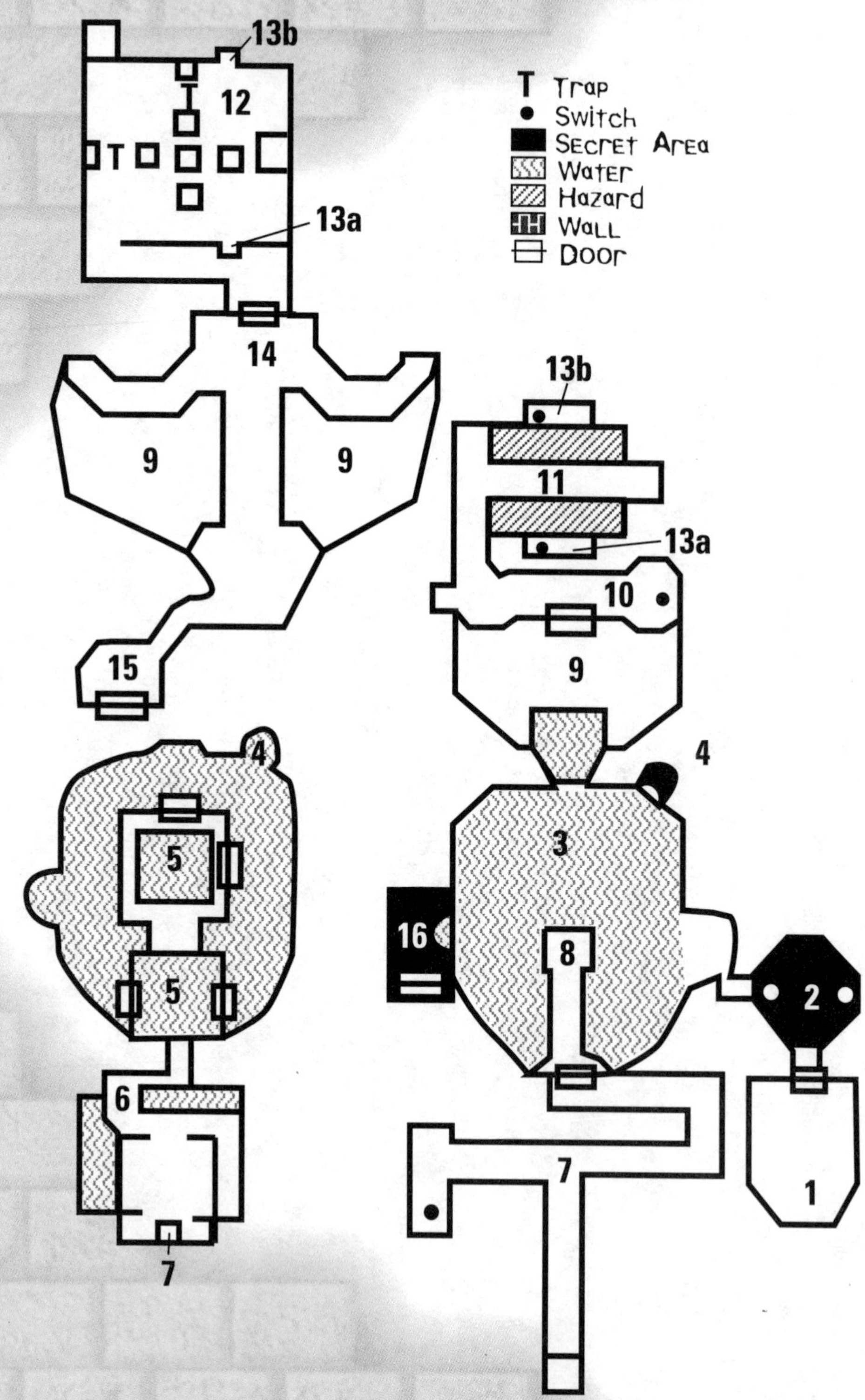
T Trap
Switch
Secret Area
Water
Hazard
Wall
Door
12
13b
T
13a
14
9
9
15
13b
11
13a
10
9
4
4
3
5
5
16
8
2
6
7
7
1
7

Mission 4: The Grisly Grotto

We didn't actually find any grottos in this mission, though we did endure a lot of grisly combat action. The mission starts off innocently enough as you wind your way to a stagnant pond—but it's all downhill (and underwater) from there.

Your mission path is quite linear—that is, once you know the lay of the Grotto. Essentially, you dive into the drink, explore some sunken houses, battle your way to the Silver Key, and endure a gauntlet of fire en route to the castle gates of Gloom Keep (i.e., Mission 5). If you follow this swim-through, and dog-paddle quickly from place to place, you shouldn't need a Biosuit.

As a bonus, this is the mission where you gain access to the "Secret Mission: Ziggurat Vertigo." It's surprisingly easy to find the entrance to this Secret Mission. Stick with us, and we'll take you there.

Mission 4: The Grisly Grotto At-a-Glance (E1M4)

1. Health, Shotgun Shells
2. **Secret Area.** Two Switches, Yellow Armor, Flechette, Shotgun Shells
3. Flechette, Health, Biosuit (can see Silver Key at 8)
4. **Secret Area.** Rockets
5. Health, Supernailgun, Flechette
6. Health, Shotgun Shells, Flechette; Flechette (underwater)
7. Flechettes, Health, Star Switch, Shotgun Shells
8. Silver Key, Health, Shotgun Shells
9. Flechettes, Shotgun Shells, Health
10. Shotgun Shells, Health, Flechette (en route to 11)
11. Shotgun Shells, Health
12. Nailgun Trap (and access to 13a and b); Shotgun Shells

13a. Rockets, First Switch to Open Secret Area 16

13b. Health, Flechette, Second Switch to Open Secret Area 16

14. Flechette (en route), Shotgun Shells, Health
15. Shotgun shells. Exit to "Mission 5: Gloom Keep."
16. **Secret Area.** Exit to "Secret Mission: Ziggurat Vertigo"; Health, Grenade Launcher

Highlights:

- Access to Secret Mission: Ziggurat Vertigo
- Three Beguiling Secret Areas
- Deep-Pond Diving for Fun, Profit, and the Supernailgun

You'd Best Grab a Snorkel, 'Cause We're Going Down!

1. As soon as you grab an item, or move toward the cellar doors, they open. Watch for Scrags—killing the first one makes another teleport in. Stop at the edge of the platform, and get ready to dodge some Ogre-thrown grenades.

2. **Secret Area.** We're not sure why this counts as a secret, but it does. Shoot both red switches (above you to the right and left). The large wooden platform supporting a suit of Yellow Armor drops to the ground, taking the Ogres with it. The platform might even crush a Knight if you're lucky. Let the Ogres fight each other for as long as you can stand it, then use your height advantage to its fullest. Heh, heh. We suggest you take the time to actually walk down the stairs. Doing so means you won't take any damage from a fall. Slip through the archway.

3. The Silver Key is so close, and yet so far. Nail the Scrags before you dive in—they have a nasty tendency to follow you. The liquid isn't toxic but there aren't any lifeguards on duty, just Ogres and Scrags. Where's the cast of Baywatch when you need them? Now, strap on the Biosuit, 'cause you're going down.

4. **Secret Area.** From the mossy beach where you enter 3, drop straight down and look right. Watch out for the swimming Scrag. When you get just about even with the top of doorway of the sunken house, look toward the surface on your right. You should see two dimly lit circles of light in the far wall. The Secret Area is the smaller one on the right. Swim up and in for Grenades.

5. Drop to the ledge below the Secret Area, then swim through either of the two closest doorways of the sunken house. Surface, get on the ledge for Health, and smoke the Ogre who guards the gleaming Supernailgun. Use your newest toy to ventilate the Ogre in the chamber in front of you. Dance over the Ogre's carcass and keep going down the passage.

6. As you emerge into a big open area, watch for a Knight attack. Beware also of an Ogre attack from the left. Dive into the water to the right of the walkway to score a box of Flechettes. Back on the walkway, go around the left side of the arched entrance for a Health box and Shotgun Shells.

See the suspicious pool of water just inside the archway? An Ogre leaps from the water as soon as you approach, chainsaw swinging. Why not lob a trio of Grenades in the pool from a distance for head-turning results? Creep forward, Grenade Launcher to the ready. A pair of Knights are hiding in the inside corners next to the lift. You should be able to see the tips of their bloody swords. Let 'em have it then step onto the lift. Turn 180 degrees as you ascend!

7. Slay the dark Knights then blast the Ogre as you haul down the T-shaped walkway. Go into the Ogre pen and press the Star switch. Tag the Knight/Scrag team that materializes when you pressed the switch, then dash toward the now-open door on the right side of the 'T.' Battle your way past the melancholy Ogre en route to the blood-soaked pentagram door.

8. At last, the blessed Silver Key—and an ugly crew of Scrags complete with an Ogre sidekick. Slay your way to the key and leap off the end of the dock. Watch for another pair of Scrags! Swim for the large patch of light dead ahead.

9. Slog out of the water and prepare to nail some Fiends. By far, the best way to survive this encounter is to pop up until you hear the Fiend's roar, then slip back down beneath the waves and backpedal into 3. The Fiend will follow you down the ramp and stop there. Only his leaping and cavorting about make him hard to down. Repeat once more to complete the sequence. If you look above you, you'll see a bridge (it leads to the last area of the mission). When you go to grab ammo or Health, the enemies above may see you. don't try to fight their from here. Step up to the Silver Key door and watch out for any sneaky Knight and Ogre attacks when you open it!

10. Turn right and step onto the floor-mounted switch. You've just opened a tiny alcove behind you containing Yellow Armor (you have to jump up and in to get it). Something nasty must be coming up...

11. As you descend the stairs, watch for an Ogre and Scrags. When you step onto the lighted circle in the middle of the bridge which spans the blue-green acid, you trigger an Ogre attack from above and both sides. Run forward toward the Health box and the lift. Turn 180 degrees as you ascend, your best Knight-killing tool shouldered and cocked.

12. Slide sideways off the lift while you slay the horde of Knights that runs to greet you. Since the Ogres below can't hurt you from this platform, take a moment to look around while they hurt each other. Note the wall-mounted Nailguns and the Quake squares on the floor. A trap? Most definitely—and more. Each square triggers both wall guns to fire. If you run across them the nails should just miss you. Step on all five of the Quake squares to open small holes in the walls that lead into areas 13a and b. Note that the wall-mounted guns will fire anytime you step on a square. That feature makes this room a way-cool Deathmatch venue.

When the doors to 13a and b are down, lob grenades onto the Ogres' heads to soothe their anxieties. Then drop into either one of the smoking holes.

13a. Press the squiggly wall plate, save your game, then jump out of the niche and (hopefully) onto the walkway below. Go back up to 12 and worm your way into the other smoking hole.

13b. Press the squiggly plate to get this message: "A Secret Cave has Opened… " Leap down to the walkway.

Now you have a choice: You can go back the way you came to find the exit toward the Secret Mission (and a handy Grenade Launcher), or you can exit directly to "Mission 5: Gloom Keep." For grins, let's go to the Mission 5 exit first. (If you want to go right to the Secret Mission exit, skip ahead to 16.)

Go back up to 12. When you approach the back wall and the staircase leading to 14, a Fiend bursts out of a hidden alcove to attack you from behind.

14. Creep up the stairs at the far-left corner of 12. Watch for Knights! Go through the door, take out the many errant Knights and a trio of Ogres. When the coast is clear scour the ledge for supplies. Cross the bridge and climb the stairs to find the exit to "Mission 5: Gloom Keep."

As soon as you step off the bridge, an Ogre attacks from the top of the stairs and a pair of Scrags take pot shots at your back. The best way to survive is to nail the Scrags as you retreat across the bridge toward the castle. The Ogre will venture onto the bridge, and if you stand on either ledge he's easy pickin's as he runs towards you.

A Knight and another Ogre wait impatiently for your presence atop the steps. Repeat the process and the Grizzly Grotto is yours to keep.

15. Exit to "Mission 5: Gloom Keep."

16. **Secret Area.** To get to the "Secret Mission: Ziggurat Vertigo," retrace your steps to 9. (If you're at 15, simply step off the walkway in 14. You'll take a little damage from the fall if you hit the ground; none of you hit the water.) Go under the water, turn right, and swim. You should see a semicircle of light near the surface on the right, past the large post. This is the secret cave you opened from the two-switch sequence in 13a and 13b.

Swim to the right around the post and head straight for the center of the light. When you reach the back wall, start going up. Yes! Don't forget to grab the Grenade Launcher. You'll need it where you're going.

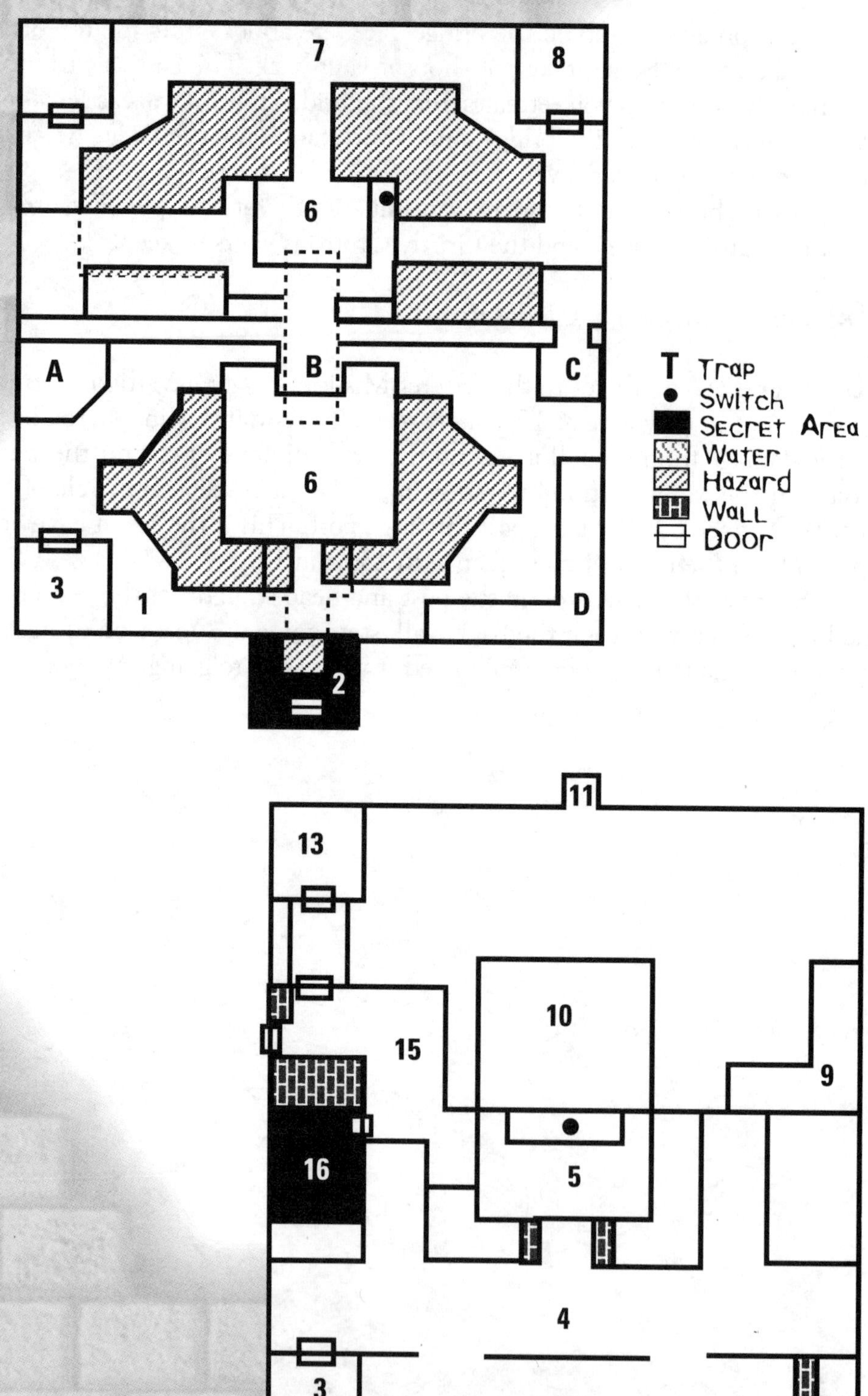
7
8
6
A
B
C
6
3
1
D
2
T Trap
Switch
Secret Area
Water
Hazard
Wall
Door
11
13
10
15
9
16
5
4
3

Secret Mission: Ziggurat Vertigo

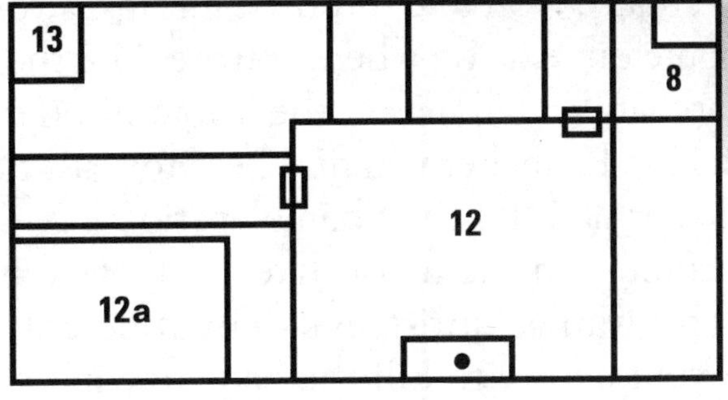

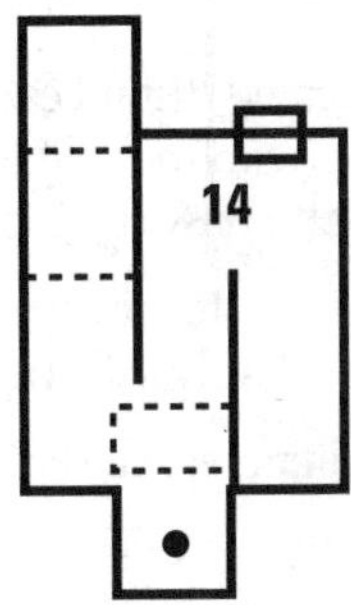

Secret Mission: Ziggurat Vertigo At-a-Glance (E1M8)

1. Health, Pentagram of Protection, Yellow Armor, Shotgun Shells; Lift (3)
   A. Shotgun Shells, Flechette, Health
   B. Flechette
   C. Health
   D. Rockets, Shotgun Shells, Health
2. **Secret Area.** Quad Damage rune, Health, Teleport Back to 1
3. Lift
4. Rocket Launcher, Health, Flechettes
5. Rockets, Yellow Armor, Flechette, Megahealth, Switch (Opens Access to 6)
6. Switch to Open Lift in 7 and Gate between 1 and 7, Rockets; Health, Shotgun Shells
7. Lift, Shotgun Shells, Health, Rockets
8. Lift
9. Flechette, Rockets, Pentagram of Protection
10. Flechette
11. Megahealth
12. Health, Switch to Open 13

12a. Shotgun Shells, Health

13. Yellow Armor, Flechettes (En Route to 14)
14. Silver Key, Flechettes, Health
15. Health, Exit
16. **Secret Area.** Flechettes

This mission consists of two major areas and one major trick—a total disregard for gravity. Both major areas are virtually identical—virtual mirror opposites, actually. Don't be surprised if it takes you a few playthroughs to figure out exactly where you are. Use the pyramid for your main landmark, and you'll master the layout in no time. We suggest you rely on the Rocket Launcher you find here to toast the Ogres, and by extension save your nails for the Shambler trio.

Mastering combat in the moon-like (lack of) gravity is another thing, however. This warped anti-gravity environment offers a few quirks that affect your ability to kill the bad guys and navigate the terrain. Briefly, they are:

- All ordnance travels increased distances—in all directions. In this environment, Grenades in particular have an incredible range. But unlike Quake's Shareware version, grenades now have the nasy habit of bouncing back into your face. You'll see.
- Being under an explosion will send you flying. If you haven't experienced a Rocket Jump yet, you probably will here.
- Ground surfaces are not slippery: All sliding, strafing, and running tactics apply here.
- When airborne, you can (sort of) control your direction and velocity. Practice with the directional keys (and your mouse) makes perfect.
- When on the offensive, get out the Rocket Launcher and pretend you're an attack helicopter. Leap up between structures, unleash your ordnance, and float back down. Repeat until all is quiet.
- You won't bounce off walls like a Superball. When trying to reach a platform, aim for a corner and use the walls to stop your flight.
- Practically speaking, lifts only work in one direction—up.
- You will never take damage from any fall—unless you land in lava.

Highlights:

- Two Secret Areas
- Swim in Lava—and Live!
- Lay Your Grubby Hands on the Fearsome Rocket Launcher
- Three Shamblers vs. One Pentagram of Protection

One Small Step for Man, One Giant Leap for PC Gaming

1. Before you run, you must jump. Whoooaa! Back up a tad as you fall, but don't fall into the lava! And don't grab the Pentagram of Protection—yet!

Once your feet are firmly on the ground, from the starting point look up to your right for two lurking Ogres. Nail them into action. If you hit the left one, he drops down—becoming an excellent candidate for Grenade fodder.

You can jump to each platform. Go to them as you need supplies. Beginning at the platform in the far left corner from the start point (we'll call it Platform A), you'll find:

A. Shotgun Shells, a Flechette, and a Health box

B. A Flechette (behind the Pyramid)

C. Health boxes (jump to Platform D from here)

D. Rockets

2. **Secret Area.** Grab the Pentagram of Protection, literally look at your feet, then gently slip off either ledge of the walkway into the lava! You should start sinking almost immediately. Swim away from the Pyramid. Look up toward the surface, and you'll see a large rectangle of red light above you. Swim for it! As you pop out into this Secret Area, you fly right into a Quad Damage rune! Dash through the Teleporter and run to the lift.

3. Enter the lift, turn around, and prepare to blast Ogres as soon as you step off.

4. Clear a path down the hall to the right. Go into the second alcove on your left to score a Rocket Launcher. Helicopter up and try it out. If you sustain too much damage from your own Rocket attacks, we suggest you switch to the Supernailgun, at least until the action settles down here. The cage in front of the lift is a Secret Area 17.

Leap up to rooftop below the Quake switch platform. This is area 5.

To soften up the Ogres in room 16, drop a cluster of Grenades through the bars in the floor to the left of the Quake switch platform (as you face the switch). You should see a Health box below. Shoot your Grenades through the door past the Health box. It's Secret Area 17 and a Flechette cache is below you to the left.

5. If you did some serious Helicopter attacks, this area should offer nothing but Ogre chunks and supplies for you to pick over. Scurry up either narrow ramp to the Megahealth and Quake switch. When you hit this switch, the bars that block the hallway through the Pyramid slide away.

Step off any ledge and soft-shoe back to where the Pentagram of Protection was floating. Go into the Pyramid and prepare for an Ogre sneak attack.

6. Smoke the Ogre in the distance before you descend the short flight of stairs into this area. From the top of the stairs point your weapon of choice to the bottom left to counter an Ogre attack. Then look above the ledge on the right. You should see a Quake switch—but you probably won't see the Ogre greeting party! Uh-oh. When you hit this switch, you not only unlock the doorway below Platform C, you take down the barrier between you and the lift in 7 and get attacked from the walkway opposite the Quake switch. Once the Ogre's gone, meander down this walkway opposite the switch for Health boxes and Shotgun ammo—but be careful not to let the Shamblers in 10, 12 and 12a see you!

7. This room is the mirror-opposite of room 1. As you enter, note the lift on your right; it takes you to 8. (We won't need the left lift in this walk-through.) You can't get into the alcove next to the crucified ghoul from here, though you can quite easily from 10. Go left around the lava for an otherwise unseen box of Rockets. Stay close to the center building so the Shamblers (especially the one in 10) won't see you!

The high ledge across from the lift is 9. You can rocket the Ogre protecting it to bits from where you stand, or you can take him out from 8. The choice is yours.

Note the now-opened hall between the two large rooms on the floor below the Ogre platform (9). Go into the lift opposite this new tunnel, turn around as you ascend, and get ready to rumble.

8. Take out the bad guy(s) in front of you. If the Ogres on 9 aren't dead yet, kill them from here. While you're at it, kill the Ogres to your right, both below and across from you. But regardless of what you do, stand close to the central structure and do not let the Shamblers see you. In other words, do not jump up! Coming even with Shambler's ledge (10, 12, and 12a in the walk-through) alerts them to your presence. You're not ready for them. Yet. Return to the front of the lift and step off the ledge to land softly on 9.

9. Quickly: Grab the Pentagram; waste the Shambler in 10; leap down to the lift and helicopter up, Supernailgun raging. Try to land on the ledge above the lift (in the corner). While the Pentagram lasts, you've got a fighting chance against the remaining Shamblers—and since you're pinned into a corner, the Shambler on 12 can't bat you around like a cat toy (and no lesser beasties will flank you and possibly knock you off a ledge, wasting precious Pentagram time). Moreover, you'll be standing on a pair of Health boxes.

Keep up the pressure. Once you've nailed the Shambler in 12, you've got one more Shambler to go! Leap onto 12 and wax his buddy on 12a. Because you're so much higher than he is, he'll have trouble hitting you with his lightning attack. Use that knowledge to his disadvantage.

Once your Pentagram runs out, and if a Shambler still shambles, drop back down to 9 en route to 10.

10. From here not only can't the Shambler(s) above you hurt you, but you can easily make a slow running leap into the alcove next to the crucified ghoul for Megahealth, area 11.

11. Once you've got that all-over glow, drop down to the ground and go back up the lift to 8 and polish off the remaining Shamblers (if necessary).

12. Pressing the Quake switch to gives you access to 14, the Silver Key room. It also releases an Ogre from a hidden platform outside the Silver Key room—that is, if you didn't already kill him back at 8. From the switch, float to the large platform immediately to the lower right (12a).

12a. From here, launch yourself toward 13 and the Yellow Armor.

13. From this platform, you should see the Silver Key door. If only you had the Silver Key… Simply face the door and drop off the ledge; turn left and face the open door (the switch at 12 opened it); drop onto the ledge (note the Flechettes behind you), and go through the door, prepped for an Ogre encounter.

14. Turn right and behold the blue steps. Duck into an alcove behind the stairs for a pair of Health boxes, if you need them. The Silver Key hangs before you in the room atop the blue steps.

Get out your Supernailgun, creep up the steps and wax the Ogre at the top of the stairs, down the right hallway. After he's dead, simply walk backward over the Silver Key. A trio of Scrags appears out of nowhere and would have given you a bad time had your back been to them. Once you've ripped them to bite-sized bits, go down the hall to the end of the walkway. Turn right and you should see the Sliver Key door. It's an easy leap from here to there. Go for it. If you miss, the lift will happily take you back up to the ledge.

15. As soon as you open the door, watch out for an Ogre attack! To your right is the Slipgate exit—but don't go there yet! Instead, get out your wimpy Axe and prance down the left hallway. At the end of the hall, turn to the right, smack the off-colored rectangle of wall, and voila! A Secret Area. If you lobbed a load of Grenades through the grating at 5, there's a good chance that this door may already be open.

16. **Secret Area.** Go in and collect your Flechettes. Now get out of here. Gloom Keep requests your presence.

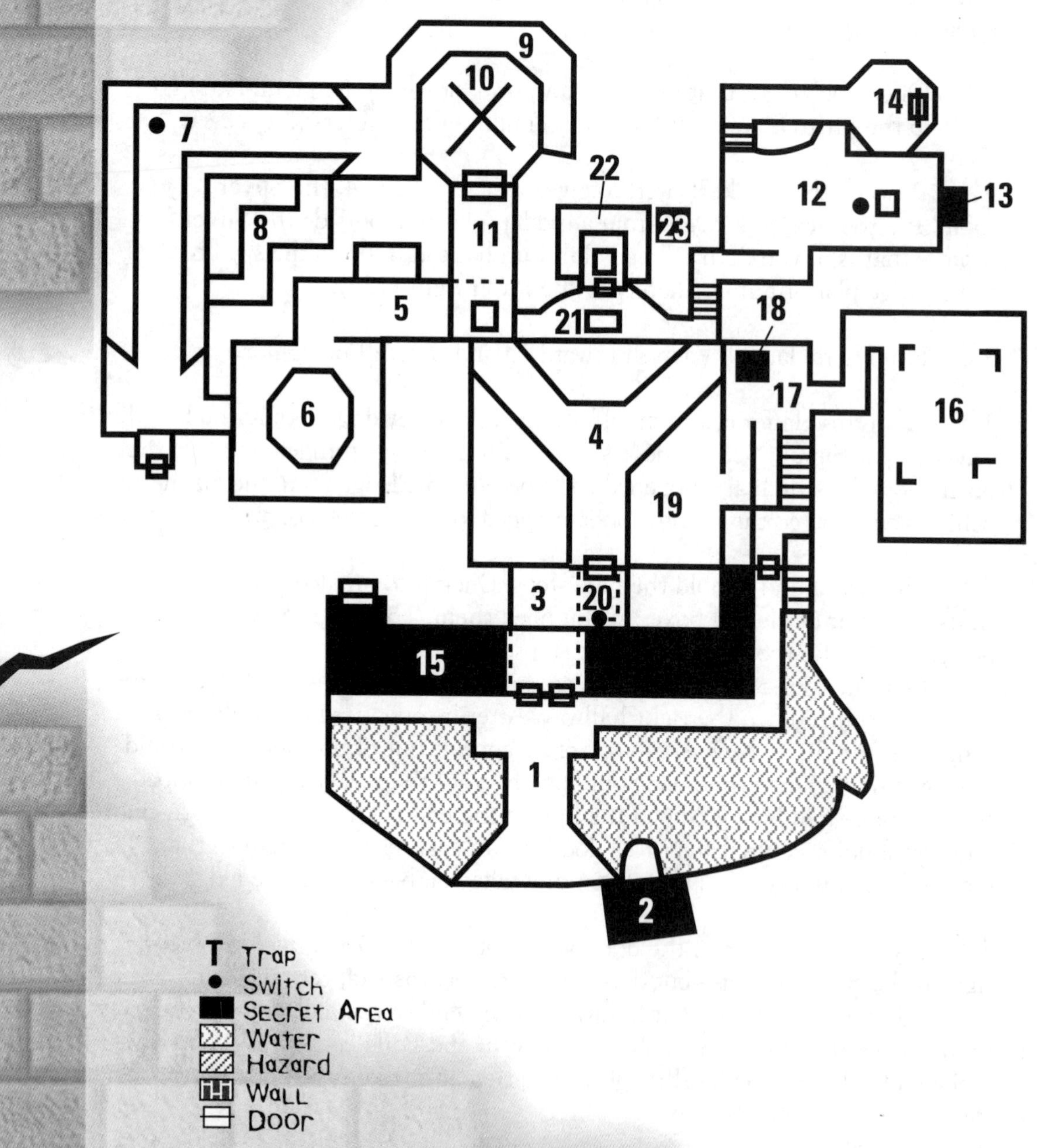
9
10
7
22
8
11
23
12
13
14
5
21
18
6
4
17
16
19
3
20
15
1
2
T Trap
Switch
Secret Area
Water
Hazard
Wall
Door

Mission 5: Gloom Keep

Gloom Keep is a creepy place, indeed, sprawling and homicidal. Underscoring the circular nature of the mission, you actually acquire two keys before you need to use them.

The combat really picks up here, especially with the difficulty mode at the Hard setting. At Nightmare skill level, things get downright nightmarish. Be conservative with that ammo, even though your enemies will be dispensing it liberally, and be sure to take the Quad Damage rune when you go to get the Gold Key.

At present, you should have all the weapons but the Thunderbolt. With the tricks at your disposal, there's no reason you shouldn't own the Keep.

Mission 5: Gloom Keep At-a-Glance (E1M5)

1. Health, Shotgun Shells
2. **Secret Area.** Flechettes, Megahealth
3. Shotgun Shells, Health, Traps
4. Rocket Launcher, Grenades, Shotgun Shells, Health
5. Shotgun Shells, Trap
6. Trap, Health
7. Health
8. Shotgun Shells, Health, Flechettes
9. Grenades, Flechettes, Health
10. Silver Key
11. Health
12. Health, Flechettes, Supernailgun
13. **Secret Area.** Yellow Armor
14. Grenades
15. **Secret Area.** Quad Damage
16. Gold Key, Health, Flechettes, Shotgun Shells
17. Health, Shotgun Shells, Grenades
18. **Secret Area.** Yellow Armor, Shotgun Shells
19. Silver Key Door, Health, Shotgun Shells, Flechettes
20. Switch
21. Gold Key Door, Shotgun Shells, Health
22. Health, Exit Slipgate
23. **Secret Area.** Green Armor

Highlights:

- Five Secret Areas
- Shambler vs. Quad Damage
- Plenty of Fiends

Playing for Keeps

1. Utilize the Health boxes beside you as the mission begins, and charge boldly through the doors of the Keep. There's two Knights waiting inside the door, but it behooves you to take a little damage from them at close quarters. As you cross the drawbridge toward the front door of the castle, a flock of Scrags teleports into the outside area. Best to strafe them, and a third curious Knight, from the relative safety of the front hallway. There are Shotgun Shells in the outside area, and another Knight on the outer walkway requiring death before you visit the nearby Secret Area.

2. **Secret Area.** Standing as you were when the mission began, jump to the right, into the water, and look below for an opening you can swim through and up. Inside the small chamber wait Flechettes and Megahealth. Swim around the side of the castle to the right to find a stairway back to land. When you come out of the water, it's possible the nearby door will open to emit another Knight. Dispose of him, but enter the castle through the front door.

3. Things should be relatively quiet if you disposed of the Knights in the front hallway earlier. There's another box of Shotgun ammo nearby, as well as Health. As you traverse the hallway, avoid the illuminated floor patches, and you'll also avoid having your hair parted by the traps above you.

4. As you approach the large room, slay the first Knight you spy and some of his friends may come running to investigate. If they do, lie in wait in the hall to take care of business. With your back to the hallway looking into the room, an Ogre will be above you on the ledge. Ignore him until the last of the Knights crumples, and he may even aid your cause. Next, run down the walkway to the left, dispatching the Ogre that comes from that direction. Afterward, the Rocket Launcher is yours for the taking, as are

Grenades, Shotgun Shells and more Health. If you look beneath you, you'll see a couple of Fiends and perhaps a Knight milling around, and it's highly advisable to punish them from this vantage point. A cautionary note, however: Your new toy does a little too much blast-radius damage to fire it at the floor below you. Go with the Grenade Launcher, then follow the walkway leading left.

5. Lob a few more Grenades down the hall to soften up the Ogre, then go and claim the Shotgun Shells, taking care not to get head-spiked in the process.

6. Hang back and wait for the Knights before entering this room, or you'll have to contend with a shower of nails from the central hub at the same time. Two large boxes of Health wait on the other side of the trap, and if you go and stand in the corner near them, you can usually draw Scrags and a Knight from the adjoining room right into the path of the nail-spitter. The trap deactivates when you exit through either doorway.

7. If the Scrags never showed up, you'll have to peek into this room, as nails whiz past you from behind, and slay them from there. You'll find Health boxes nearby. Run past the first ramrod, stand on the floor switch, and turn to see a small hallway opening in the wall behind you. Jump through.

8. From the hall, you can turn and dispatch the Fiends with impunity, and without using any of your more valuable ammo. In the area beneath the walkway you'll find a box of Shotgun Shells, and, in the small hallway itself, more Health. If you bother to use the Teleporter, you'll find it only goes to the ramp above, and a nail trap whacks you in the head in the bargain. Instead, take the lift at the far end of the small hall. You'll find more Knights, more Health, Shotgun Shells, and a box of Flechettes.

9. Ascend the stairs, looking quickly above you to snuff a Scrag, then dropping a Knight near a box of Grenades. Lob a few through the doorway to dispose of the Ogre, en route to more Flechettes and Health. Step on the floor switch to open the door.

10. Slay the Knight and claim the Silver Key, then hop through the hole in the floor, ready for an Ogre ambush.

11. Run straight forward when you hit the ground, and you can avoid the Ogre's initial backside attack. You'll find Health in the room where he was hiding. Now explore the other side of the walkway in this familiar large room.

12. Whip out the heavy weapons and dismember a Knight and three Ogres. Nearby lie plenty of Health, and Flechettes to go with that shiny new Supernailgun. When you grab the big gun, pause to acquire the secreted stash of Yellow Armor.

13. **Secret Area.** From the spot where you took the Supernailgun, hop up and bonk your head on the overhead torch fixture. The wall behind the column opens to reveal a small room with Yellow Armor and a switch that unseals the room should the door close behind you.

14. Climb the stairs and perforate the Knights and their Scrag buddy. A niche with an Ogre opens behind you as you reach the top of the stairs, but you can stand in this room and only a lucky bounce will allow one of his Grenades to reach you. Take a box of Grenades and inspect the Teleporter as part of your victory celebration. If you enter the Teleporter through the front, you travel directly to the Gold Key room. If you walk around and go in from the back side, you get to take a side trip to a Secret Area.

15. **Secret Area.** As you materialize on the roof of the castle, a Fiend bears down on your left shoulder. You'll also have to contend with a pair of teleporting Scrags and then a Knight as you traverse the walkway, but the payoff is big: Around the corner waits a Quad Damage rune, which you can activate before returning to the Teleporter and heading for the Gold Key.

16. When you grab the Gold Key, the walls drop and a serious ambush ensues. If you acquired the Quad Damage previously, and ready the Supernailgun, you can pretty much laugh it off, though you must be quick and accurate to hammer the Shambler, Ogre and Fiends into submission. You might even sprint into the adjoining rooms while you're still in Quad mode so that none of that impressive power goes to waste. Along with the Gold Key, this room and the adjoining hallway boast plenty of Health, Flechettes and Shotgun Shells.

17. In the room next door, expect serious resistance from Ogres and Knights, and maybe even the Fiends from room 19, if you didn't hammer them from above earlier. There's a goodly supply of Health boxes about, as well as Shotgun Shells and Grenades. There's also a Secret Area in plain sight.

18. **Secret Area.** To reach the Ogre's sniper nest, hop onto the handrail, then across to the other wall. Use the torch as a stepping-stone if you need to, but a good half-step and jump will make it. From there, run and leap to the small platform from the very end of the wall, and defend yourself against the arriving pair of Scrags while acquiring a new suit of Yellow Armor and some Shotgun Shells.

19. If the two Fiends never showed up, and you neglected to kill them earlier, then they're waiting in the Silver Key room. Otherwise, the coast is clear, and you can safely gather Health, Shotgun Shells, and Flechettes.

20. Push the switch on the other side of the Silver Key door, and a lift arrives behind you. Ride up.

21. Near the Gold Key door you'll find Shotgun Shells and Health—and most likely the body of the Ogre you slew from ground level earlier. Beyond the Gold Key door lies a hole in the floor, and you should lob down a few Grenades unless you want to be at the mercy of the Ogres waiting below. When the coast is clear, jump down.

22. You land near a Health box, the exit Slipgate, and a couple of lukewarm Ogre bodies. And, of course, the mission's last Secret Area.

23. **Secret Area.** Shoot the wall opposite the Slipgate and it slides away to reveal a suit of Green Armor and a Teleporter back to the front of the Silver Key door. Return to the Slipgate and take the plunge.

7
6
4
3
5
8
1
9
2
15
12
10
12
13
16
17
14
11
T Trap
Switch
Secret Area
Water
Hazard
Wall
Door

Mission 6: The Door to Chthon

After hammering your way through the winding halls of Gloom Keep, this compact mission is a welcome relief. With more bells and whistles than a New Year's Eve party, "The Door to Chthon" features a multilevel combat situation replete with falling floors, moats of lava, a crushing wall, Zombie commandos, four cleverly placed Secret Areas, Slipgates a-plenty, and a pair of surprisingly easy-to-nail Shamblers. The circularity of the mission, in addition to the plethora of nooks, shadows, and Slipgates, makes this slayground an excellent choice for smaller Deathmatch encounter groups.

Mission 6: The Door to Chthon At-a-Glance (E1M6)

1. Health, Rockets, Shotgun Shells
2. Flechette, Health
3. Health, Rocket Launcher, Switch to Secret Area 4; Switch to Access 6
4. **Secret Area.** Quad Damage Rune
5. Yellow Armor, Quake Switch; Megahealth, Flechette (accessed from 8)
6. Rockets, Health; Silver Key, Flechette, Shotgun Shells, Slipgate to 2
7. Megahealth, Slipgate to Secret Area 8; Lift to 6
8. **Secret Area.** Supernailgun, Flechette
9. Health
10. Rockets, Health, Flechettes, Quake Switch, Secret Area Switch, Slipgate to 1
11. **Secret Area.** Rockets
12. **Secret Area.** Megahealth
13. Health, Floor Switch to Access Gold Key
14. Gold Key
15. Quake Switch, Shotgun Shells
16. Health, Flechette, Floor Switch
17. Yellow Armor, Mission Exit

Highlights:

 Four Fabulous Secret Areas

 Spiked-Wall Crushing

 (Yet More) Shambler Surprise Attacks

Knock-Knock-Knocking on Chthon's Door

1. From the start, the Gold Key and the Gold Key door (the exit) taunt you. Grab the goods, then look over the ledge into 2. A pair of Ogres wait for a dance. Remember what we said about using high places to your advantage?

2. Try as you might, you can't quite make the jump over the lava to the Gold Key. Looks like you'll have to explore the entire mission. (At least you know where it ends). Don't go into the dark passage beneath the starting point—at least, not yet. This passage lights up the moment you grab the Silver Key. Stand on the pentagram floor switch. The far corridor lights up. (That's 3.) Get out your Supernailgun and watch for an Ogre attack from the left and from dead ahead. (Note: The Supernailgun and ammo above the left-attacking Ogre is Secret Area 8.)

3. The Ogre who frontally attacked you lurks next to the switch. Take him out and claim your prizes. Look up at the far, far wall opposite the Quake switch; you should see a blood-red Quake symbol. Shoot it and a panel in the wall to your right opens, revealing a lift. Hop on and ride up.

4. **Secret Area.** Look over the ledge and to the left. That protruding lip of a ledge is the Secret Area. Drop onto it to collect your Quad Damage rune. Get out your Rocket Launcher; step off the ledge into 3; hit the big wall-mounted Quake button; turn right, and dash down the hall into 5.

5. Grabbing the Yellow Armor doesn't trigger a trap; pressing the Quake switch does. Three things happen:

- A bank of panels to your left (with your back to the switch) drops, triggering an Ogre attack.
- A section of floor before you falls away.
- The door you came in through seals back up—locking you in.

While the Quad Damage is raging through your veins, blast the Ogres, drop through the hole, and take out three more Ogres in 6. Note: You'll be able to get the Megahealth and Flechette on the Ogres' ledge in 5 from Secret Area 8.

6. Use your trusty Rocket Launcher to chunkify the Ogres. There's one on each ledge. You can't jump across the lava to the Ogres' ledge from here. That Silver Key remains a dream—for now. We'll pick it up from 7. Note that the blocked-off Slipgate on the left ledge takes you back to 2. (The bars drop once you grab the Silver Key.)

Go down the steps, get out your Supernailgun, and prepare for yet another trap—and a nifty Secret Area.

7. As soon as you step into the bloody hall two major events occur:

- The moving wall-spikes are forever set in motion.
- Three Ogres burst out, grenades flying—two behind you and one in front of the Megahealth.

Turn right. Murder the Ogre and run past the barred lift to snag the Megahealth at the end of the hall. Shoot the Ogres between you and the lift—only when the Ogres are dead will the bars blocking the lift open. Ride the lift to the Ogres' ledge at 6. Go through the Slipgate (to 2), or leap down to the stairs. Either way, get back to the entrance of the bloody hall. Wait for the spiked wall to go past (moving to the right). Turn left and run through the Secret Slipgate.

8. **Secret Area.** Grab your swag. Then try out your new Supernailgun and ammo on some hapless Scrags. From this ledge you can jump into the closest opening in the alcove on the right for yet another Megahealth boost and some nails. This dark area may not be an official Secret Area, but as you might imagine it's a great Deathmatch power-up and hidey-hole.

Go back to 2 and face the now-lit passage beneath the start area.

9. A double-jump is usually enough to get you over the pit. If you fall in, wall-mounted Nailguns will perforate you until you get to the Slipgate (in another Nailgun pit behind you). The Gate takes you back to 2.

As you hit the ledge past the pit, a wall in front of you drops and an angry Ogre comes out swinging. As a bonus, two more bad young cannibals and a Fiend attack your left flank from 10 if you get too close to the doors.

10. To painlessly murder the Fiend, open the doors and flee into the Nailgun pit. Where you go he follows. He probably won't come through the Teleporter which means he's shotgun fodder from the pit's edge. Take out any dancing Ogres, then hop back into 10 to down the remaining Ogre(s) and claim your goods.

When you hit the pulsating Quake switch three things happen:

- A bridge spans the lava to the red-paneled door.
- A glowing red switch appears on the pillar opposite the aforementioned door. (As you face this button, the Slipgate at the top of the stairs will be to your left.)
- A pack of Zombie commandos falls from compartments hidden in the ceiling. A group awaits you in each section of 10.

We suggest you hit the switch and immediately run to the relative safety of 9 to rocket attack your undead friends.

Once the Zombies are dead, pull out your trusty Single-barreled Shotgun and shoot the secret red switch mentioned above. When you shoot the button, the stairs leading to the Slipgate to your left invert. Hurry down them.

11. **Secret Area.** Grab the box of Rockets, turn around, and wait for the staircase to reassemble above you. When it does, a Slipgate appears. Go on in for the fourth—and final—fabulous secret of this mission.

12. **Secret Area.** You're on a ledge overlooking 10. Megahealth waits on the opposite ledge. Jump across to score big-time. Drop down to 10 and cross the bridge over the lava into 13.

13. Get out your most trusted Fiend-killer and open the red-symbol doors. He leaps out claws first the moment you open the door. Once you've put him down, pass through the doors and step on the floor switch. Look through the bars: A very helpful plank emerges from the Gold Key platform. Do you hear the gurgling chainsaw? It's an Ogre in 2 (and more), just waiting for you. Go back to 1 via the Slipgate in 10. This allows you to take out the Ogre safely from above.

14. Whip out your Supernailgun and walk the plank for the Gold Key. As you snatch it, a Shambler appears in 2 to give you some hell. Go ahead and get close—you're out of paw-range at the end of the plank, but too close to allow him to unload a lightning attack, especially when your Supernailgun roars. Even so, you'll take some damage during this encounter, but the Megahealth should keep you alive.

You know where the Gold Key door is. Prepare for a surprise attack and let's go.

15. As predicted, a gang of Ogres leaps out at you from behind the Gold Key door. Backpedal with Rockets bursting in air. Run to the lift up to 1 to get completely out of harm's way. Once inside, the Quake switch opens the opposite wall. Only one monster trap to go. But make no mistake—it's a big one.

16. Grab Health and ammo as needed. Get out your Supernailgun and save your game. Step on the floor switch when you're ready.

17. The floor switch opens the door in front of you. As the passage lights half way, you'll see a suit of Yellow Armor. When the passage lights completely, a Shambler bursts out of the exit hole toward you, fangs first.

Fire as you run to grab the armor. Remember: Shamblers and Nailguns mix very well. Get snuggly close and send him to hell. He may smell bad, but when you're this close he can't unleash his deadly lightning attack—especially when you're doing the death dance in this oddly-shaped tunnel. That location seems to prevent him from fully bringing his arms up, thus dampening his ability to heave lightning. Even if you run out of Nails before you kill him, a few up-close-and-personal shotgun blasts should put him down for good. Shambler killin' don't get no easier than this.

Now that you've entered Chthon's door, go through the gate to visit his cheery house. You've earned it.

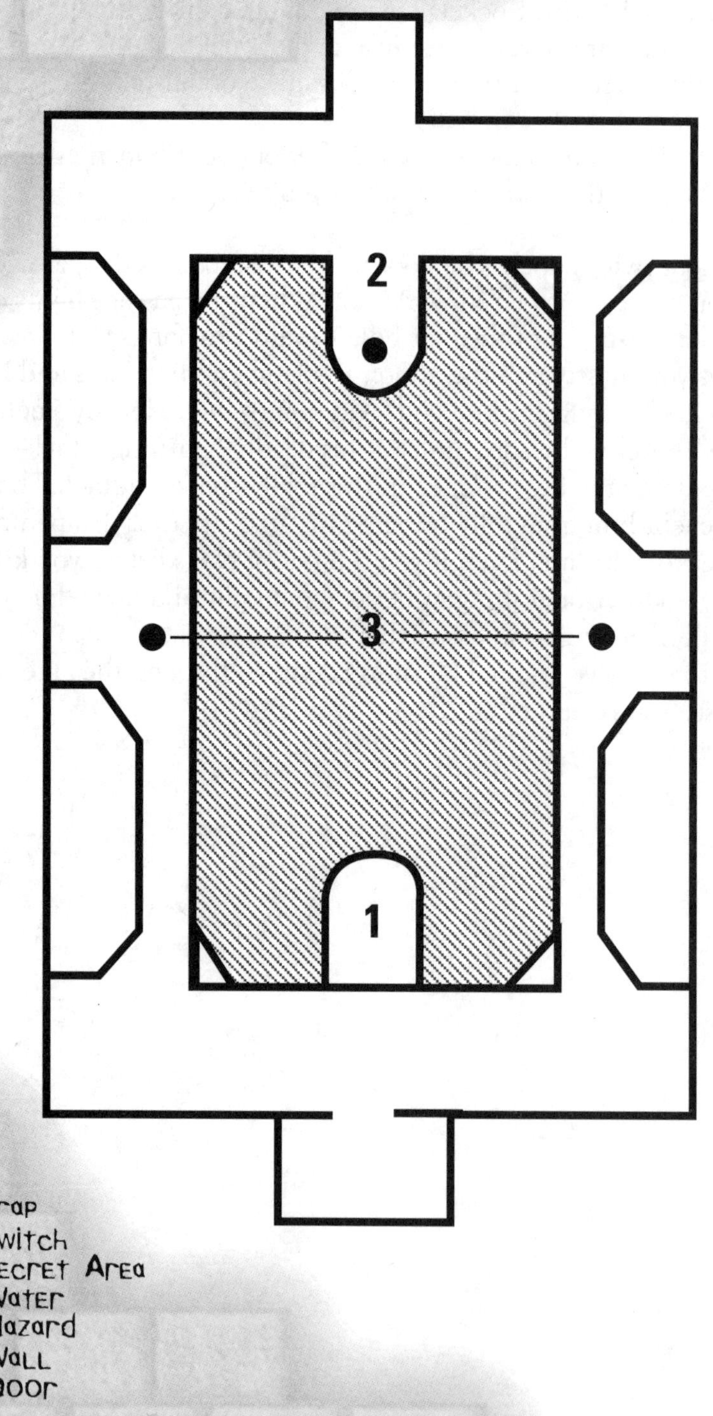
2
3
1
T Trap
Switch
Secret Area
Water
Hazard
Wall
Door

Mission 7: House of Chthon

One last battle to go, and we're sorry to say it's a little anticlimactic. The final Boss comes with a king-sized Achilles' heel to match his bad attitude. Save that Megahealth pack in case you really need it, but taking care of business seldom has been so easy.

Mission 7: House of Chthon At-a-Glance (E1M7)

1. Rune Key
2. Arc Switch
3. Prong Switches (2)

Highlights:

- Major Monster Barbecue

Burnin' Down the House

Prepare for the end-of-the-episode Boss Monster when you grab the Rune Key, which you can see as the mission gets underway. He'll rise out of the lava, and he'll be in a foul mood. Hurling ammo at the big freak does little to help his disposition—or, for that matter, to dampen his resolve. Luckily, you've got serious firepower you didn't even have to bring with you.

Run around to the far end of the room and ride the lift up. Upstairs, you'll see a floor switch as you exit the lift. Before it can do you any good, however, you must run a complete loop around the upper tier and step on two more floor switches you find along the sides of the room.

Once you've stepped on those switches, two huge prongs extend from the ceiling to either side of the monstrous demon. Next, stepping on the switch near the top of the lift sends a huge jolt of electricity between the prongs—arcing through the center of the bad guy.

The prongs reset after every burst, so you have to keep running around and stomping the switches to deliver jolts of juice. Three tends to be the magic number, though it may take four or more shots at the higher difficulty levels. As the monster dies, he sometimes gets off a tremendous parting shot, so prepare to sidestep or your moment of glory will be short-lived, indeed.

When the beast collapses in defeat, a walkway bridges the lava, and you can drop down a tunnel to the episode's final Slipgate.

Episode 2

The Realm of Black Magic

The second Episode of *Quake* cranks up the game a notch from the shareware levels, and that's a good thing.

Most of the bad guys are here in abundance, though you won't see a Vore until the final room of the last mission. Don't worry. If it's any consolation, Episodes 3 and 4 more than make up for the lack of spikeball-throwers.

While we're quibbling, it's also a little disappointing not to lay hands on the Thunderbolt any sooner than you do—mission 5. At least there's a Shambler nearby. You'll be itching to give one of those big freaks a taste of its own medicine by then.

Minor points of contention aside, the missions here work very well as a collective Episode, increasing the pace of the game in a nice even manner, while still humbling you once in a while with some major monster ambushes. Hey, a little blind panic is good for the soul, we always say.

By now, you should have a feel for some of the finer points of the game… when it's prudent to take on supplies (only when you're truly in need), when to save your work (only when you've done a decent job), etc. As Episode 2 gets underway, you'll also need to be more mindful of using the rarer power-ups for achieving some vital strategic goals. Don't worry: That's what we're here for.

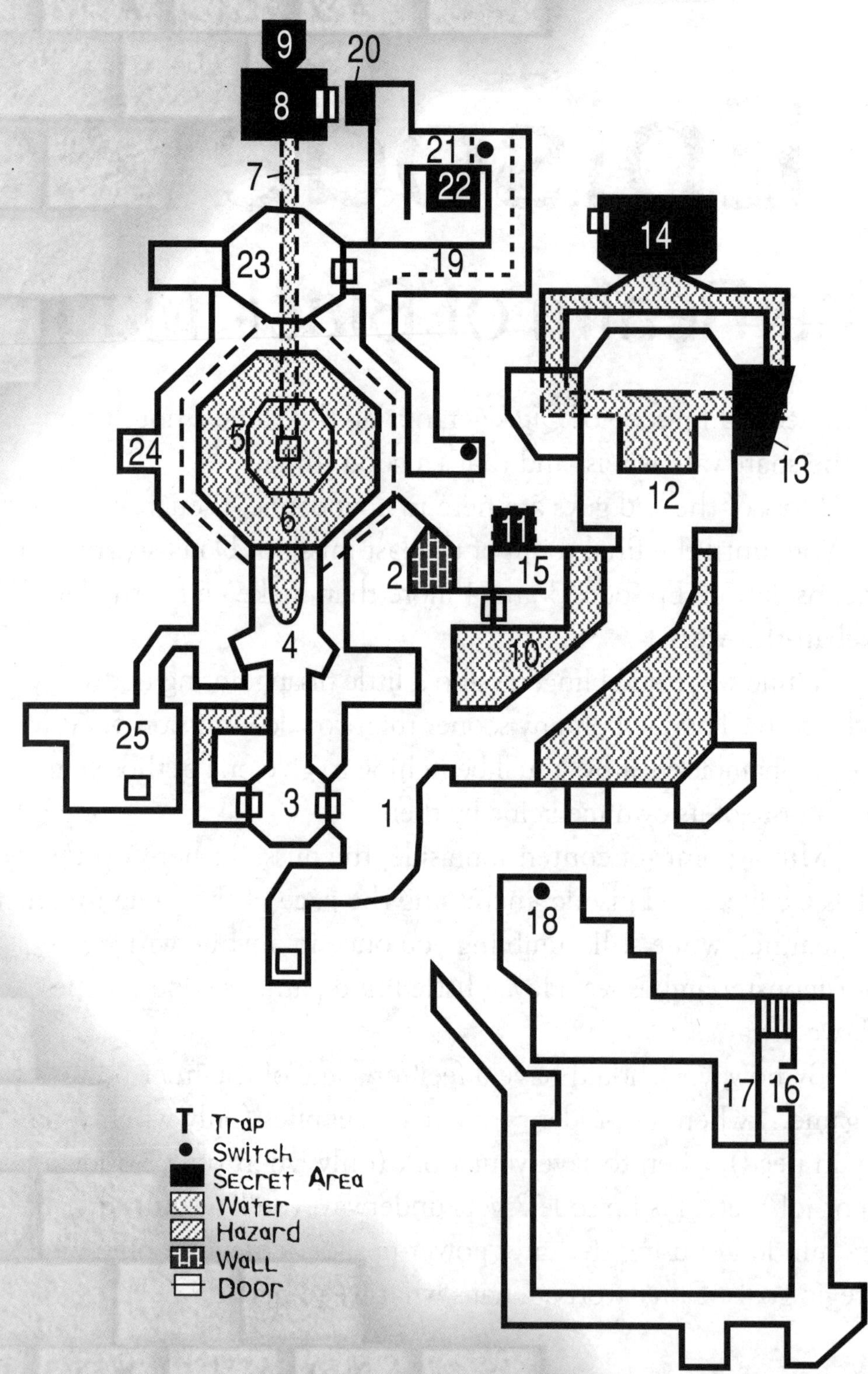

9
8
20
21
22
7
14
23
19
24
5
13
12
6
11
2
15
10
4
25
3
1
18
17
16
T Trap
Switch
Secret Area
Water
Hazard
Wall
Door

Mission 1: The Installation

The first mission of Episode 2 eases you into a new realm, as you might expect. The Installation is crawling with Enforcers, however, so be cautious venturing into large open areas—there's usually cross fire just ahead.

Mission 1: The Installation At-a-Glance (E2M1)

1. Shotgun Shells, Health
2. Health, Gold Door
3. Silver Keycard
4. Shotgun Shells
5. Megahealth
6. Underwater Gazebo, Switch
7. Biosuit, Switch
8. **Secret Area.** Flechettes, Health, Shotgun Shells, Grenades, Grenade Launcher
9. **Secret Area.** Pentagram of Protection
10. Shotgun Shells, Health, Green Armor, Flechettes
11. **Secret Area.** Red Armor
12. Flechettes, Health, Gold Keycard
13. **Secret Area.** Megahealth
14. **Secret Area.** Health, Shotgun Shells
15. Nailgun, Flechettes, Health
16. Flechettes, Shotgun Shells
17. Green Armor
18. Health
19. Switch
20. **Secret Area.** Shotgun Shells, Quad Damage rune
21. Health, Shotgun Shells
22. **Secret Area.** Yellow Armor
23. Double-barreled Shotgun
24. Health, Shotgun Shells, Flechettes
25. Health, Flechettes, Slipgate

Highlights:

- Seven Secret Areas
- Pentagram of Protection
- Red Armor

Ease of Installation

1. Slay the Grunts and their puppy, and gather Shotgun Shells and a box of Health. The large portal is sealed for the present. Stick to the left wall as you enter the next area.

2. Buttonhook around the corner to your left, hugging the wall. Bars extend across the entry behind you, preventing a hasty retreat, so take up a position on the left wall or the Enforcers across the way will make short work of you. At that point, the bars preventing your exit will slide aside, and you can beat feet to a better battle vantage point.

3. The large portal is now unsealed. Slay the Enforcer beyond, and gain the Silver Keycard. Before venturing through the other sealed door, explore the large rooms containing pools of water.

4. Pick up the box of Shotgun Shells. If you move to the right, past the partition, you can slay the crowd that was picking on you in room 2.

5. Hug the right wall and circle the room to the far end, where a box of Megahealth awaits you. From here, you can dispose of the Enforcer and Grunt sniping at you from the ledge above.

6. Dive down and spy the switch at the bottom of the underwater gazebo. Shoot it, and sink into a hallway.

7. Traverse the hall as quickly as possible, picking up a much-needed Biosuit as you begin to take on water. Once you've suited up, return to the area where you originally sank down and blast the grate-like switch on the wall. You may have to shoot it several times with the ordinary Shotgun. Now double back and ascend the angled hallway to visit two Secret Areas.

8. **Secret Area.** The first secret room of Episode 2 is worth the trouble. Inside, claim Flechettes, a box of Health, Shotgun Shells, and Grenades. The Grenade Launcher is also present. The Teleporter drops you back into the room where you acquired the Silver Keycard.

9. **Secret Area.** Shooting the switch in the underwater tunnel opens this small room containing a Pentagram of Protection. Grab it and go.

10. Run across the walkway between the two bodies of water and grab the box of Shotgun Shells. You'll find Health and Green Armor on nearby ledges, and a box of Flechettes partially submerged in one corner. If you jump into the smaller body of water, on your left as you enter the room, you'll sink to discover a small room with a significant Flechette stash.

11. **Secret Area.** Facing the entrance to the underwater room contains Flechettes, look to your right and up, and you'll see a small area where you can surface. That room holds a shiny new suit of Red Armor.

12. Hug the left wall as you enter this area's foyer, and it's relatively easy to draw out the Enforcers and Grunt. They also have a Rottweiler with them, though the pup may lag. In the room proper, you'll find more Flechettes, a box of Health, and the Gold Keycard. Be ready for an Enforcer ambush from behind when you claim the precious metal.

13. **Secret Area.** After acquiring the Gold Keycard, investigate the alcove where the light flickers. You'll notice something approximating a stairway to the right of the alcove, and if you climb to the ledge you can pass through the wall for Megahealth.

14. **Secret Area.** If you jump down into the small pool of water in front of the sniper's room, you'll find two hallways leading to the same small room. Inside, you'll find boxes of Health and Shotgun Shells, and a Teleporter that returns you to the foyer outside the Gold Keycard room.

15. Access the Gold Door and claim the Nailgun, then ride the lift to the room's upper tier. After you clean out the snipers' perch to the right, gathering Flechettes, circle the walkway around the room. As you near the far side, Enforcers arrive via Teleport. Hammer the bad guy in front of you, then turn and shoot out into the large room without enduring nasty cross fire. Another Enforcer lurks below, and there's plenty of Health nearby to see you through the battle.

16. Shoot the large box resting just inside the doorway, and you won't even have to meet the Grunt hiding in this small room. Inside find Flechettes and Shotgun Shells; exploring herein opens the barrier at the top of the stairway outside.

17. Upstairs, drop the Enforcer and strap on the Green Armor.

18. Indulge in a Health box or two and catch the lift downstairs.

19. Hammer the Enforcers waiting in the hall, and clear the area beyond of Grunts and Rottweilers. Throwing the switch provides access to a lift guarded by more bad doggies and an Enforcer; and also leads to a Secret Area.

20. **Secret Area.** Cross the lift, without elevating it, and acquire the Shotgun Shells. If you shoot the wall in that small alcove, it slides to reveal a room with a Quad Damage rune.

21. Up the lift, slay the Grunt and the Enforcer, and collect boxes of Health and Shotgun Shells. Before proceeding, check the framework on your right—just as you start descending the stairs—for an opening large enough to fit through. You have to hop up to reach it.

22. **Secret Area.** Inside the framework, drop down and acquire that tantalizing Yellow Armor.

23. Through the Silver Door, grab the Double-barreled Shotgun and ride the lift down.

24. Plenty of Enforcers and a Rottweiler greet you when the lift descends; luckily, you'll find two large boxes of Health nearby. Ahead, collect the Shotgun Shells and Flechettes, and clean the corpses you created shortly after the mission began.

25. An Enforcer goon squad guards the room with the exit Slipgate, and you can check behind the boxes on your right for Health and Flechettes before you take the final plunge.

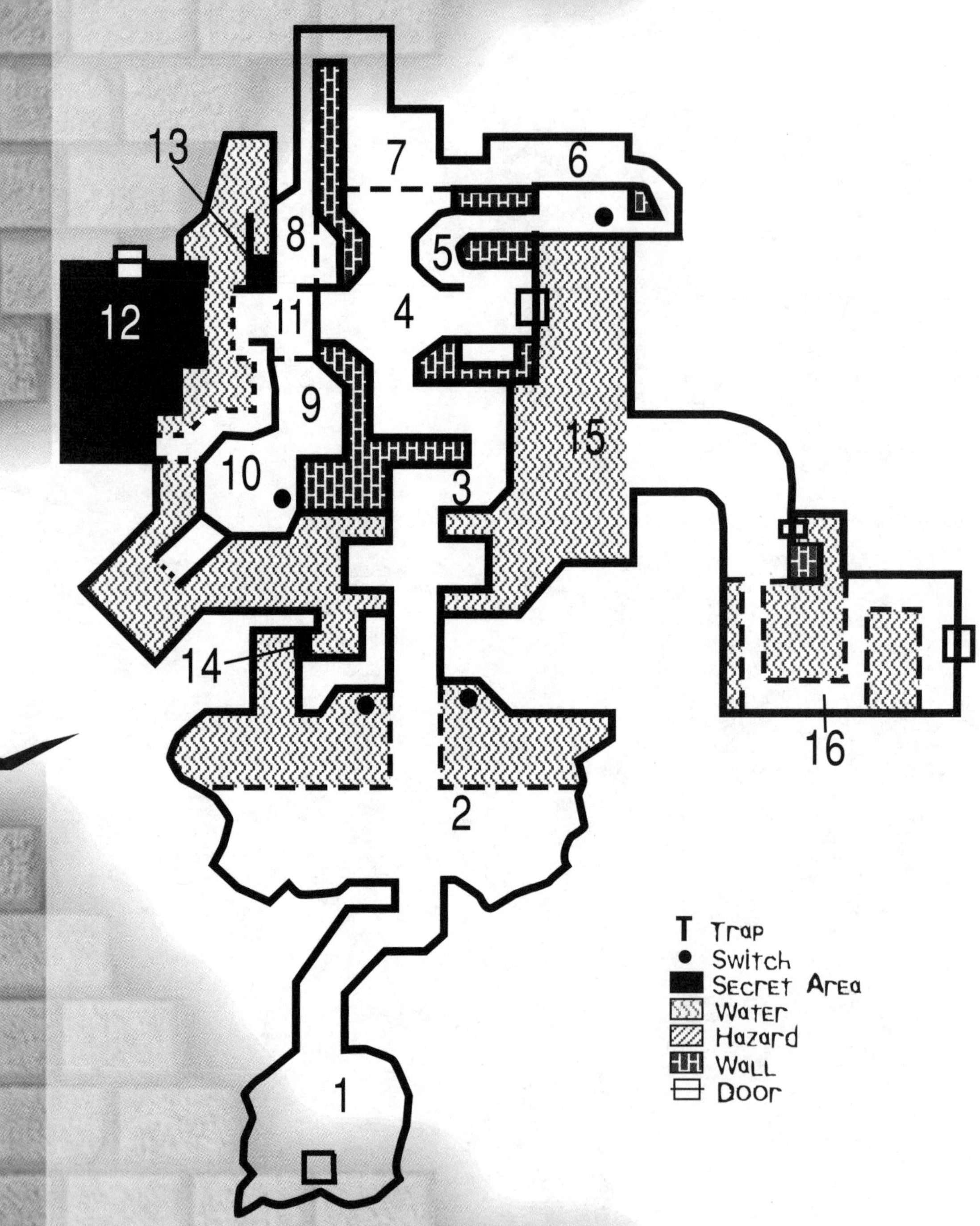

1
2
3
4
5
6
7
8
9
10
11
12
13
14
15
16
T Trap
Switch
Secret Area
Water
Hazard
Wall
Door

Mission 2: The Ogre Citadel

As Episode 2 gathers steam, the scum-filled Citadel of the Ogres requires a good housecleaning. Watch your step near the edge of the waterways, and be sure to put that Quad Damage rune to the best possible use—namely, disposing of the Shambler guarding the Gold Key.

Mission 2: The Ogre Citadel At-a-Glance (E2M2)

1. Shotgun Shells, Health
2. Shotgun Shells, Green Armor
3. Grenades, Shotgun Shells, Double-barreled Shotgun, Health
4. Health, Shotgun Shells, Gold Door
5. Ogre Trap
6. Shotgun Shells, Floor Switch
7. Nailgun, Quad Damage Rune
8. Health, Flechettes
9. Switch, Health, Shotgun Shells
10. Health, Flechettes
11. Yellow Armor
12. **Secret Area.** Megahealth
13. **Secret Area.** Grenade Launcher
14. **Secret Area.** Megahealth
15. Shotgun Shells, Health
16. Mission End

Highlights:

- Three Secret Areas
- Quad Damage Massacre
- Gratuitous Moat Bombing

Eviction Notice

1. Get the Knight's attention and gather up a box of Health before descending the stairway. To get the Shotgun Shells, you'll have to leap from near the Slipgate to the top of the nearby box.

2. A knot of Knights waits at the bottom of the stairs. Most of them will rush conveniently toward you if you back up. If you enter the courtyard, the passage seals behind you. It won't open again until you shoot the switches on either side of the castle door. In the courtyard, collect Shotgun Shells and Green Armor. Shoot just one switch to open the large door without extending the drawbridge. When the castle door opens, an Ogre and a Fiend confront you, though the Fiend generally winds up in the moat. Pause before entering the castle and lob a few Grenades down on the unfortunates below you.

3. Inside, claim Grenades and Shotgun Shells, and stick to the left wall in the hallway to avoid the nail trap behind you. Thin out the local Knight population and grab the Double-barreled Shotgun. You'll find Health nearby.

4. Slay the Ogre flipping Grenades from the ledge—you can take up a position in one of the alcoves for cover, or rush up beneath him. You'll find a couple of Health boxes nearby, and a load of Shotgun Shells in front of the Gold Door.

5. Just around the first curve in the staircase, an Ogre waits. If you lob a couple of Grenades in his direction before you descend, it's much easier to deal with the second Ogre—which comes screaming out of a small hidden chamber near the Gold Door the moment you set foot on the steps.

6. Traversing the staircase, battle Ogres and Knights, and pick up more Shotgun Shells. At the top, a floor switch raises a platform across the water. You can stop and lob Grenades from the window, much to the dismay of the Fiend below. Perhaps he'll take out some of his aggressions on the neighborhood Ogres...

7. When the walkway terminates on the previously deceased Ogre's ledge, grab the Nailgun and spy a Quad Damage rune. You'll want to put the rune to good use in the rooms just ahead, especially with regard to the Shambler, so keep moving and firing as long as you're empowered. Plenty of Ogres and Knights wait in the hall, and if you enter the Shambler's room, you must shoot the switch behind you on the wall to get out again.

8. In the small system of halls rests Health and a box of Flechettes.

9. Pressing the switch in the small upper room opens the barrier between you and the Gold Key, and trips a trap designed to push you unexpectedly into the Shambler's den. You'll also find boxes of Health and Shotgun Shells nearby.

10. In the Shambler's room there's Health, and more where that came from—plus some Flechettes—in the small Gold Key area.

11. Out the window, blast the Knights and trade shots with the Ogres across the water. If you hop onto the window sill and step out ever so lightly, you'll be standing on a narrow walkway, with Yellow Armor nearby.

12. **Secret Area.** Cross the bridge where you pick up the Yellow Armor, and enter the Ogres' hideout. Inside is Megahealth, and a Teleporter that returns you to the window across the way.

13. **Secret Area.** Jump out the window, over the ledge, and wade through the water to your right. Buttonhook around to the right through the entry, and climb the stairs to receive a Grenade Launcher.

14. **Secret Area.** Jump from the window where you traded shots with the Ogres and circle the castle to the left. Before you pass through the large archway, look to your right and you'll see an opening with a box of Megahealth. Behind it is a lift which lowers you to the moat outside, featuring a lonely Zombie.

15. The Gold Door opens onto the huge steel platform you previously elevated with the floor switch. You can also swim below the platform and it'll lower to water level. Inside the hall, slay the Knight and Ogre and gather Shotgun Shells and Health.

16. Between you and the end of the mission lies a nasty room of Zombies, requiring you to jump along the top of stone pillars while you do battle. Below lurks a Fiend, while an Ogre protects the mission exit. Bomb the first Zombies you see, and leap to their ledge. Two other Zombies will begin to hurl themselves at you, and they should be your next priority. Meanwhile, the Ogre and the Zombies nearest him usually begin to sort out some childhood issues, at which point you can close to attack range and bomb the lot of them into oblivion. Polish off the Fiend below, and you can hop down into the water to locate a lift if you'd like to backtrack without pillar jumping.

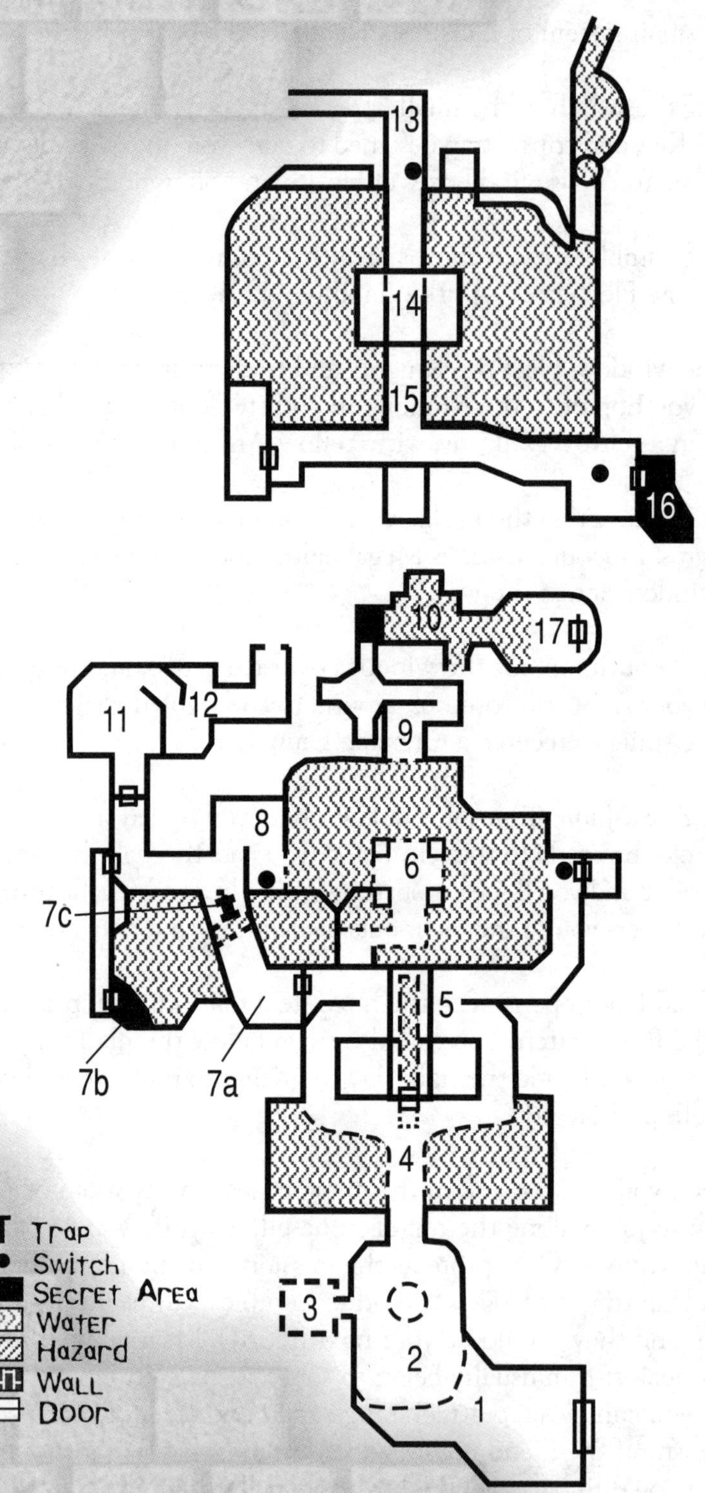
13
14
15
16
10
17
11
12
9
8
6
7c
5
7b
7a
4
3
2
1
T Trap
Switch
Secret Area
Water
Hazard
Wall
Door

Mission 3: The Crypt of Decay

The "Crypt of Decay" mission can be hazardous, as Shamblers and Death Knights now show up with alarming regularity. Fortunately, you'll find plenty of ammo and Health to scoop up, and the entrance to Episode 2's Secret Level waits at the end of the battle.

Mission 3: The Crypt of Decay At-a-Glance (E2M3)

1. Nailgun, Health, Flechettes
2. Health, Shotgun Shells
3. Flechettes
4. Green Armor
5. Shotgun Shells, Health, Switch
6. Shotgun Shells, Nailgun, Switch

7a. Flechettes, Health, Gold Door, Switch

7b. **Secret Area.** Grenades

7c. **Secret Area.** Red Armor

8. Shotgun Shells
9. Spiked Doorway, Shotgun Shells, Grenades, Grenade Launcher, Gold Key
10. **Secret Area.** Megahealth, Yellow Armor
11. Supernailgun
12. Health
13. Nail trap, Switch
14. Health, Grenades, Quad Damage Rune
15. Health, Grenades, Flechettes, Switch
16. **Secret Area.** Flechettes, Megahealth, Switch
17. Teleporter to Secret Level: The Underearth

Highlights:

- Four Secret Areas
- Nail Trap of the Gods
- Secret Level Entrance

Nails in the Coffin

1. Dispose of the Ogre and lay hands on another Nailgun, as well as Flechettes and a Health box. Back onto the lift for the trip upstairs, and be ready to defend yourself.

2. Nail the Death Knight and his Ogre buddy, and gather the Health and Shotgun Shells. Expect more Death Knight trouble when you stick your nose out of room 2, in the direction of the Armor. When you cross that threshold, you may hear a distant door slide. If you hop back down to room 1, you'll see that a portal has indeed opened up.

3. A small room has opened in your absence, revealing two big boxes of Flechettes.

4. In the outer moat area, claim the Green Armor. An underwater entry exists, but unless you clean out some of the bad guys first, you'll dodge Grenades while you tread water. Take the door on the right.

5. Down the stairs, the hallway turns to the left and then back to the right, giving you a good deflection angle for dealing with the lurking Ogre and Death Knight. Two more Ogres wait just ahead, near Shotgun Shells, a box of Health and a switch. Throwing the switch raises a bridge to the central tower outside—and, after a short delay, unleashes a horde of Zombies to claw at your back. Wait for the door to open, opposite the door leading to the tower, and Grenade them to pieces before proceeding.

6. Approaching the tower, expect more Death Knight and Zombie resistance. Claim the Shotgun Shells in the tower and watch for another Death Knight, near where you can see the Nailgun and the switch. Throwing the switch opens the doorway on the other side of the wall, which you can see through the window. Don't bother returning sniper fire in the large tower area.

7a. Through the Pentagram Door, be ready for Ogres and a Death Knight, followed closely by a Fiend. A platform full of Zombies hurl themselves futiley in your direction, though you'll be able to close the gap when you're good and ready. The walkway features Flechettes, several Health boxes, the Gold Door, and a switch that raises more walkways. Once you bomb the Zombies, a narrow hallway opens leading to their ledge.

7b. **Secret Area.** Detonating a Grenade on the Zombie ledge opens a hallway for easy access, netting you a box of Grenades.

7c. **Secret Area.** Explore the water ponds, rife with Rotfish, to find several Health boxes and some Grenades. There's also a small room—through a quite obvious doorway beneath a bridge—containing Red Armor and a Teleporter. The trip leaves you on the ornate pad outside the Pentagram Door.

8. From the area where you press the switch and raise the walkways, race back through the center of the tower and make a left turn, toward the box of Shotgun Shells. If you linger, enemies above will make you pay. Be ready for an Ogre near the box of ammo, and another beyond the spiked doorway.

9. Approach the spiked doorway with caution, ready to back away when the trap trips. Once the spikes extend, press up against them. When they retract, you'll pop unscathed into a room with another Ogre, as well as Shotgun Shells, Grenades, a Grenade Launcher, and the Gold Key. When you grab the Gold Key, Death Knights pour out of the three alcoves to punish you. Upon their demise, shoot the back of the lit alcove to reveal a Secret Area.

10. **Secret Area.** Shooting the back of the alcove slides the wall to reveal a box of Megahealth, most likely just in time. There's also a suit of Yellow Armor under the water, and a sealed entry—more on that later.

11. Through the Gold Door, be ready for the resident Shambler. If you step into the narrow hallway nearby, you'll discover you can strafe him into submission, and his girth prevents him from giving chase. Beyond the door is your prize: the Supernailgun.

12. Upstairs beyond the Gold Door waits a Death Knight, and usually when you dispose of him, the Ogre and Death Knight below take the wind out of each other's proverbial sails. Show the victor how much you appreciate his efforts, and claim the Health boxes nearby.

13. Stick to the right wall and ride the lift up to a nail-filled hallway—unfortunately, they're all flying in your direction. Round the corner and slay the Ogre, hugging the walls as much as possible. The switch on the wall (gasp!) raises the walkway, and if you can endure that nail sound a little longer, the trap actually polishes off a couple of distant Death Knights.

14. The tower itself contains a box of Health, and you should expect an ambush from behind when you finally venture in that direction. Once inside the tower, the nail trap ceases, and you can turn and dispose of the Ogres on the ledges nearby. You can also leap to those ledges, claiming Grenades and a Quad Damage rune.

15. When you venture down the walkway out the other side of the tower, you attract the attention of still more Death Knights, a pair of Shamblers, and some Ogres. If you retreat back through the tower to near the switch that lifted the walkway, your enemies will have an uphill battle just getting close to you, as the nail trap hammers them from one end of the walkway to the other. Any that do actually make it within striking distance are guaranteed to be a shadow of their former selves. In the room opposite the exit door collect Health, Grenades, Flechettes—and then shoot the overhead switch.

16. **Secret Area.** Shooting the overhead switch opens a small passage behind the boxes, leading to a room with Flechettes, Megahealth, and yet another switch. When activated, that switch informs you that an underwater barrier has lowered. If you backtrack to the Secret Area near where you found the Gold Key, you'll see that the barrier beneath the water has indeed lowered.

17. Through the unsealed portal in the Secret Area, behind the panel in the Gold Key room, you'll find the gigantic Teleporter to Episode 2's Secret Level: The Underearth.

Note

From the ledge where you acquire the Quad Damage rune. notice a small catwalk, about six inches wide, running along the face of the cliff. If you follow the narrow path, you'll discover a hallway full of Health, and a pool you can jump into. Welcome to the Well of Wishes! Below… Naw, we don't want to spoil it. Look to the left of the room's billboard, and you'll find an alternate avenue to the Episode's Secret Mission entrance, room 17.

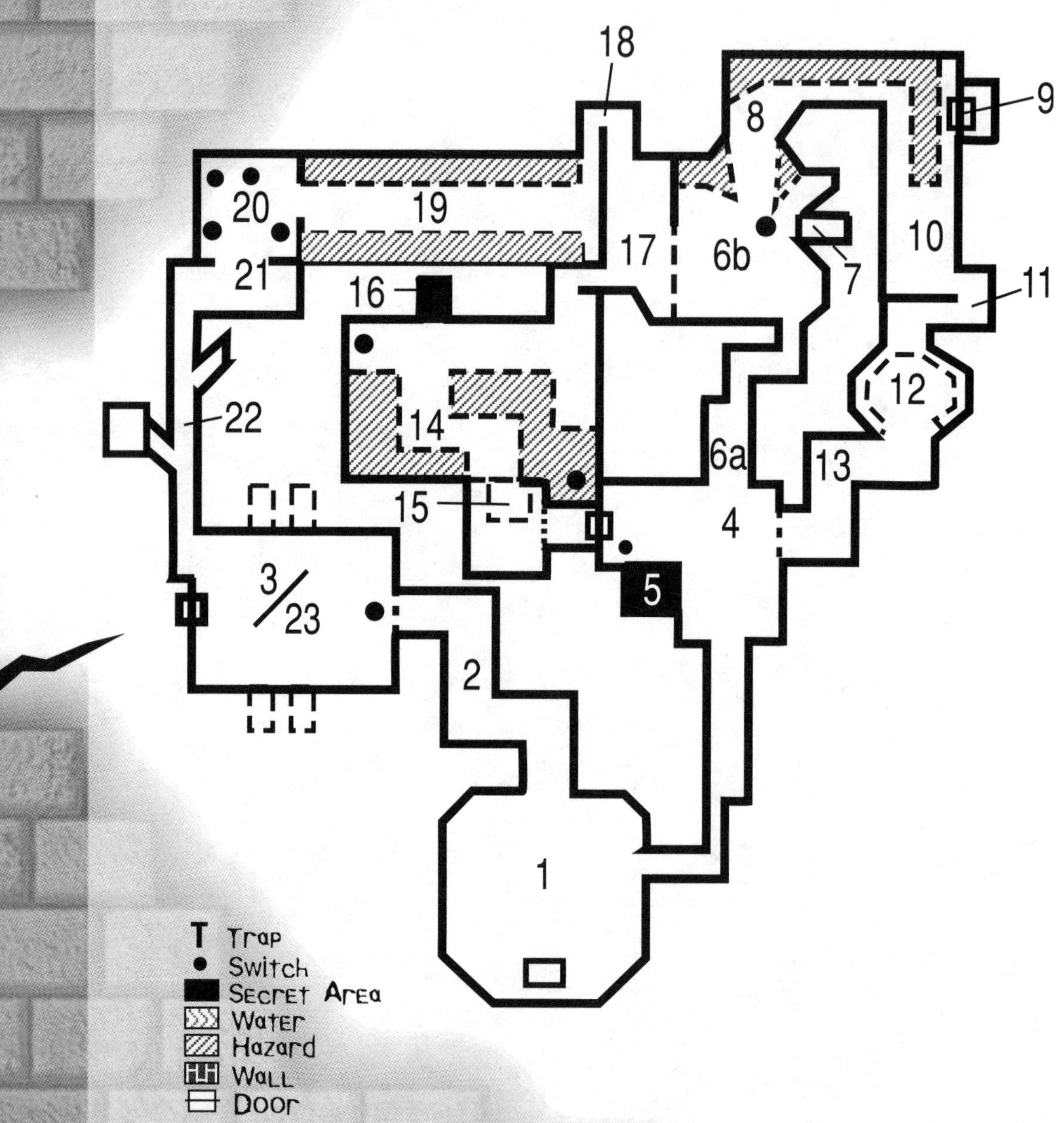

18
8
9
20
19
10
17
6b
21
7
11
16
12
22
14
6a
13
15
4
3/23
5
2
1
T Trap
Switch
Secret Area
Water
Hazard
Wall
Door

Secret Mission: The Underearth

The Underearth mission is a long, elliptical trek full of Death Knights and far too many Scrags. Ammo, too, is plentiful— fortunate, because you often must engage in a little overkill just to thin out a crowd. Save the Quad Damage rune until you really need it, and cross each threshold prepared for an overhead ambush.

Secret Mission: The Underearth At-a-Glance (E2M7)

1. Shotgun Shells, Health, Flechettes
2. Flechettes, Health
3. Grenades, Shotgun Shells, Flechettes, Health
4. Flechettes, Health, Shotgun Shells, Gold Door, Grenade
5. **Secret Area.** Quad Damage Rune

6a. Grenade Launcher, Grenades, Flechettes, Shotgun Shells

6b. Shotgun Shells, Health

7. Shotgun Shells, Green Armor
8. Flechettes, Shotgun Shells, Megahealth
9. Flechettes, Health
10. Shotgun Shells
11. Health, Shotgun Shells
12. Flechettes, Health, Shotgun Shells
13. Shotgun Shells, Health, Gold Key
14. Flechettes, Shotgun Shells, Health
15. Flechettes, Biosuit
16. **Secret Area.** Red Armor
17. Shotgun Shells, Health
18. Shotgun Shells, Flechettes, Health
19. Flechettes
20. Shotgun Shells, Health
21. Health, Shotgun Shells
22. Health, Flechettes
23. Health, Grenades

Highlights:

- Two Secret Areas
- Angry Ogre Shish Kebab
- Plenty O' Nails

Deeply Disturbing

1. As you explore the outer area at the start of the mission, expect an Ogre to welcome you aboard. Stand to the right of the entrance to dispense Grenades, then collect Shotgun Shells, Health boxes, and Flechettes.

2. Venture in, and a Fiend rushes you just inside the doorway, while farther along the passage an Ogre and a Death Knight guard more Flechettes. Keep the Supernailgun handy. You'll find Health boxes nearby.

3. When you step into the room where you can see the large barred door, Scrags appear on your left and right. For that reason, you might pause before crossing the threshold and deal with the seriously disadvantaged Death Knights from a distance with Grenades. In the large room, lay claim to Grenades, Shotgun Shells, Flechettes, and Health. Then heed the door's advice, and return to the outside area for a little swim.

4. Following the underwater passage beneath the bridge, and surface on the left side of the room, across from a large box of Flechettes. One Ogre waits in the area ahead, and another will bail from a ledge on the left when you engage. If you then move along the right wall, you can dispatch a Fiend without getting the attention of the Ogre near the Gold Key. There's also a Death Knight up there for you to bomb before collecting the Health and Shotgun Shells.

5. **Secret Area.** Approach the Gold Door and turn to your left. You'll notice a brick protruding slightly from the wall. Push it, and the barner drops allowing access to the Quad Damage rune. Save the rune until you come back to open the Gold Door.

Note

Note that when you jump over the side of the bridge into the water, you won't be able to get back out again. Load up before you take the plunge. Also, in the area beyond the pool, you'll start to notice large gargoyle faces on the walls. Make sure you shoot each one you see (they'll splatter blood on the first shot, unless they've already been tagged during combat). Later, a small room will open if you shot them all. There's at least one Gargoyle in the rooms or areas of 4, 9, 17, 19 and 21 that must be blasted for the trick to work.

6a. Grab the Grenade Launcher and pulverize the Zombies. Hop off the stairs near where you grab the box of Grenades, and you'll also discover more Flechettes. Gather the Shotgun Shells and get ready for trouble as you traverse the pipe.

6b. When the tunnel terminates, hammer the Zombies and the Fiend, followed closely by a Scrag. Sprint into the room and stomp the floorplate to spike the nearby Ogre, then press up against the other Ogres' ledge to Shotgun them from below. Nearby waits Health and Shotgun Shells, and there's more Health beneath the slime near the front door. If only you had a Biosuit…

7. In the room with the skewered Ogre, pocket more Shotgun Shells, and strap on the Green Armor while avoiding the big spike.

8. Cross the drawbridge and draw out the Scrags. A nasty Ogre and Death Knight ambush ensues when you begin gathering up Flechettes—don't be shy about dispensing some of those nails, though you can also retreat to the outside area for a moment and see if the locals don't soften each other up a little bit. You'll find Shotgun Shells and Megahealth nearby, but the Megahealth can be decided unhealthy: A wall drops to your right and a pair of Fiends appear to rend flesh when you claim the prize.

9. If you grab the Megahealth and beat a hasty retreat to the outside area, the Fiends are Grenade fodder coming through the small entryway in pursuit. In their room Flechettes and Health await you.

10. When you pass into the area through the two arches, a Scrag attacks from above, while a Death Knight rushes from your left. Drop back to dispense justice, and the Knight may aid your cause. You'll find Shotgun Shells nearby.

11. When you round the corner in the hall expect a Fiend and a Death Knight to take exception to your presence. An Ogre perches above you, as well, ready to do what comes naturally. Stand to one side of the boxes of Shotgun Shells and you can peg him quite effectively, while his Grenades generally bounce away from you.

12. Kill anyone left alive at floor level, and try to get the attention of the Ogre that you can see above and in front of you. You need to kill him quickly, so that he doesn't stand and lob Grenades down into your hallway. Another Death Knight usually takes up a position on the plank overhead during this time, and you should execute him as you did the Ogre—notice you can reach the ledge easily with the Grenade Launcher. If you avoid the blue flooring, you won't set off the nail trap while collecting Flechettes.

13. If you didn't kill the Death Knight near the Gold Key from room 4, then do so now. On the ledge above room 12 you'll find still more Flechettes, as well as Health and Shotgun Shells. In the room at the top of the lift wait more Shotgun ammo, Health, and the Gold Key.

14. If you were prudent enough to leave the Quad Damage rune alone when you first found it, you'll want to activate it before you open the Gold Door. A Fiend waits inside, followed by a herd of Scrags. There's plenty of nails for dealing with them and the Ogre, and if you push the switch in the far left corner, you can hurry ahead to inflict Quad Damage before the spell dissipates. In the room, you'll discover Flechettes, Shotgun Shells, and Health, as well as the means to explore the slime underfoot.

15. In the slimy area below the entrance to room 14, an alcove beckons. Inside wait Flechettes and a Biosuit, which you can use to discover the nearby Secret Area. The switch at slime level raises stairs up from the muck, though you have to hop up them.

16. **Secret Area.** Exit the Biosuit alcove straight forward, then turn left when you hit the far wall of the slime pool. Advance forward slowly, and you should sink down and spy a tunnel and a suit of Red Armor. Make haste for the stair switch once you acquire the prize.

17. An Ogre guards Shotgun Shells between you and the landing you saw from room 6b. As you approach the archway leading to the landing, expect Scrags to teleport into the room outside. On the ledge waits more Health.

18. As you approach the two boxes of Shotgun Shells from the ledge outside, stop and use the wall as a backboard to Grenade the Fiend and Ogre waiting up ahead. Flechettes and Health are also readily available.

19. Scrags and Death Knights attempt to knock you from this room's walkway into the slime below. If they succeed, you find only an empty pool, but some steps allow you to hop back out and face a more noble death… Aim high to polish off the Scrags initially.

20. When you step onto the threshold of this room, a nasty revolving nail trap activates, peppering the vicinity. If you stand in the center of the doorway, however, the nails crash harmlessly into the wall on either side of you. Let a nail strike to your right, and then run in that direction, pushing the four switches on the wall as you circle the room. You're bound to take a little damage, but you'll live. You'll find Shotgun Shells and Health on the floor, and hitting all the switches unbars the exit.

21. Through the door, quickly slay the Ogre, and don't go near the other doorway until you're ready to attract the attention of the Fiends up ahead. Health and Shotgun Shells await your collection.

22. Grenade the Fiends and Death Knights lurking in the hall, and gather up Health and Flechettes. The second niche, on the right, is the one that'll open if you've been blastering gargoyle heads.

23. Where the passage emerges, expect plenty of Zombie fun. You'll find Health and Grenades nearby, and the switch on the wall invites more Zombies to the party. In the alcoves from which they emerge you'll find two more switches that open the bars to the room above—3. Clean the upper area of anything you might have left behind, and go through the large door to exit the mission.

Note

The gargoyle faces in room 21 are the last you need to blast to open the small room nearby. If you've gotten them all, you can now shoot the back wall of the right-hand niche in the flickering hallway, and enter a small empty room that someone must be very proud of. Who knows why.

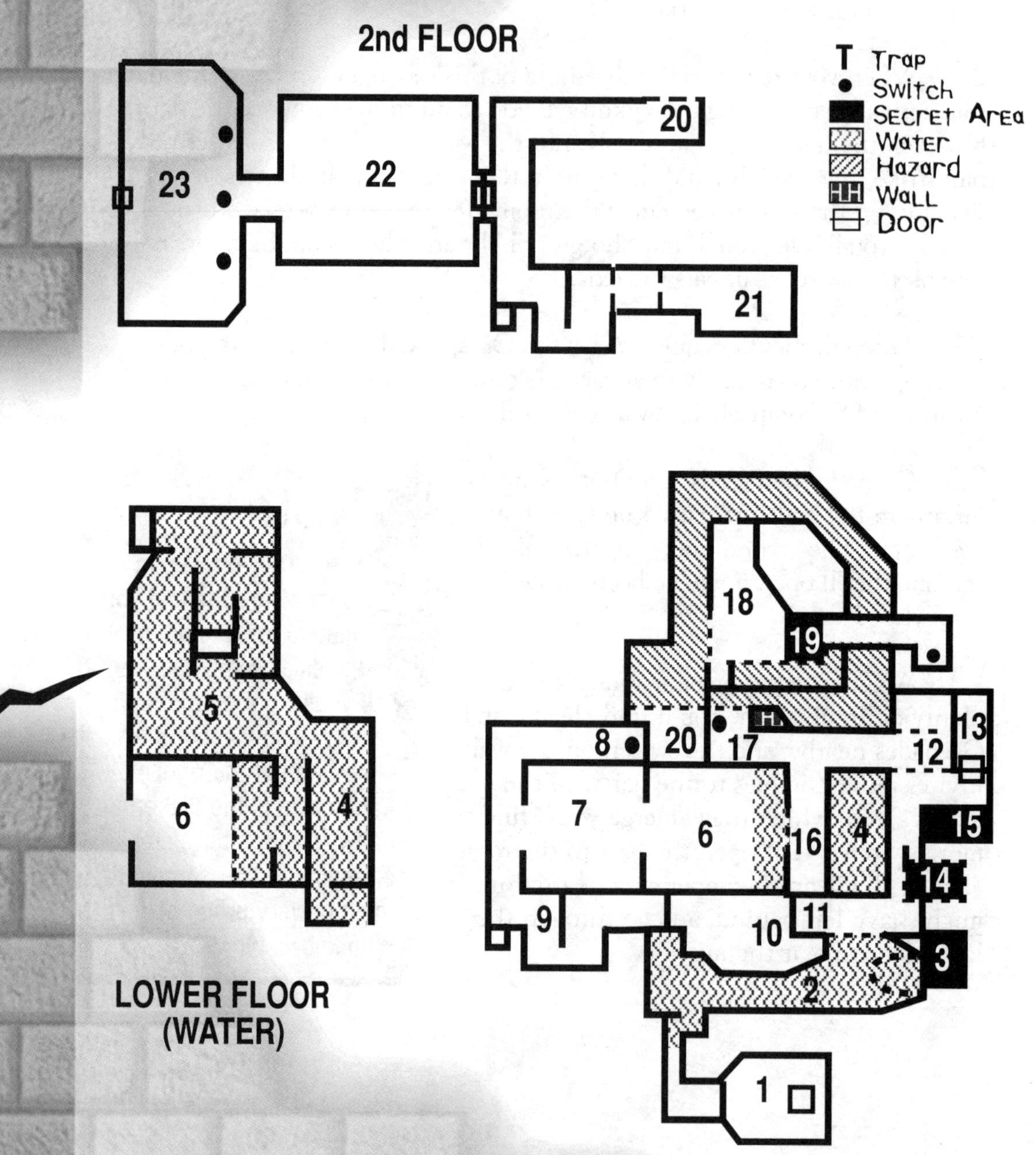
2nd FLOOR
23
22
20
21
T Trap
Switch
Secret Area
Water
Hazard
Wall
Door
5
6
4
LOWER FLOOR
(WATER)
18
19
8
20
17
13
12
7
6
16
4
15
14
9
10
11
3
2
1

Mission 4: The Ebon Fortress

The grim and foreboding Ebon Fortress is enough to test even the heartiest adventurer, as huge crowds of monsters conspire to soak up your ammo at an unprecedented rate. The key to getting out of this mission with more than lint in your pocket is to prudently apply the many runes at your disposal. And, failing that, run like hell…

Mission 4: The Ebon Fortress At-a-Glance (E3M4)

1. Shotgun Shells, Health, Flechettes
2. Health, Shotgun Shells, Grenades, Flechettes, Supernailgun, Nailgun
3. **Secret Area.** Shotgun Shells, Flechettes, Yellow Armor, Quad Damage Rune
4. Ogre and Scrag Ambush
5. Health, Grenades, Yellow Armor, Gold Key
6. Grenades, Health
7. Rocket Launcher, Health, Shotgun Shells, Green Armor
8. Health
9. Health
10. Health, Grenades, Flechettes
11. Health
12. Health, Flechettes, Grenades, Gold Door
13. Yellow Armor, Flechettes
14. **Secret Area.** Megahealth, Grenades
15. **Secret Area.** Pentagram of Protection
16. Shotgun Shells, Health
17. Switch
18. Shotgun Shells, Health, Silver Key, Green Armor
19. **Secret Area.** Biosuit, Red Armor (Quad Damage Rune)
20. Health, Ledge Trigger
21. Flechettes, Megahealth, Quad Damage Rune
22. Health, Grenades, Shotgun Shells
23. Health, Shotgun Shells, Switches

Highlights:

- Four Secret Areas
- Finally: The Rocket Launcher
- The Episode's Sneakiest Non-Secret

Black Death

1. Shotgun Shells and Health welcome you as the mission begins. Grenade the Death Knight below you and hop down to his landing, where you'll gather Flechettes.

2. Traversing the underwater passage, you enter a large room; notice that Health, Shotgun Shells and Grenades, Flechettes and the Supernailgun lie beneath the waves. Stick to the castle wall, and slay the Zombie near the Nailgun quickly, then bomb the Ogres above from his platform. About halfway down the short section of the wall, near the well-lit area, you'll find a sinkhole to a Secret Area.

3. **Secret Area.** Sink slowly into a room with Shotgun Shells, Flechettes, Yellow Armor, and a Quad Damage rune. Pop back up and hurry to the next room, dispatching a Zombie in the hallway.

4. Strafe the ledge above the room without entering, mindful that the Ogres will make short work of you should you linger too long in the doorway. You'll also proabably attract attention from the local Scrags, who generally gather above and to your right.

5. Pass beneath the Ogres' ledge and break up the Zombie party. Just into the small system of canals there's an immediate left turn—avoid that avenue until the other area is cleared. In addition to the meat-tossers, you should lay hands on Health, Grenades, Yellow Armor, and the Gold Key. Don't overlook the underwater Grenades, in the small alcove to the left as you stand facing the Gold Key.

6. Retracing your steps to the avenue near where you first entered the canal system, dispose of any Zombies you meet and strafe the waiting Ogres and Death Knight with Grenades from the doorway. Find Grenades and Health on their ledge.

7. Finally, and at long last, Episode 2 serves up the Rocket Launcher. Expect the standard Fiend rush from the doorway when you clutch your new toy…Hell, give the trigger a couple of squeezes, since the opportunity presents itself. You also find Health, Shotgun Shells, and Green Armor in the room.

8. Through the doorway, more Health waits. Hang a right, rounding the corner to discover two Death Knights, and a switch. Tripping the switch opens a portal down the hall in the other direction.

9. Make your way down the passage, beating the occasional hasty retreat to better deal with the Fiends. A Death Knight lurks up ahead, as well, and Health abounds should you be in need of a boost.

10. As you pass through the portal the switch unsealed, watch your back—an Ogre snipes from a ledge above... unless you say otherwise. You find Health, Grenades, and Flechettes in the room ahead, and draw the attention of another Fiend in addition to more elevated Ogres.

11. Nail the Fiend and then stand so you can peek around the corner and Grenade the Ogre above. His Grenades generally sail over your head and bounce away. Ride the lift upstairs to claim the Ogre droppings and a big box of Health.

Note

Now that you have the Rocket Launcher, don't be afraid to lean on it a little. No other weapon in the game provides as much deadly force with the Launcher's degree of accuracy, and there's a goodly supply of shells between here and the end of the Episode.

12. Through the door on the other side of the ledge, expect immediate trouble from Scrags, followed closely by the ever-popular angry Ogre troupe. A pair of Fiends and a Death Knight wait at floor level, as well as Health, Flechettes and Grenades. At the end of a small nook at floor level, you'll spy the Gold Door.

13. Beyond the Gold Door lies naught but a short hallway. Therein, discover Flechettes, and a suit of Yellow Armor. You'll want to clear a path to the slime outside before you suit up, of course.

14. **Secret Area.** Buttonhook around the edge of the staircase, to the left as you descend into room 12, and discover a room with Megahealth, and Grenades.

15. **Secret Area.** Past the Gold Door, a flight of stairs curls upward to the right. Stop on the first landing, before you have to make a harder right, and climb the final few steps. You should face a relatively dark wall, top half stone, wood below. Notice the small wooden panel on the right side of the stone section, about the size of a small door. Shoot it, and the panel slides aside, granting admittance to a room with a Pentagram of Protection.

16. Follow the stairs up and dispose of any straggling Ogres while you claim the Shotgun Shells. When you climb the stairway, a panel slides for ease of access to room 4. Upstairs, watch for a lurking Scrag, and wax the Ogres standing guard over Health, Flechettes and a Biosuit.

17. Blast the Scrag near the switch, then go grab the Pentagram from room 15 before activating the platform. Angle your aim upwards to dispose of Scrags and Ogres as the ride crawls along.

18. Before you reach the end of the line, hop through the doorway on your left, where Ogres and a Shambler clamor for your hide. Stick close to the Shambler's parapet as you spend the last of your Pentagram time with the Ogres, and the furry freak will be unable to get in any licks. Once the Ogres succumb, gather the Shotgun Shells and Health nearby, and peek from below the parapet to slay the Shambler before heading across the short bridge.

Press the switch you find to lower the bars protecting the Shambler's perch. Grab up the Silver Key and the Green Armor, and investigate a Secret Area before proceeding.

19. **Secret Area.** Hop into the small body of slime across from the Shambler's nest and spy the top of a doorway. Surface to discover a Biosuit and Red Armor. You can use the Biosuit to locate a Quad Damage rune in the moat outside, before using the steps to climb to the landing where the moving platform makes its final stop.

20. Health greets you on the landing and more waits in the hall. There's also far too many Scrags. Where the hallway terminates, past the Silver Door, a ledge provides a glimpse of an extremely hard-to-access area. Step onto the ledge, and you'll hear a mechanism functioning in the distance. Walk back down the hall and look through the windows opposite the Silver Door into room 7; you should see a switch high on the wall to the right. If you shoot it, a platform extends, and the bars retract, allowing entrance to the following room.

21. Back where you previously stood on the ledge and faced an impressive gap, now you stroll easily into the room–disposing of the lone Zombie—and claim Flechettes, Megahealth, and even a Quad Damage rune. Beyond the Silver Door lurks a Shambler, and you might consider bringing the rune along to impress the killer carpet.

22. Beyond the Silver Door, flatten the Fiends and Death Knights, and don't forget the Ogre near the distant wall. You'll have to hurry to the switch beneath the stairs if you want to have any Quad time left with the Shambler. Collect the Health, Grenades, and Shotgun Shells. Once the Shambler succumbs, advance to the end of his ramp, then turn and shoot the switch that's been revealed behind you. Turn back around, introduce yourself to the Ogre, and use the switch therein to access a downward lift.

Note

Notice that a lift is now operational between the upper and lower hallways. In Deathmatch, of course, that comes in very handy, and it also allows you to back-track for goodies without delay.

23. Stay on the lift when it descends, and deal quickly with the closest Ogre. The Fiends, in their enthusiasm, will be unable to get at you beneath the lift's overhang. Usually, the distant Orge and a Fiend will take exception to each other. Once you've stopped the Fiends from bouncing off the walls, gather Health and Shotgun Shells. To unlock the mission's exit door, stand in front of the portal and turn to face the castle. Shoot the three switches you spy to drop the massive barrier.

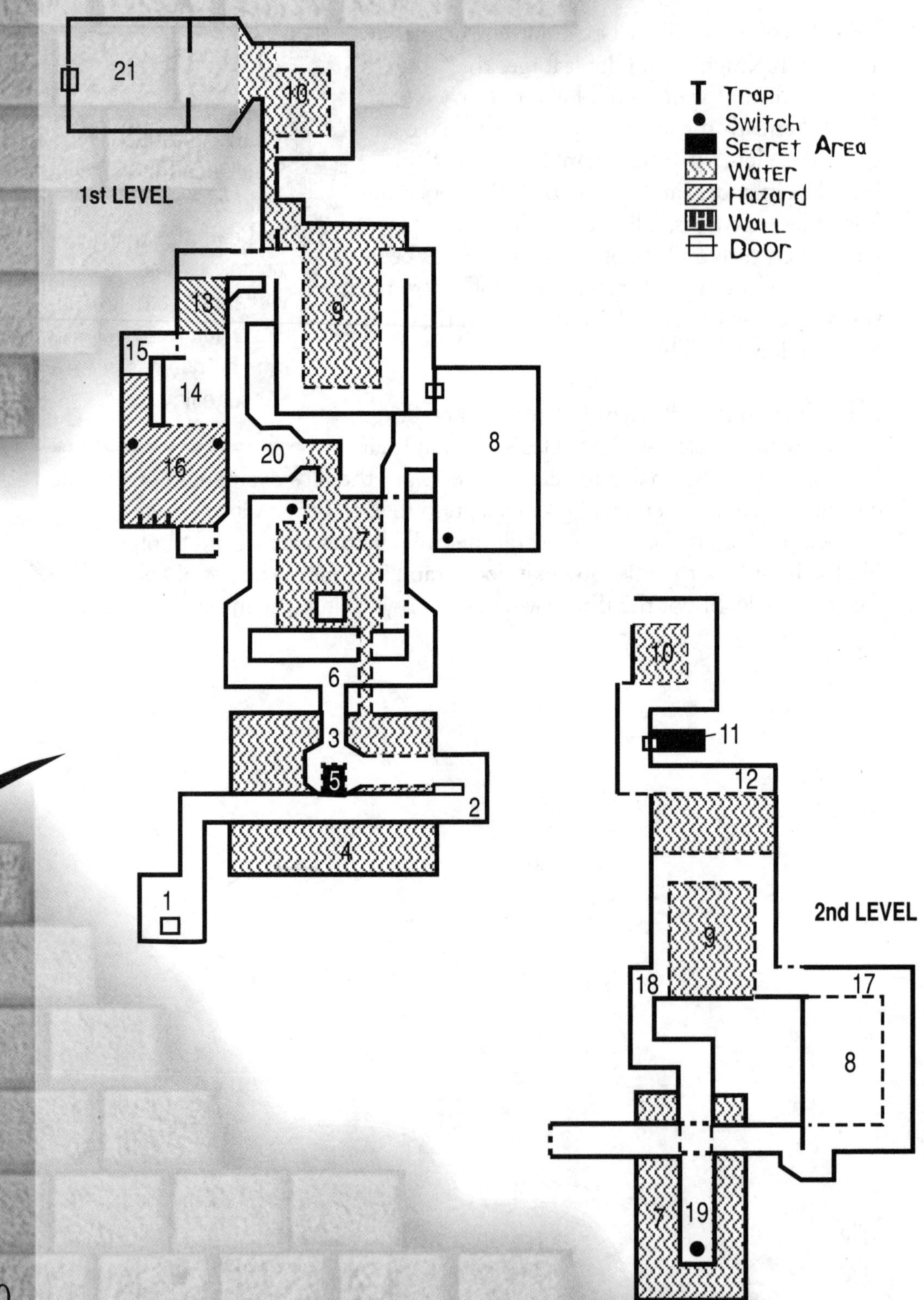
1st LEVEL
2nd LEVEL
T Trap
Switch
Secret Area
Water
Hazard
Wall
Door
21
10
13
9
15
14
8
16
20
7
6
3
5
2
4
1
11
12
18
17
19

Mission 5: The Wizard's Manse

As Episode 2 screams toward its conclusion, you often find yourself in dire straits. "The Wizard's Manse" is one of the game's grimmest missions, as gangs of bad guys gather in your honor with alarming frequency. Use the two Quad Damage runes wisely, and anticipate dropping back to take up a defensive position on a moment's notice.

Mission 5: The Wizard's Manse At-a-Glance (E2M5)

1. Shotgun Shells, Health
2. Rocket Launcher
3. Shotgun Shells
4. Flechettes
5. **Secret Area.** Shotgun Shells
6. Flechettes, Health
7. Shotgun Shells, Flechettes, Health
8. Flechettes, Health, Shotgun Shells, Red Armor
9. Shotgun Shells
10. Grenades, Flechettes, Quad Damage Rune
11. **Secret Area.** Red Armor, Quad Damage Rune
12. Health, Grenades, Gold Key
13. Shotgun Shells, Megahealth
14. Thunderbolt, Cells Blosuit Grenades
15. Health, Flechettes
16. Shotgun Shells
17. Shotgun Shells, Flechettes
18. Shotgun Shells, Health
19. Health, Switch
20. Health
21. Health, Grenades, Exit

Highlights:

- Two Secret Areas
- Two Epic Battles
- Finally: The Thunderbolt

That Old Black Magic

1. Shotgun Shells and Health lie nearby as the mission gets underway, and you can expect to attract the attention of an Ogre and a whole horde of Death Knights when you move in front of the hallway. Break out the heavy artillery and deal with them before they close the gap.

2. When you emerge from the cave onto the bridge, Ogres hurl Grenades at you from above. Don't pause, but sprint to the center of the bridge and grab the Rocket Launcher. From that spot, punish the Ogres above, then continue to the lift.

3. Grab a reload for your Shotgun. When you approach the right turn in the walkway ahead, a Fiend generally leaps out of the doorway to greet you. Backing along the walk, it's easy enough to dispose of him as he bounds in your direction. A couple of Scrags also wait inside to make your acquaintance.

4. Jump in the water below, and grab up the Flechettes. One of the large columns has a marker pointing you toward an underwater passage; avoid it for the time being. Instead, look inside that column and discover a lift to a Secret Area.

5. **Secret Area.** Ride the lift up the center of the column and collect the Shotgun Shells. A door opens to deposit you back outside, on the lower ramp.

6. Through the doorway where you previously pegged the Fiend and Scrags, the halls left and right intersect in a large room. The right-hand avenue probably provides the best vantage point for starting the battle, and you can gather Flechettes on that landing. Both directions offer boxes of Health.

7. From the landing at the end of the right hall, concentrate on the Ogres, then double back to the other side of the room if you need to polish off the Death Knight. On the ledge near the switch rest Shotgun Shells and Flechettes, and the switch extends the walkway along the other edge of the room, admitting an Ogre in the process. Beneath the water, you discover more Shotgun Shells, Flechettes, and Health; you must take the underwater tunnel to the outside area to exit the pool.

8. This room can be absolutely grim, especially if you go waltzing blindly into the initial ambush. As you crest the stairs, Ogres bail from the walkway above, and Death Knights rush you from floor level. Retreat to the large room behind you, and Rocket anyone who gives chase. When you finally creep into the room, go in gunning, but save some nails for the Shambler who appears when you throw the switch.

Collect Flechettes, Health, and Shotgun Shells before tripping the trap. The door to the room seals when Shaggy makes his entrance, but it opens again when you claim the newly revealed Flechettes opposite where you push the switch. You can also strap on a shiny new suit of Red Armor once things finally quiet down.

9. After that last room, this area probably looks like the last thing you want to see… Fortunately, this battle is nowhere near as overwhelming. Use the walkways above for cover once you've drawn out the Death Knights, and the Ogres are easy targets. If you enter and run along the wall to your left, you'll find that the far corner of the room makes a good vantage point once the initial Ogres are cleared. Nearby lies a box of Shotgun Shells, and if you traverse the walkway to the exit, you can peg the Orge that's been hurling Grenades from afar. Afterward, hop into the water (as opposed to continuing through the hallway).

10. Traverse the waterway to discover a room with a wide staircase. An Ogre usually waits at the foot of the stairs, and sometimes others come down to play if you get their attention. Otherwise, you'll have to angle your attack almost directly up to clear the way. Grenades, Flechettes, and even a Quad Damage rune lie underwater, near the bottom of the stairs.

11. **Secret Area.** When you reach the top of the stairs and turn left into the hall, look to your left and notice that part of the passage is devoid of decorative trim. Shoot that section, and it slides to reveal Red Armor. If you walk to the back of that room, you'll drop to another area where you have to claim a Quad Damage rune to exit. You can grab the Armor now, but save the Quad Damage. To get it, you have to drop to the water below upon exiting the room, and there's no one nearby to kill until you open the Gold Door.

12. Continue down the hall onto the ledge above room 9, collecting Health, Grenades, and finally the Gold Key.

13. Once you have the Gold Key, hop down to the room below and continue through the hallway, acquiring more Shotgun Shells en route. From the ledge where you can see the Biosuit, get the attention of the Fiends below, and kill them mercilessly. Don't stand right near the edge when they leap towards you, or you'll pay the price. In the slime pool they came from lies a box of Megahealth. Jump over near the Biosuit, but don't use it yet!

14. From the corner outside the room, just to the right of the Biosuit, slay the Scrags, then hop out to deal with the Death Knight and finally the Ogre you can see through the doorway. Grab the Thunderbolt, Cells and Grenades, and then suit up. Claim the aforementioned Megahealth, then dive into the slime near the recently deceased Ogre to locate an underwater passage.

15. Pass through the slime-filled corridor, back onto the lift, and ride up, blasting the Scrag as you climb. A short hallway at the top of the lift holds Health and Flechettes, and drops you back near where you found the Biosuit.

16. In the slime pool room where you swam through the underwater passage, shoot both wall switches to extend precarious ledges to bridge the distance. Each step up the wall extends as you hop along. At the top, gather more Shotgun Shells.

17. Follow the walkway back across room 7—collecting Shotgun Shells, battling Death Knights—and onto the upper ledge of room 8. There you find still more Shotgun Shells—and endure a Scrag ambush—before acquiring an impressive load of Flechettes.

18. Continuing on the walkway, you cross the upper ramp in room 9, then enter a small stairway where you spy Shotgun Shells ahead. A Shambler waits at the top of the steps, and you should pause to soften him up by bouncing a few Grenades before switching to some other weapon more suitable for close combat. You'll find Health nearby.

20. Finally, cross the upper ramp in room 7, collecting Health on your way, and press the switch to ride a huge lift down.

21. The lift encases you in a small cell, which wouldn't be so bad except that it travels underwater, and you'll be gasping for air when you're finally released. Hammer the two nearby Ogres, then the one on the ledge to your right. The small lit alcove provides an avenue through which you can backtrack to the floor of room 7. Gather the Health, and ascend the lift ready for a sneaky Scrag.

22. You emerge into a familiar water-filled hallway, and if you swim into room 10, you'll see that the previously barred portal is now open for business. Beyond is the Gold Door, and beyond that a truly grim confrontation. Hopefully, you saved one of those Quad Damage runes… Note that if you want to use the one upstairs, you have to go and get it before opening the Gold Door. A barrier rises around the stair landing when you use the Gold Key. Open the door and back quickly into the water, as Fiends, Death Knights and a Shambler clamor to keep you from reaching the mission's end. Submerge and retreat to the hallway, and the locals will battle amongst themselves for a while. Gather Health and Grenades before you make your exit.

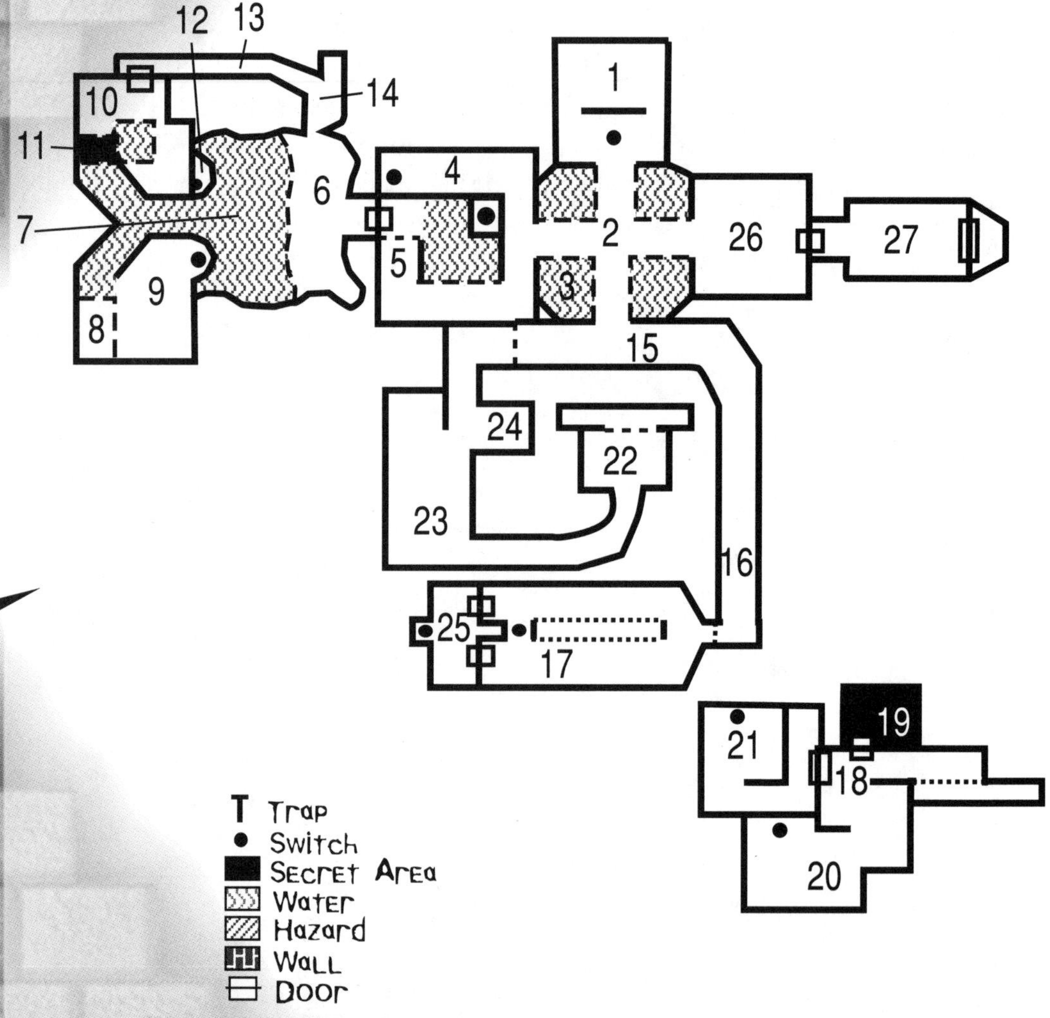

1
2
3
4
5
6
7
8
9
10
11
12
13
14
15
16
17
18
19
20
21
22
23
24
25
26
27
T Trap
Switch
Secret Area
Water
Hazard
Wall
Door

Mission 6: The Dismal Oubliette

They don't call it dismal for nothing. The final mission of Episode 2 is probably the sternest test, which is as it should be. It features a load of bad guys unlike any you've seen up to this point, and some combinations of monster that'll leave you begging for mercy. Unless, of course, you use this walkthrough as your guide…

Mission 6: The Dismal Oubliette At-a-Glance (E2M6)

1. Box Switch, Shotgun Shells, Health, Green Armor
2. Shotgun Shells, Green Armor, Flechettes
3. Health, Yellow Armor
4. Health, Flechettes
5. Grenades, Health
6. Grenades, Cells, Health, Shotgun Shells
7. Shotgun Shells, Health
8. Ledge Ascent
9. Health, Flechettes, Grenades
10. Shotgun Shells
11. **Secret Area.** Quad Damage Rune
12. Grenades, Box Switch
13. Health
14. Shotgun Shells, Flechettes
15. Cells, Yellow Armor, Flechettes
16. Shotgun Shells, Flechettes
17. Health, Gold Door
18. Health, Shotgun Shells
19. **Secret Area.** Flechettes, Grenades, Megahealth, Pentagram of Protection
20. Flechettes
21. Shotgun Shells, Health
22. Thunderbolt, Flechettes
23. Flechettes, Health
24. Gold Key, Flechettes
25. Cells, Health, Grenades, Shotgun Shells
26. Yellow Armor, Megahealth, Flechettes, Grenades, Cells
27. Flechettes, Health, Rune Key

Highlights:

- Two Secret Areas
- Plenty of Angry Enemies
- Rune Key Showdown

Bleak Outlook

1. Shotgun Shells, Health, and a new suit of Green Armor bid you welcome. Bounce a few Grenades around the room's partition to get things started with the local Ogre and Fiend, and then push the large square switch-box to lower the barrier. At the same time, a bridge rises in the room outside, and some Death Knights to your right beg to be introduced to your Rocket Launcher.

2. Cross the elevated bridge, gathering Shotgun Shells, and Flechettes.

3. Below, in the water, lie Health, Cells and Yellow Armor. You have an easy chance to pick up the Armor nearer the end of the mission, so you might consider saving it for now. Lifts near the bridge's central hub raise you from the drink.

4. Through the entrance, hang a right and fry the Fiend in the small room. He was keeping company with Health, Flechettes, and a switch. The switch on the wall raises a stairway in the room you can see nearby, but it only lasts a minute, so you'll need to clear a path through the large room.

5. Down the other branch of the hall, a Fiend cringes below. Dispatch him and his Scrag buddy, then follow the tunnel to find Grenades and Health. You'll want to strafe out of the tunnel in the area of the Health boxes to slay an Ogre on a nearby ledge, then return to room 11 and throw the switch. Make haste back to the Health area, and climb the stairs to the Ogre's resting place. Activating the switch there opens a large door behind you.

6. Blast the Fiend through the open doorway, and approach with caution. The Ogres above can flip Grenades through the portal with depressing accuracy, and just inside and to your right lurks a Shambler. Draw the shaggy abomination into the outer area, and use the narrow corridors to bring him down. On the ledge inside the room you'll discover Grenades and Cells, and it's prudent to stand near the Cells and mine the water before you go diving. You'll need to disassemble the Zombies below before you can collect the Health, Shotgun Shells, and Grenades at the bottom of the briny deep.

7. Up the underwater ramp, blast the poor oblivious Zombies into oblivion, then bear right to draw out the Fiends. If you back down into the underwater passage once again, the leaping losers are pretty much at your mercy. Grab the Shotgun Shells and Health, stirring up the locals in the process, then double back down the other branch of the hall.

8. Aim high as you enter this small room, first disposing of the Scrag, then firing through the upper portal to dispatch the Death Knights and Ogre. Lob a Grenade or two up there before you go climbing, just to make sure no one interrupts your ascent. Hop along the narrow steel ledges to reach the summit.

9. In the area above, you'll dispatch a Fiend (in the corner to your left) while collecting Health, Flechettes, and Grenades. You can also check out the angry denizens nearby before you hit the switch. You'll find they have some personal issues they're trying to work out… The switch draws back the bar that blocked the other passage.

10. A Fiend still may linger, but, if you were even remotely helpful, the Ogres have been reduced to bite-size morsels. Before you venture to the top of the stairs, claim a big box of Shotgun Shells, and meet the Ogre in the tower, take time to rid the water below of Zombies, and discover a soon-to-be-very-important Secret Area.

11. **Secret Area.** In an underwater alcove waits a Quad Damage rune, and that's a good thing. When you slay that Ogre in the tower above, a Shambler teleports in literally right behind you, at which time you should bail from the ledge to the water below, claiming the Quad for its intended purpose. Notice that to exit the water, you have to step out near the wall, where the floor is lower.

12. Once you take care of the Shambler, drop down into the Ogre's tower and gather Grenades. The switch there unseals the room and opens another doorway, on your right as you emerge.

13. Blast the Ogre in the doorway and prepare for the Fiend in the hall beyond. You'll find Health near a point where you can launch Grenades quite effectively into the next room.

14. Dispose of any lingering adversaries—or merely pause to appreciate the chunks of Zombie and Ogre you have wrought—then gather Shotgun Shells and Flechettes before dropping back into room 13, below.

15. When you reemerge in room 9, you'll see that the walkway has pivoted, and you're free to claim Cells and Yellow Armor. Well, alright, the Death Knight might have a little to say about it, but see if you can convince him. Bear left in the hallway after a quick side trip to grab those Flechettes.

16. Slay the Ogre and ride down the lift for more Ogre fun, this time with a side order of savory Scrag. You'll find Shotgun Shells and Flechettes nearby.

17. Both hallways, which hold boxes of Health, lead to a room where a Death Knight guards a switch near the Gold Key door. Hit the switch, and ride upstairs on the nearby lift, ready for the Ogre that awaits your arrival. As you face the switch, if you head to your right to enter the elevator, you'll be facing the Ogre above.

18. Hammer the Ogre and watch for the Fiend who'll come leaping from your left. Also in that direction, Ogres lob Grenades through a barred portal. Deal with them from a distance, then advance slightly into the hall, backing off to draw out the Death Knight. Suck down the Health on the floor, and perhaps a load of Shotgun Shells, but make a right turn as you face that barred portal and locate a Secret Area.

19. **Secret Area.** Shoot that wall to the right of the barred Ogre room, if you haven't already, and ride down the lift to a room with Flechettes, Grenades, Megahealth, and a Pentagram of Protection. Gather the goodies before you explore the other branch of the hall above.

20. Waste the Death Knights, Zombies, and their overzealous Fiend friend. Grab up the Flechettes, and punch the switch to unbar the portal in the hall outside.

21. Clean up the Ogre debris and stop shy of the doorway to lob Grenades at the Fiends. In their room wait Shotgun Shells, Health, and the switch that accesses the third floor.

22. Ride the lift up to the third floor and hammer the Ogre with unbridled glee. The Thunderbolt beckons, not to mention some Flechettes for good measure. Save those Cells for the end of the mission—you'll need them.

23. Continuing up the stairs, drawing out the Fiends and Death Knights. Plenty of Flechettes await, as do several Health boxes.

24. Through the small doorway you'll discover a Friend and the Gold Key. Claiming the key unbars the nearby doorway leading to familiar Flechettes, unless you picked them up earlier.

25. Drop the Gold Key door and retreat back down one of the hallways while the Shambler and Fiend get better acquainted. Give the Shambler a little of his own medicine—namely a Thunderbolt upside the head, then grab up a Cell box, Health, Grenades and Shotgun Shells. Activating the pillar switch pivots the bridge one last time.

26. Cross the bridge, claiming the Yellow Armor now elevated from beneath the water. In the room beyond the bridge you'll see your stock for the battle ahead: Megahealth, Flechettes, Grenades, and several boxes of Cells. A Zombie lurks, too, and another is nailed to the wall. When you go to check out the wall-mounted version, two Shamblers teleport in near the door, and you should Thunderbolt them in a big hurry. As the floor drops, a Fiend teleports in, and the central hub becomes a nail trap. Take up a position in the corner, and the nails will miss you while you dispatch the Fiend. Next, you can expect company from teleporting Zombies, and the floor stops dropping. Finally, a portal opens onto the last room of the Episode.

27. A pair of Vores rushes to protect the Rune Key you covet, though you can rocket them into pieces effectively enough by using the pillar in the previous room as an obstacle to their counterattacks. Notice Flechettes and Health on the floor of their room, though collecting once the battle is over is a moot point. Procuring the Rune Key grants you access to the huge Teleporter nearby, and it's on to Episode 3.

Episode 3
The Netherworld

Episode 3 is *Quake*'s version of baseball's "7th Inning Stretch;" and it's make or break time for players and fans alike. Faster and more furious than Episode 2, only an itchy trigger finger and exceptional puzzle-solving savvy will keep you from an untimely demise.

The only drawback of Episode 3 is its sameness in regard to how the missions unfold. All but the first mission in Episode 3 were designed by the same individual, and his predilection for tight encounter areas with strings of triggered events shows. Spend a little time in all but the first and last mission (which was co-designed) and you'll see what we're talking about.

Though single-player action is more interesting elsewhere in *Quake*, you'll no doubt delight in bombing Ogres while surfing and thrill to riding the wind, your Rocket Launcher leading the way. Single-player limitations aside, we're certain small bands of Deathmatchers will flock to Episode 3 precisely for its exceedingly circular, multi-dimensional mission maps.

If you yearn for sprawling maps, long hallways, and multiple (successful) routes through a mission, this isn't the episode for you. If, however, you enjoy the thrill of heavy firepower in your hands during boot-to-cloven-hoof slugfests, excellent power-up placement to make mincemeat out of your opponents, and multilevel encounter areas to rain down death from above, look no further.

T Trap
Switch
Secret Area
Water
Hazard
Wall
Door
12
11
10
To 13
7
7
5
6
13
10
4
3
2
1
9
8

Mission 1: Termination Central

Like the other first missions in a *Quake* episode, the combat here is of the Grunt goon squad-lying-in-wait-around-the-corner variety. The path to victory is also linear, though a few well-placed Quad Damage runes and Megahealths make for satisfying play. Knowing the locations of these items makes you tougher than any Terminator—a decidedly unfair advantage. Now aren't you glad you bought this book?

Mission 1: Termination Central At-a-Glance (E3M1)

1. Health, Double-barreled Shotgun, Shotgun Shells
2. Shotgun Shells, Green Armor
3. Shotgun Shells, Nailgun, Flechette
4. **Secret Area.** Red Armor
5. Health, Yellow Armor, Shotgun Shells
6. Quad Damage Rune, Rockets, Flechette
7. **Secret Area.** Rockets, Yellow Armor, Health
8. **Secret Area.** Health, Rockets, Flechette
9. Green Armor, Megahealth
10. Heath, Gold Keycard
11. **Secret Area.** Megahealth
12. **Secret Area.** Quad Damage Rune
13. Exit. Health, Shotgun Shells

Highlights:

- Five Fabulous Secret Areas
- Taking an Acid Bath without a Biosuit
- Only One Gratuitous *Terminator* Reference

Searching for Sara Conner

1. You get a couple of free shots into the back of the Enforcer. Nab the Health box (if necessary), go around the corner, grab the weaponry, and take the lift down. Face the button as you descend.

2. Before the platform drops all the way, start dumping Double-barreled death into the Grunts, Enforcers, and their furry friends. Getting under the perched Enforcer also nullifies any height advantage he otherwise has.

Note the tantalizing Megahealth through the rectangular window to your right—that's area 9. Unfortunately, you can't get there from here. Watch for a Grunt/Enforcer/Rottweiler ambush en route to 3!

3. In this room-like hallway, you have to hit a pair of linked buttons to progress. Watching for Grunts as you move down the right hallway. Hit the red button. Return to the room's entrance and dash down the left hallway for your first Secret Area of this episode—and an all-important Nailgun. Once you've got it, immediately test out your new toy on the rabid doggie and the Enforcer to the right. Any enemies on the catwalk above (they're in 10) will be lucky if they land a shot within 10 feet of you. You can snipe them from here, or wait until you get your mits on a Quad Damage rune in 6. It's tons more fun if you wait.

The wall next the first red button and the wall to your left drop when you hit the second button. Now, step back, get some cover and let the platoon of Grunts, Enforcers, and rabid Rottweilers in 5 come to you.

Note that the buttons also drop a platform-style lift in 2 that allows you access the area where the perched Enforcer was standing. Once all's quiet, how about peeking into the first Secret Area of this episode?

4. **Secret Area.** The parabola-shaped shadow on the right wall under the catwalk hides this secret area. Shoot the wall and slip in for a suit of Red Armor. Of course, if you've still got lots of Green Armor protecting you, why not leave this Red Armor alone and come back to it when you're in dire need?

5. Watch out for *Quake's* version of *Doom's* toxic barrels. Luckily, you should have killed most, if not all, of the bad guys in here from a safe area near the second red button—except the Grunts on the catwalk above the exploding boxes.

Go behind the ramp for a box of Shotgun Shells and a Grunt sneak attack. After you grab the Yellow Armor, you've got to waste another gang of subhumans to get to 6.

6. The steel Dutch (blast) door drops as soon as you step up to it. As a bonus you also trigger an angry goon collective into action. Besides living to tell the tale, your goal in this area is to activate the red button on the far side of the center structure. Drawing the bad guys across the catwalk and blasting them from the entrance works well. However, a headlong rush for the Quad Damage rune is bloody fun. Quicksave before going in and try 'em both. Even so, we suggest you save the Quad Damage rune for mounting an attack on 10.

Take out the soldier who guards the switch. Hit the switch to unleash a pair of Enforcers to the right of the switch, or ride up the lift in 7 to accomplish the same task. Your choice.

7. **Secret Area.** Peer over the ledge between the stairways. See the lip of ledge below? Drop down to collect the Yellow Armor, Rockets, and Health box. Ride the lift up to get the Shotgun Shells. Riding the lift opens the same pair of doors the switch on the platform does. If you didn't hit the switch in 6, it's quite easy to waste the Enforcers from your perch up high. When sounds of peace ring throughout the area, drop down to the main platform and put your back to the switch and your toes over the ledge. It's time for an acid bath.

8. **Secret Area.** Jump off the platform and swim for the opening cut into the bottom of the far wall. Oh, that slime hurts so good! Swim through the tunnel and flop onto any of the steel-decked piers. Once you've scoured the area, head up the Slipgate and you're off to 9.

9. On the ledge, you have no choice but to grab the Green Armor and wax the lurking Grunt. Go down the passage and leap to the platform below—that's the area visible from area 2. Take the Slipgate return to the Green Armor passageway. The Slipgate here takes you back to the start. Go back to 6 and the Quad Damage rune you should have been saving. Let the games begin!

10. If you didn't kill the goons from your Nailgun niche in area 3, now's your chance. Grab the Quad Damage rune in 6, hit the switch, and battle your way down the hallway. What a mess! Watch out for the bad guys hanging to the right of the lift. The Gold Keycard and a few more Grunts are to left of the lift, as is a hefty collection of Health boxes.

Note

Deathmatch players: If you jump into the slime, go through the niche in the wall below the Slipgate, turn right and follow the passage. You'll wind up on a lift that delivers you to area 2. Ifyou've got a Megahealth going, you'll probably be down to a fine 100 Health points at the end of your swim.

11. **Secret Area.** In area 10, go into the center of the stacked crates. Watch out for a Grunt attack! Jump on the brown one and continue your jumps until you're on the very top. Once on top, turn left and shoot the wall panel. Follow the passage to the lift. A Megahealth and a bird's-eye view of 5 and 10 await.

12. **Secret Area.** In front of the lift in 10, turn left. You should see a Quad Damage rune quietly spinning to the right of the catwalk. Getting there is surprisingly easy: Face the lift and angle a step onto a dark ledge—no jumping required. Follow the ledge around and claim your prize. Return the way you came, jump onto the catwalk,(if you miss a lift graciously brings you back up to the catwalk), run through the Yellow Key door, and Quad Damage blast your way to the exit room.

13. End. Watch for an Enforcer and Grunt once you descend the steps. Jump up the two boxes in front of you—leap across to the other set of boxes for a Health box. Watch out for the Grunt in the shadows! If you miss the jump when going for the Health box, you'll land next to a crate of Shotgun Shells.

Battle your way up the steps. As soon as you get close to the exit Telepad, a pair of Enforcers appear to give you a bon voyage party. Spoil their celebration and make sure to go behind the Telepad for yet more Shotgun Shells before you terminate this mission.

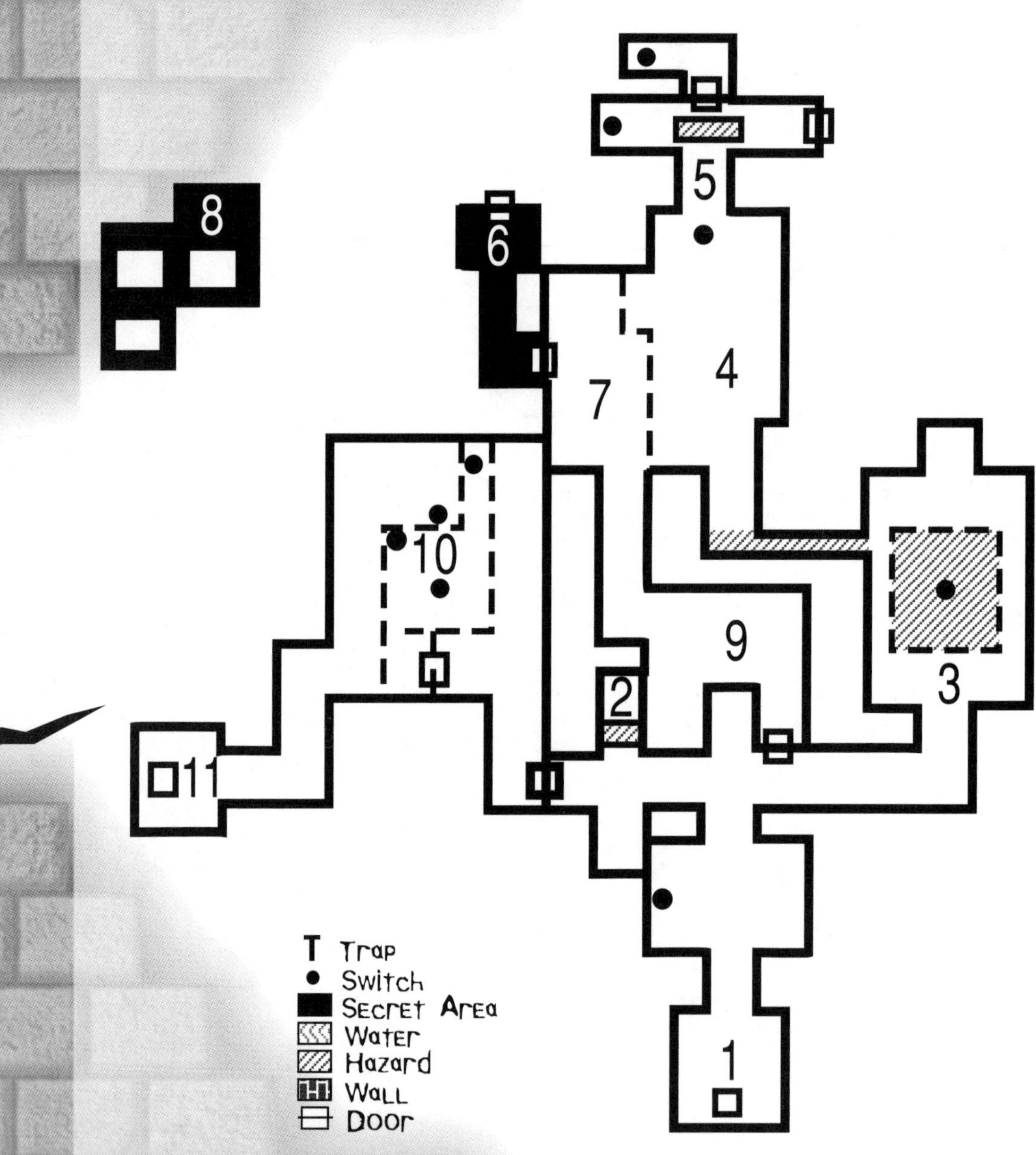

8
6
5
4
7
10
9
3
2
11
1
T Trap
Switch
Secret Area
Water
Hazard
Wall
Door

Mission 2: The Vaults of Zin

"The Vaults of Zin" essentially consists of three large encounter areas (or "vaults," if you like). Each vault contains an insidious trap, where you literally trigger a series of events with every button push. Each trap is deadly if you rush blindly into action, but easily defusable if you bide your time and read this walkthrough. In fact, if you defuse the traps, there's no reason not to finish the mission with almost a full complement of armor and 100 Health points. Last, if you like blasting Zombies, Ogres, Scrags, and Shamblers (and who doesn't?), you'll dig the action here.

Mission 2: The Vaults of Zin At-a-Glance (E3M2)

1. Health, Rockets
2. Grenade Launcher, Megahealth
3. Health, Flechettes, Quad Damage Rune, Rockets, Yellow Armor
4. Health, Flechette
5. Rockets, Health, Shotgun Shells, Flechette
6. **Secret Area.** Ring of Shadows
7. Quake Switch
8. **Secret Area.** Shotgun Shells, Rockets, Health
9. Silver Key, Rockets, Flechette, Health
10. Shotgun Shells, Health, Flechette, Zombie/Scrag/Shambler trap, Gold Key, Rockets, Double-barreled Shotgun
11. End. Health

Highlights:

- A Pair of Nifty Secret Areas
- Claim Your Very Own Grenade Launcher
- Shooting Shamblers in a Barrel

Zinful Fun for the Whole (Undead) Family

1. The Silver Key glints in the distance. Could it be this easy? Of course not. Dash toward it anyway. Coming even with the second set of devil-head panels causes them to drop—releasing a quartet of moaning Zombies.

The Silver Key drops through the floor (to 9) the instant you even come close to it. At least you know where you'll be going. Turn left where the Silver Key was, dodge the Zombie, and feast your eyes on a Grenade Launcher.

2. **Secret Area.** Leap across the pit for your lovely Grenade Launcher. Once the upper deck is clear, lob a bomb or two on the Zombies playing in the lava below. Then follow your shot, angling for the lip of floor next to the lava pool. You may get a little toasty, but the Megahealth more than makes up for it. The ledge is the Secret Area.

Take a right off the lift and chunkify the remaining Zombies you unleashed in 1. Hit the Quake switch in the Zombie pen to open the doors opposite the Silver Key Door. Area 3 awaits.

3. Watch for a Scrag attack from the right as you murder the Ogre from the doorway. Shoot the section of skull on the wall (it's to the right if you're on top of the stairs) for a Zombie and Quad Damage rune surprise. We suggest that you save the rune for when you mount an attack against the baddies in 4.

The box in the lava (the one with crosses on it) has a Quake switch on top of it that opens a door to 4. Try as you might, you can't jump on this switch from the ground floor… but you can fall on it. This room has two levels and one nasty trap—one that's surprisingly easy to survive absolutely unscathed. Here's how:

> **Note**
>
> If you want to soften up the Silver Key room (9), lob a grenade at the Ogre and Fiend in the pit below the barred window. One of the bad guys typically runs through a Slipgate, appearing in the hallway to attack you! To put Quake environment to work for you, we suggest you stand on the telepad in the hallway after you've stirred up the bad guys. You never know who you might telefrag.

- Keep your Nailgun at the ready and run to the lift on the far side of the room.
- Nail the Scrag and run around the right ledge (toward the box of rockets). Nail the other Scrag in the back from a distance—just aim between the railing (he's above the Yellow Armor).

- Hit the Quake switch and turn around—the column in the center of the walkway ascends, leaving a hole just big enough for a guy your size to fall through.
- You'll land squarely on the famed Quake switch. Doing so unleashes an unholy horde of Ogres. Run back up the lift and snipe them at your leisure. When all's quiet, get out your Nailgun, grab the Quad Damage rune, and dash into harm's way.

4. As soon as you engage the first Ogre, three more drop from the ceiling. Keep up the close-range Nailgun pressure so they don't have a chance to toss grenades into your face. Watch for the Ogre lurking on the crossbeams that make up the ceiling! (That's Secret Area 8.) Battle forward to 5, Quad Damage power urging you on.

5. This room is really a lift going down. Here's how to survive and escape:

- As the lift drops, turn left and take down the first Ogre you meet up close and personal. The lift goes back up, hopefully whisking away an Ogre that was running to saw your back.
- Hit the Quake switch. A panel to the left of the lava opens. Lure out the Ogre, take him down, and hit the switch he died to protect.
- Back in the lava room, the second switch opened a set of doors to your left, revealing a Slipgate that takes you back to 4—and the Ogre who went up the lift. Get out your Grenade Launcher and run through the Slipgate. The open area makes killing the last Ogre positively easy.

6. **Secret Area.** From 4, Shoot the wall to the right of the crucifix-like wall art. A panel slides away. Jump through the opening and keep going to claim a fabulous Ring of Shadows. The Slipgate takes you back to 4. Note that the pit below the naked lady wall art is 7.

Note that the second switch in 5 opened a section of wall below you in 7, letting a class of Fiends out to play. They won't take the lift up to you, so smoke them from above at your leisure.

7. With the Ring of Shadows burning, drop down, and pick off the remaining Fiends one at time. Use that lift to your advantage. When it's completely safe, hit the Quake switch. Not only do the bars blocking the hallway to 9 drop, but a trio of Zombies emerges from the floor at the hallway's entrance. One clean grenade shot and the undead are forever dead.

Before you go, shoot the off-colored section of wall opposite (and a little to the right) of the Quake switch. It reveals a Slipgate that gladly takes you to this mission's second, and final, Secret Area.

8. **Secret Area.** Once you've claimed your prizes, drop off any of the beams at 4, then drop to 7 and slog over the Zombie chunks en route to 9.

9. If you didn't kill the Ogre and Fiend here while in 2, now's your chance. Claim the Silver Key and the other items then ride the Slipgate back to 2. The Silver Key door beckons dead ahead.

10. A pair of Zombies and a Fiend greet you the moment you open the door. There's more where those came from, and then some… Here's what we feel is the best way to survive the string of events waiting for you in this room:

- Turn left down the first isle and topple the Ogre standing guard by the Gold Key door.
- When he's down, get out your Grenade Launcher and approach the Quake switch from the left. Hit the Quake switch to both unleash a herd of Zombies and uncover another Quake switch in the center of the room. DO NOT WALK OVER ANY GRATING IN THE FLOOR AND DO NOT STAND ON THE SWITCH YET! Use only the perimeter to cream the Zombies. Don't forget to score the box of Rockets in the Zombie pen closest to the Gold Door.
- Get out your Nailgun or Double-barreled Shotgun, and peer down into any of the floor gratings. A few seconds of standing around is usually all it takes to trigger a wild Shambler and Scrag party into action. Drop a grenade into the pit to kick off the festivities if no one seems otherwise interested in your presence.
- Snipe the Shambler and Scrag from between any of the floor grates; just make sure to stay clear of the floor-mounted Quake switch—easy to do.
- Once he's dead watch out! Another Shambler teleports in for some action. Use the entire mission map to your advantage. The Zombie pen in 1 seems to work well for a game of nail-n-seek, as does the loft in 3. Keep moving and good luck.
- Finally, step on the Quake switch in the center of the 10. Like magic, the floor around you drops away, leaving you on a pedestal—with a thankfully dead Shambler to fall onto.
- Drop into the pit and grab the Gold Key; hit the Quake switch; go into the now-opened alcove behind you to nab the Double-barreled Shotgun and hit yet another Quake switch. Go through the previously barred passageway to ride the Slipgate back to 10. Waltz straight ahead to 11.

11. The Gold Key grants you access to the exit room and its lovely Slipgate. Watch out for an Ogre sneak attack from the far left corner. Once he's down, you have our congratulations: You've conquered a sinfully bloody mission.

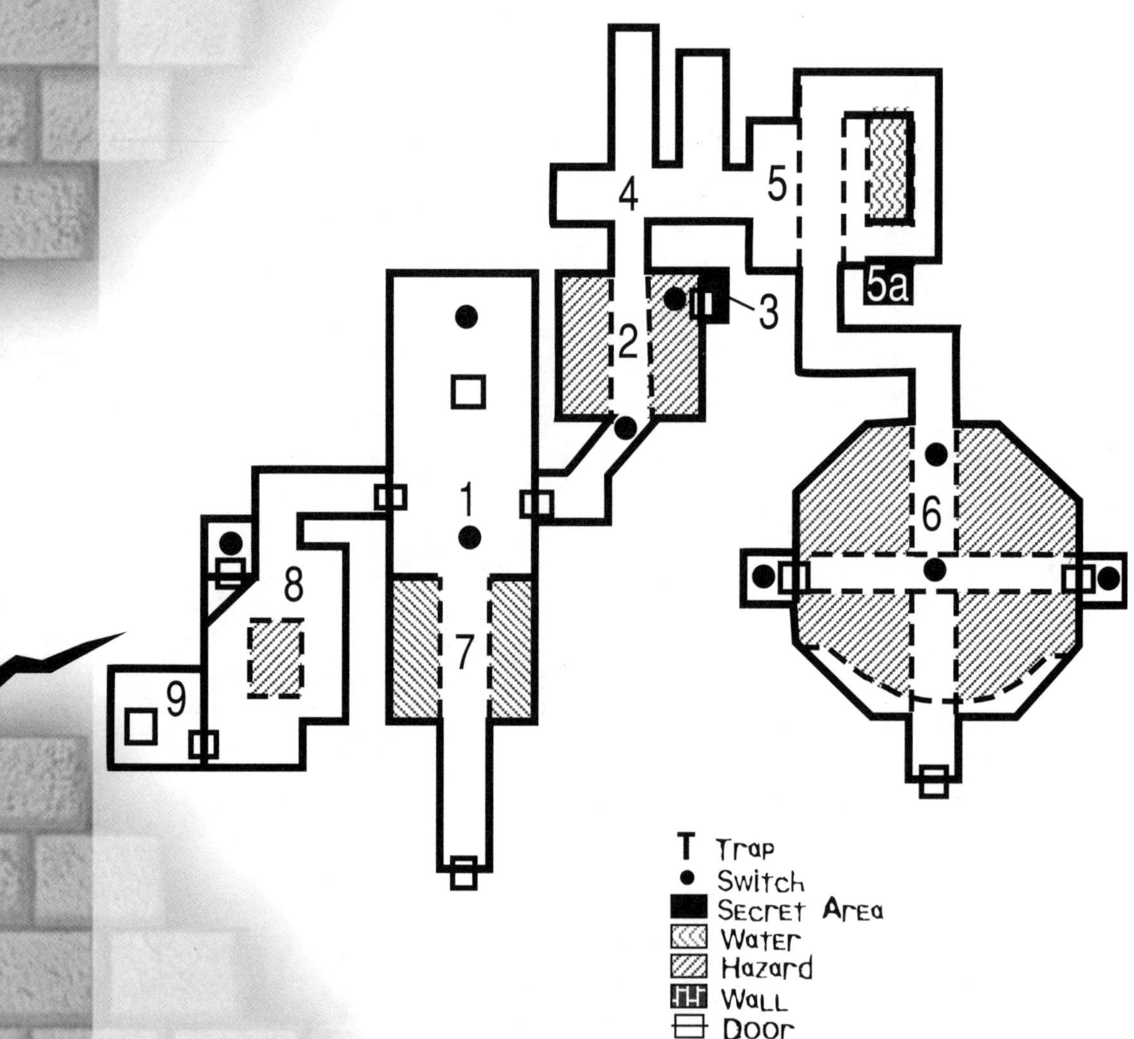
1
2
3
4
5
5a
6
7
8
9
T Trap
Switch
Secret Area
Water
Hazard
Wall
Door

Mission 3: The Tomb of Terror

Compact and tricky, this mission delivers traps aplenty and non-stop action. Depending on your point of view, this mission is either a warm-up for bigger and better things to come, or a breather from the test-of-endurance missions in Episode 2.

In essence, this mission map centers around a central hub (area 1 in this walkthrough). This design feature, in addition to a pair of Nailgun traps and many lava hazards, makes this an ideal slaying ground for a small party of Deathmatchers.

Mission 3: The Tomb of Terror At-a-Glance (E3M3)

1. Shotgun Shells, Health
2. Yellow Armor, Health
3. **Secret Area.** Red Armor
4. Supernailgun, Shotgun Shells, Health, Flechette
5. Shotgun Shells, Flechettes, Rockets, Nailgun Trap, Health

5a. **Secret Area.** Megahealth

6. Flechettes, Shotgun Shells, Health, Rockets
7. Megahealth, Nailgun Trap, Flechette, Health, Silver Key
8. Health, Flechettes, Rockets, Shotgun Shells, Switch to Open 9
9. Exit. Health, Green Armor

Highlights:

- Two Easy-to-Find Secret Areas
- Relentless Ogre Killing
- NBA-Style Grenade Bank Shots

This Tomb's for You!

1. Paste the Ogre in front of you; run past his smokin' corpse and hit the Quake switch hidden behind the stairs. Watch for the Death Knight who comes roaring from the hallway you just opened. Also beware of his grenade heaving buddies on a platform above the stairs (area 7). All foes in this area can be killed quite handily from below. Get out your favorite Ogre killing apparatus and go through the doorway you opened.

2. Scoop up the Yellow Armor and send the perched Ogre packing. Stand on the Quake floor switch to bring a flight of stairs out of the lava. They only appear for a few moments, so you'd better hurry up. Get out your shotgun, turn right, and look up.

3. **Secret Area.** From the top of the stairs you should see a Quake switch high above. Shoot it and a section of wall directly below it (and directly in front of you across the lava) opens to reveal a Slipgate. Leap toward the Slipgate and let it take you to the rafters above 2 and a shiny suit of Red Armor. Drop off the catwalk to the right of the armor, and you'll land safely on top of the platform. Select your Grenade Launcher and prepare for a warm Zombie welcome wagon.

4. Grabbing the Supernailgun and immediately jumping back often gets an Ogre to your right and a Zombie to your left to trade body parts for grenades. To end the spat, use the angled walls to make trick bank shots even Michael Jordan would envy. Snatching the Rockets or Health at the end of the hall brings a trio of Zombies to their feet. They limp out of an otherwise hidden alcove down the left hall (as you face the top of the lava stairs). Going into their fetid pen alerts a Death Knight patrolling 5 to your unwanted presence. We suggest you grab the Flechettes, get out your new Supernailgun, and punish him for disturbing the peace.

5. A Death Knights leaps out from the left to behead you as soon as you creep in. Nail him while keeping an eye on his canned buddies lurking on the catwalk over the water. As a reward for securing the area, you now have unmolested access to another Secret Area.

5a. **Secret Area.** Dive into the water, turn right, and sink down for a juicy a Megahealth.

Slog up the stairs and follow the walkway to the lift, and get ready to confront yet another herd of Zombies. As soon as you make the left turn down the hall, a nail trap erupts from the floor. Get out your Nailgun and run down the center of the hall or hop and hug the walls. As soon as you finish running the nail-trap gauntlet a Death Knight materializes. Cut him down to size, turn left, and lay waste to the Ogre at the bottom of the steps. Thank id for the Megahealth.

6. The Slipgate across the lava pool is your ultimate destination here (it takes you back to 1). As in the previous mission, only a successful completion of an ordered series of events allows you to continue. Here's how:

- Nail the Scrags that menace the sky (there are two); step onto the pulsating Quake switch.
- Run down the plank, spin around, and take care of business with a Death Knight and his Zombie pals.
- Run down either side plank and stand on the Quake switch. Don't let the Scrags pin you into a corner or you'll be mercilessly smushed!
- Run down the other plank and stand on its Quake switch. The last plank emerges, granting you access to the Slipgate. But there's a catch.
- As soon as you step on the Slipgate platform, a Fiend teleports in your face (preventing you from making a clean escape through the Slipgate), and yet another pair of Zombies appear. Punish them for their insolence and dive into the Slipgate.

7. Welcome back to 1, young warrior. Backpedal as you climb up the stairs, killing the Ogres as you go—unless, of course, you already banished them to hell at the beginning of this mission.

Spin around at the Megahealth and make the Death Knight bow down before you. Walk down either ledge toward the tunnel. When you step on the floor-mounted Quake switch two events happen: A plank extends across the lava pit (briefly), and a section of far wall pulls back to reveal a pit containing the Silver Key, a Death Knight, and a Slipgate that takes you back to 1. Stepping on the plank activates a vicious nail trap—putting you in the midst of a hellacious cross fire. Moreover, if you loiter the plank retracts, dunking you in the firewater. Simply put, we suggest you run like hell down the plank once it appears, bushwack the Death Knight from above for a few moments, then drop down for a manly toe-to-toe. In short, don't hesitate and look back.

8. Get out your most trusted Fiend killer and open the Silver Key door. When the leaping Fiend leaps no more, help yourself to a pair of Health boxes.

Grabbing the heap of nails and rockets springs a trap from the left in the form of a Death Kight dynamic duo and their Scrag sidekick. Backpedal and let them have it.

When you enter the large open area, watch out for the Death Knight directly above and behind you. He's in an alcove in the wall. A few Grenades quiets him for good.

The set of doors on the second landing is all that keeps you from the exit. The switchs to open these doors are at the bottom of the stairs—protected by (surprise, surprise) an angry Death Knight and a gang of Ogres.

Watch out for an Ogre as you descend the stairs en route to the first

Quake switch. Get out your Supernailgun and save the game. Hitting the switch drops a set of wall panels across the lava pool, unleashing the first wave of attack. We suggest you battle the closest set of bad guys (a Death Knight and an Ogre) from the relative safety of the Quake switch area. Once you go half way down the pen the far wall drops away, releasing yet another Ogre. At the end of this hall and left is your goal—the final Quake switch that opens the doors to the exit room. Down the remaining pair of losers and Health, ammo, and Final Quake swith are yours.

Beware of one last batch of bodies (who do their best to get in a parting volley from above), as you ascend the stairs en route to the exit. A Double-barreled Shotgun/Supernailgun combo is usually quite effective for serving up a quick death to your foes—that is after they've done their best to kill each other.

9. End. Grab the Green Armor and health and go. Your work is done here.

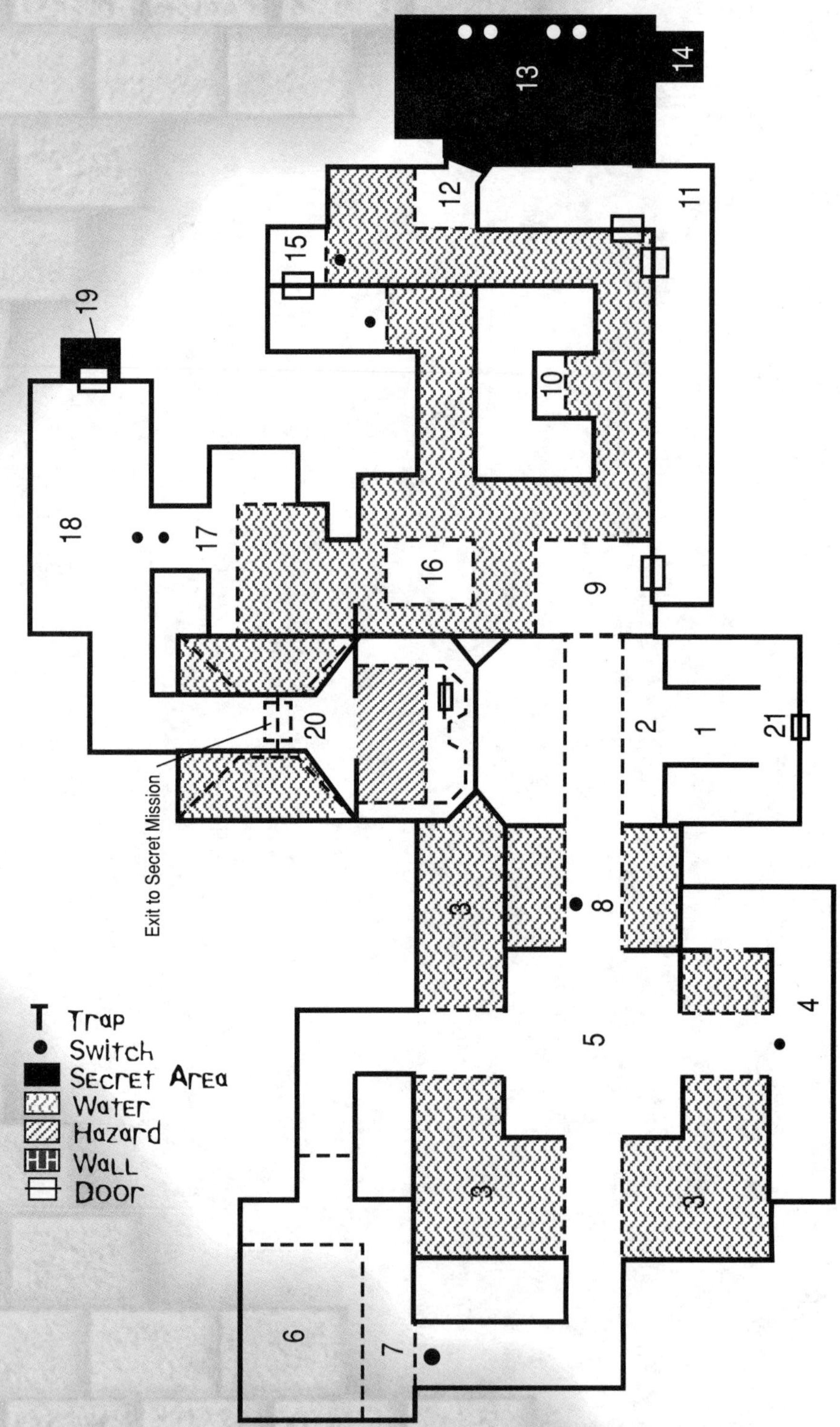
T Trap
● Switch
Secret Area
Water
Hazard
Wall
Door
Exit to Secret Mission
1
2
3
4
5
6
7
8
9
10
11
12
13
14
15
16
17
18
19
20
21

Mission 4: Satan's Dark Delight

Lean on ammo, big on water, this mission scores big on the novelty scale. If you yearn to slay your way through a mission without playing the Easter Key hunt, look no further.

Even without keys, your progress through this mission is exceedingly linear, but this feature only becomes apparent once you finish this foray into Satan's realm.

If you follow our lovingly crafted walkthrough, not only will you get your grubby hands on the blessed Rocket Launcher and Thunderbolt, you'll also vanquish your foes while under the influence of three separate power-ups. And if that isn't cool enough, follow us and gain unmolested access to this episode's Secret Mission: "The Haunted Halls."

Satan's Dark Delight At-a-Glance (E3M4)

1. Health
2. Flechette, Health
3. Flechette, Health, Rockets, Yellow Armor, Shotgun Shells
4. Flechette, Health
5. Rocket Launcher, Health
6. Cells
7. **Secret Area.** Flechette, Rockets, Health
8. Supernailgun, Flechette, Health, Shotgun Shells
9. Health
10. Switch
11. Health, Flechette
12. Access to 13 and 14
13. **Secret Area.** Health, Megahealth, Yellow Armor, Flechettes
14. **Secret Area.** Pentagram of Protection
15. Shotgun Shells
16. Platform
17. Health, Flechette
18. Health, Rockets
19. **Secret Area.** Pentagram of Protection
20. Thunderbolt, Health, Access to Secret Mission
21. Exit

Highlights:

- In-Yer-Face Shambler Zappin'
- Way Rad Platform Surfin'
- Gratuitous Ogre Smushin'
- Four Generously Stocked Secret Areas

A Delightful Chocolate Box Full of Death

1. Sidestep right or left off the telepad into the caged hallway and shoot the waiting Ogre in the back. This stirs a pair of his Ogre brethren into a vengeance fit above you (they're in area 21). Dodge their grenades and repeat this nifty move in the other caged hallway. He'll just stand there and take it. You can try to kill the Ogres above you from here, but you'll waste a lot of ammo and time.

2. The sliding floor panel to the left takes you to 3. The strangely shaped metal plate on the floor against the right wall is a lift. Ride the lift to 21, the Ogre pen. You can't get in, but your grenades can... Note the telepad directly opposite the cage. That's where you'll come in from 20.

Now, switch to your favorite Rotfish and Scrag killer, drop to the floor and approach the sliding floor panel. Save your game, read our notes on area 3, then dive in and prepare for a major ass-kicking session.

3. The ceiling at the end of the watery passage slides open to let you up, and closes behind you once you pass through. Move to the right to get out from under the metal overhang. If you feel like a fish in a barrel, you're not alone. Exterminate the Rotfish, then surface and nail the curious pair of Scrags. It helps to swim under the Zombie ledges to waste the Scrags—this way you won't be caught in a rotting-flesh cross fire.

Once you take out the Scrags, whip out your Grenade Launcher, and cream the Zombies on the ledges above. Hook around the large center structure (area 5). As soon as you partake in the great Health box giveaway (past the Shotgun-Shell-Zombie platform), an Ogre roars into action above and to the right from a niche high up in the far wall (area 4). Stay under the niche and lob grenades in his general direction. He won't know what hit him.

Under the water, past the Ogre niche, you face a steel door. Could this be the door to Davy Jones' Locker? Better open it and find out.

4. Opening the door brings down a lift—and an Ogre sneak attack! Turn him into Rotfish food, ride the lift up, and follow the passage to the Quake switch. If you didn't kill the Ogre from 3, you have your chance now. Get out your favorite Ogre-killing firestick, then hit the switch to extend a plank to the now-opened door leading to 5.

5. As soon as the door drops, an angry Ogre comes charging toward you. Fortunately for you he has to wait for the plank to fully extend before he can reallyhurt you. Those few moments of hesitation give you the precious time you need make Ogre mincemeat. Exit the structure and walk across the next plank. You can leap to the Zombies' ledges from here.

Note that you can leap from the Yellow-Armor ledge to the walkway that is 8. But then you'd miss a fabulous Secret Area and some superb Ogre killin'. Skip to 8 if you decide to wimp out.

6. Grab the Cell and jump back. An Ogre leaps off a ledge from the left. Flatten him with rockets—you'll want to save any nails and shells for an impending battle after you hit the Quake switch.

Turn the corner and trade rockets with yet another Ogre. Now's your chance to enjoy the distance and height advantage the Ogres always seem to hog for themselves. Approach the Quake switch, get out your Supernailgun, and save your game.

If you're low on Health or ammo, skip ahead to 7. If not, hit the switch now, this seals off all exits and brings down a trio of Ogres. Have fun. We suggest you aim high and hit the switch with your back. Every little bit helps. The doors open once the last Ogre is dead. As you face the switch, exit out of the left ramp, then turn around.

7. **Secret Area.** At the top of the ramp, turn around and shoot the yellow light. Hitting it brings three stair steps out of the wall, granting you access to this item-laden ledge. Collect your goods and return to 5.
If you didn't already set off the Quake switch/Ogre trap in 6, leap down and do it now. Of course, you can always skip it, girly-man.

8. Go through 5 and hit the Quake switch. Turn right as you ascend and prepare for a nasty trap. Suppress your greed once you reach the top. When you grab the Supernailgun, a pair of Ogres drops from the rafters in an effort to make a hero sandwich. We suggest you step only as far as the edge of the first rafter to trigger the trap (you'll hear the Ogres scream); then jump back and take them one at a time. As a bonus you'll get a few free shots at the first Ogre's back. You may take some heavy damage during this melee, but the gobs of Health lying around this mission should keep you out of the jaws of death. To sustain a minimum of damage, drop down the lift shaft when they attack and unleash a rockets from below—the Ogres like to hang out at the edge of the ledge.

At the end of the hall is a deep pit. Take out the Ogre brothers in 9 from here, then drop onto the now-quiet platform.

9. You must make a lot of floating platform connections here, and missing your ride means a long fall into the drink. If you fall, swim back toward this beginning platform—a set of stairs and a Slipgate wait to whisk you back to 9. Before you set off, why not paste the Zombie and his Ogre pals in 17? They're on yonder ledge, through the opening to your left.

Without further adieu, here's what to do and see on your tour of this area:

10. Ride the platform in front of you until it gets to the beam/ledge where the Ogre's carcass lies. Step onto that ledge and take out the Ogre in the niche below you to the left. Don't shoot the Quake switch in 10 yet! As soon as he's dead, drop down to his platform and wait for another water taxi. Get on and shoot the aforementioned Quake switch as you move out back to 9.

11. In a few moments a set of doors at the far end of the pool open, unleashing three testy Ogres and a Fiend. Aim your rockets below and beyond the aforementioned beam, and bring death to as many enemies as you can from 8. Then get out your Supernailgun just for the waiting Fiend, and ride a water taxi to their platform to finish the job. (You'll get a face full of grenades if you battle these bozos from 10.) Resist the urge to nail the Ogre in 15 as you wait for the next water taxi. (Note that the lift at the end of the hallway, past the Health, takes you down to 9. It's good to know for Deathmatch play.)

12. As your ride turns right, shoot the Ogre on the platform below. Drop off onto his corpse, and the walls around you drop away, granting you free access to the goods in 13 and 14.

But before you go in for your swag, turn and shoot the Quake switch above the Ogre in 15. Doing so puts a grisly Ogre press into action. Now you know why the walls are so bloody...

If you rocketed the Zombie and Ogres in 17 already, you now have unfettered access to 18.

13. **Secret Area.** Do not take the Quad Damage rune, the Megahealth (or the Pentagram in 14), until you're ready to go to 18. To open 14, shoot each of the white light bars in the wall behind the Quad Damage and Megahealth. When you've shot the fourth light, a niche next to the Quad Damage opens to reveal the glorious Pentagram.

The lift takes you to 11; you'll use it to get to 18 once you're powered up. Here's how to set the stage to maximize your powerup time:

- Return to 12 and hop onto a water taxi as it goes toward 15, the Ogre press.
- Go through the left doorway and step onto the waiting taxi. Shoot the floor switch and the taxi spirits you to 16, a now-waiting island. Cream your enemies from here if you didn't from 9.
- Ride the taxi to 17 to sweep up any Health or nails you might need. DO NOT go into the Quake switch alcove in 17 yet.
- Drop into the water and swim to the Slipgate under 9.
- Take a water taxi back to 13.

14. **Secret Area.** Stand in 13, select your Rocket Launcher and save your game. Nab the Quad Damage, Megahealth, and Pentagram, then run onto the lift. Leap down into the water and swim as fast as you can for the Slipgate. Leap from 9 to 16 and wait impatiently for the water taxi to take you to 17.

15 & 16. See the list in 13.

17. Hit the Quake switch in the alcove to ride a lift up to 18—and get ready to rumble!

18. Waste the Fiends and Ogres who leap into your arms of death. Don't forget to whack the Ogre hiding in the left hallway. You probably will have depleted your powerups by the time the fun stops.

The floor switch at the top of the lift is like an elevator call button. It's a swell feature and all, but since you can only access this room from 9, it's all but useless.

Go to the far right corner and look up at the yellow light in the ceiling. Why don't you shoot it and see what happens?

19. **Secret Area.** Shooting the yellow ceiling light opens a wall panel, revealing yet another Pentagram of Protection. Don't take it until you've read 20. Grabbing the Pentagram depends on how confident you are at making lava jumps or nailing Shamblers. We'll pause here while you read ahead.
Get out your Supernailgun, step backward over the Pentagram (if you want) and run like hell toward 20. The Shambler will be down before he knows it.

20. Halfway down the ramp, just before you lay hands on the awesome Thunderbolt, a Shambler appears. If you're burning the Pentagram, just stand there and make him take it like a good monster. If not, you can leap to either side of him, grab the Thunderbolt, dive into either of the Health-box-laden hallways for cover, and fry his ass. When he's dead (and if you haven't yet used the Pentagram), go back to 19 for way-cool swim in the lava—and a virtual guarantee that you'll make it to either exit.

No matter what Pentagram course you take, drop onto either ledge next to the ramp and peer deep down into the firewater. You should see a conspicuous hole in the lava. That's the exit to the Secret Mission: "The Haunted Halls."

If, however, you'd rather skip the Secret Mission, return to the Thunderbolt perch and look down at the landing that holds the Slipgate. Sticking a landing is child's play. Once through the Slipgate you'll find the bars that once kept you from 21 have vanished.

21. If you killed the Ogres in 21 from 1 or 2, simply prance through the Slipgate, much to Satan's dark disgust.

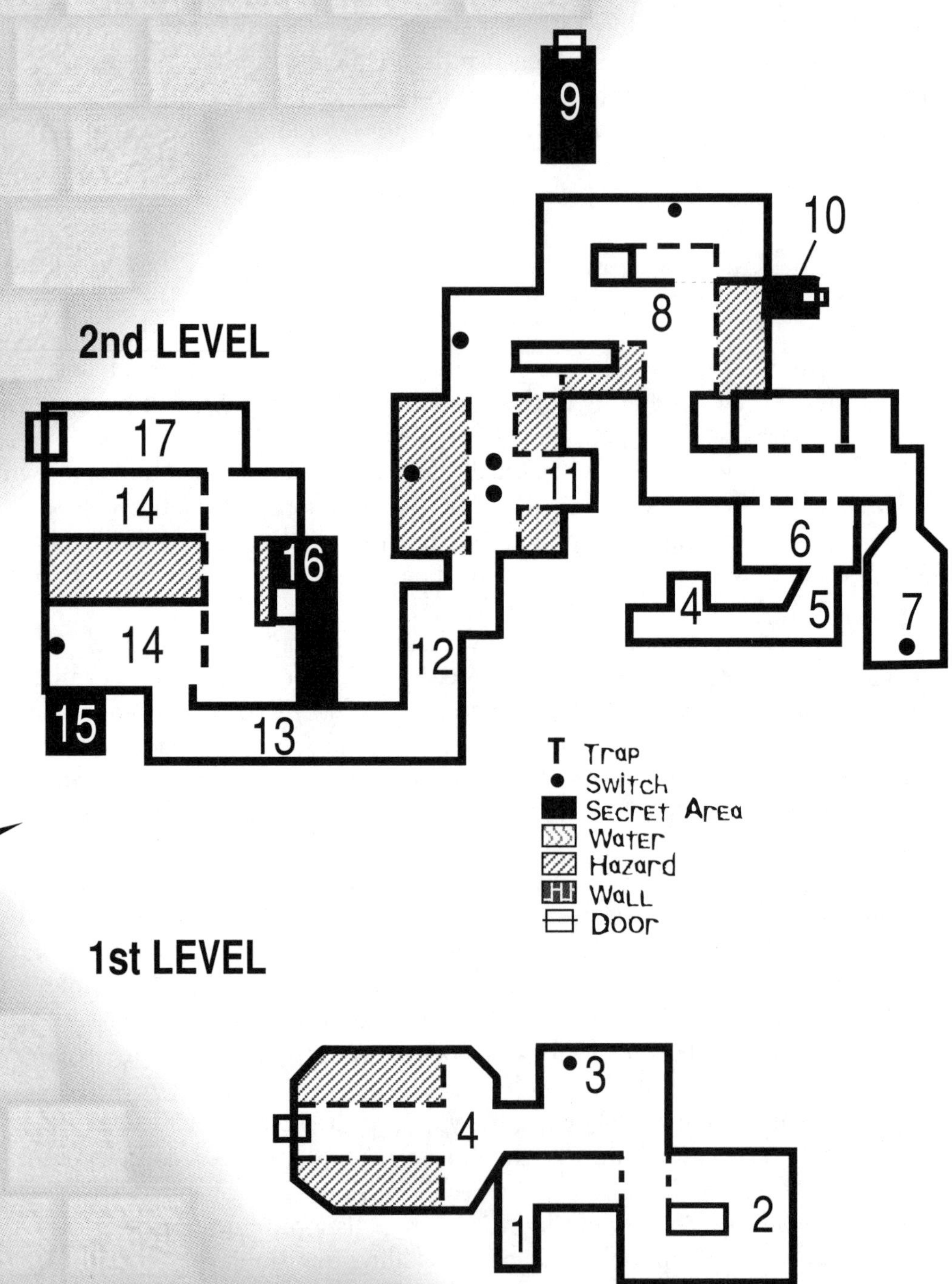

2nd LEVEL
9
10
8
17
14
16
11
6
14
4
5
7
12
15
13
T Trap
Switch
Secret Area
Water
Hazard
Wall
Door
1st LEVEL
3
4
2
1

Secret Mission: The Haunted Halls

You'll find a lot of halls here, but they aren't very haunted. This is undoubtedly the straightest Secret Mission in the game, bound to disappoint fans who demand that Secret Missions have bizarre quirks or physics-defying flair. Such is not the case, however, and perhaps this is why the Haunted Halls is a bit of a letdown.

Battling your way through this tightly designed mission shouldn't take much for those who use the environment to their advantage. A few shrewdly placed powerups make short work of its only potentially overwhelming combat area. At the end of the mission you get more powerups than the monsters warrant—a nice change of pace.

Secret Mission: The Haunted Halls At-a-Glance (E3M7)

1. Health, Rockets
2. Rockets, Green Armor
3. Switch
4. Flechette
5. Health
6. Health, Rockets
7. Switch
8. Shotgun Shells, Yellow Armor, Health, Flechette, Rockets
9. **Secret Area.** Megahealth
10. **Secret Area.** Quad Damage Rune
11. Health, Flechette
12. Health, Flechette
13. Nail Trap
14. Health
15. **Secret Area.** Yellow Armor, Quad Damage Rune, Megahealth
16. **Secret Area.** Flechette, Pentagram of Protection
17. Exit

Highlights:

 Four Swell Secret Areas

 Gangs of Goon Squads

 Caged Vore Slaying

Deck the Halls with Ogre Bodies...

1. Turn the corner and show the Ogre above and the Zombies below no mercy. Three rockets later, it's all over. Scoop up the goods on the way to the lift. Face right as you ascend.

2. Follow the passage until you get to the bridge. Stepping on the bridge drops the steel door on the other side, allowing a Fiend to come out to play. Backpedal over the walkway, rocket trails clouding the air. Keep your Rocket Launcher out as you creep over the bridge. Stop before you go past the left corner.

3. You should see a pair of Zombies wobbling before you. As soon as you paste them, a Scrag and an Ogre leap down to quarrel over the barbecue. Let them fight it out and sentence the winner to death. The steel door opens the moment you hit the Quake switch. Relax. Nothing leaps out to attack you—yet.

4. The Flechette is yours to keep. Get ready to backpedal as soon as you leap through the Slipgate!

5. An Ogre tosses a grenade upside your head the moment you appear—but not if you're already backing up. Lob a grenade or three down his hallway to soften him up, then follow up with some nails or shells, if necessary. Don't cross the threshold into 6 yet!

Note: You can leap off the ledge and fall back into 3 and Rocket the Ogre to pieces—but battling him from 3 means you're giving him a tremendous height advantage.

6. As soon as you breech the doorway, a Fiend rises out of a pit in the center of the room and a bar slams across the entrance, locking you in. It only retracts after you've downed the Fiend. Why not stand in the doorway, before triggering this trap, and lob a few grenades into the pit? Then when you enter, the Fiend's head rises to you as if on a silver platter.

Grab the rockets and immediately retreat to 5. An Ogre in 7 runs from his post atop the lift to the edge of the bridge above you. Rocket him down, get out a weapon that won't hurt you in close-quarters combat, and ride the lift to 7.

7. If you smoked the Ogre at the bridge already, you've only got two more to go. They're both hiding in the Quake switch room. Get out your Rocket Launcher and back up into the Quake switch. As soon as you hit it, a family of Zombies appears from the floor at the room's entrance. A flock of Scrags

hovers over the bridge past the Zombies to the left. Three or four rockets later the coast should be clear.
As soon as you cross the bridge and stick your nose into the passage proper, three Ogres leap out, grenades flying and chainsaws singing. Battling them toe-to-toe is a manly gesture, but why not backpedal and waste them from the safety of 7, or drop off the bridge and rocket them from the entrance to 5? If the third Ogre doesn't appear as promised, he could be lurking about in the shadows near the lift in 8. Draw him out with a few well-placed shots and deal with him as you did the others.

8. The Ogres on the faraway sniper's nest in 8 have deadly aim. Their accuracy and your poor line–of–fire combine to make this a bad spot for you to do battle. Instead of trading rockets for grenades, run down the walkway (under their grenades) and into the safe haven beneath them. Scoop up the Yellow Armor, return to the walkway, and run right. You'll see a lift on your right once you're safely away from the lava. Lob a load of grenades onto the platform, switch to a less explosive weapon, then ride the lift to finish the job. Hit the switch to open the steel door to 11—but before you go, how 'bout some Secret Area powerups?

9. **Secret Area.** Stand on the edge of the lifts and as it ascends step back and drop into the lift shaft; like magic, a Megahealth is yours to keep. Dive through the Slipgate and keep running.

10. **Secret Area.** Shoot the grate in the wall in front of you. It slides away and a small beam rises out of the lava. Grab the Quad Damage rune and backpedal as fast as you can to 11.

11. You're about to encounter a Shambler, some Ogres, and a Vore. The door slams shut as soon as you enter. It's kill or die, baby. The monsters 'port in as soon as you shoot the Quake switch near the top of the right wall. Here are some honest (and not-so-honest) ways to make your enemies go boom:

- Run past the Quake switch and the obvious trapdoor where the walkways meet. Stand about halfway between the trap door and the door to 12. Shoot the Quake switch.

- The Shambler should appear on your head. Congratulations on the telefrag! Pummel the Ogres dancing in the lava and then turn your attention to the Vore in the cage below.

- Standing on floor switch in the Vore pen opens the doors to let you out of 11. Shooting the wall-mounted Quake switch activates a hidden Teleporter, and anything inside the cage materializes on the walkway near the door to 8. If you have trouble nailing the Vore from above, shoot this switch and bring him to you.

- You'll find Flechettes under the catwalk next to the lava, as well as some Health boxes. It's an easy jump to the ledge near the lift to get back up to the walkway.

If telefragging the Shambler grates against your sense of fair play, then why did you buy this book? Seriously, if you'd rather kill the Shambler with your weaponry, stand on the ledge that leads to the lift when you shoot the Quake switch. The Shambler leaps down the walkway from left to right. Good luck—and may the Quad Damage power be with you.

12. When you reach the Flechette, a Death Knight storms up to greet you. Bring him to his knees and descend the stairs, wary of yet another Death Knight hiding to the immediate right at the bottom of the stairs. You could lob a grenade on his head from the top of the stairs, but only if you have no qualms about ambushing your foes.

13. Just peeking into the nail trap hallway forces an Ogre to leap to his death. Back up when you hear his roar (and before you set off the nails) and waste him before he gets off any grenades. Get out your best Vore- and Ogre-killer, dodge the nails as best you can, and prepare for a slugfest.

14. While nails still fly into your back, an Ogre attacks from the left while a Vore heaves spikeballs from across the lava pit. No real words of advice here, except to say that the faster you kill them the healthier you'll be. When the area is quiet again, hit the Quake switch to lower the lift. But after all that we'll bet you could use a Health and Armor boost. Stand next to the Quake switch and look up.

15. **Secret Area.** Stand in front of the lift-lowering Quake switch and look straight up. Shoot the tiny Quake switch and a panel of wall to your left drops away. Obliterate the Zombies inside and claim your swag.

Ride the lift in 14 and murder the Ogres at the top. This is also the time and place to wax the Ogre in the cage. A Grenade or two works nicely. After you've given the Ogres their beating, stand on the edge of walkway and get ready to jump onto the cage.

16. **Secret Area.** Landing on top of the cage opens a wall panel before you. Go in for your Pentagram and ammo. Drop off the far ledge back into the nail trap (13) and return to where you leapt to the cage—only this time drop off onto the ledge where the Vore corpse rests.

17. The steel door slides open as you approach. An Ogre comes out to play, but your Pentagram and firepower are no match for him. Sweep up any riches you may have left behind: It's time to find out what the Wind Tunnels are all about.

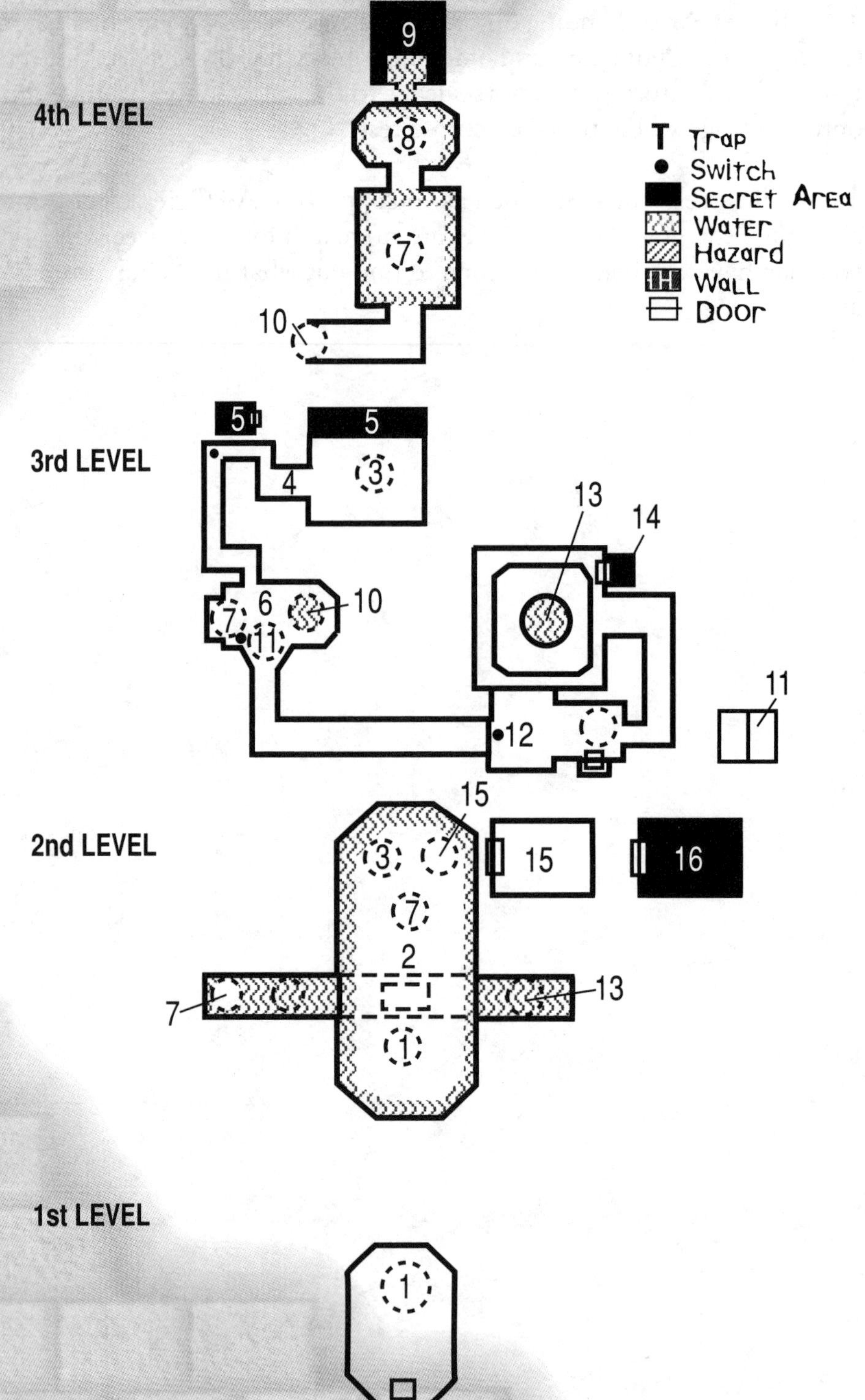

4th LEVEL
9
8
7
10
T Trap
Switch
Secret Area
Water
Hazard
Wall
Door
3rd LEVEL
5
5
4
3
13
14
6
7
10
11
11
12
2nd LEVEL
15
3
15
16
7
2
7
13
1
1st LEVEL
1

Mission 5: Wind Tunnels

Not only do you score a Thunderbolt and Rocket Launcher here, you'll find them complemented with two well-placed Quad Damage runes. Mix in a liberal helping of Flechettes and an extra-bouncy atmosphere, and you've got the makings of satisfying, blood-spouting fun for Deathmatch and solo players alike.

There really aren't any big tricks for navigating the wind tunnels. Simply, if you point in the proper direction before you leap, you'll be one gun up before the action starts. And if you rely on your Supernailgun and save your game before each jump, we suspect you'll enjoy the action here as much as we do.

Mission 7: Wind Tunnels At-a-Glance (E3M5)

1. Health, Shotgun Shells, Flechettes
2. Health, Flechettes, Cell
3. Health, Flechette, Shotgun Shells, Thunderbolt, Rockets
4. Health, Shotgun Shells, Flechette
5. **Secret Area.** Flechette, Quad Damage Rune, Health
6. Health, Rockets, Biosuit, Flechette
7. Shotgun Shells, Flechette, Health, Rockets
8. Green Armor, Flechettes
9. **Secret Area.** Flechettes, Rocket Launcher, Health
10. Shotgun Shells, Health
11. Quad Damage Rune, Health
12. Nail Trap, Cells, Health, Rockets, Flechettes, Green Armor
13. Health, Flechettes, Shotgun Shells,
14. **Secret Area.** Biosuit, Flechette, Health
15. Exit, Health
16. **Secret Area.** Flechettes, Health

Highlights:

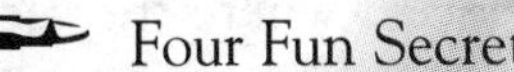

- Four Fun Secret Areas

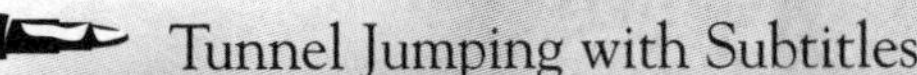

- Tunnel Jumping with Subtitles
- Air Strikes and Quad Damage Runes Aplenty

Everyone Knows It's Windy

1. Sweep up all the supplies you can. Once you leave this area you can't come back. Get out your Supernailgun and get ready to jump up into the tunnel. A dastardly bunch of enemies awaits.

2. A pair of Fiends and three Scrags begin their attack while you're still crashing and careening like a pinball against three main tunnels. Watch out for the third Fiend behind the tunnel you entered! He probably won't partake in the initial attack. Kill him now or he'll put the hurt on you just when you don't need it.

You'll return to this room via the turgid water surrounding the platform. Ignore the urge to explore the deep (you can't really go anywhere, anyway), get out your Rocket Launcher, step under the only open tunnel, and jump.

3. A pair of perched Death Knights, and one on the floor, fan their firebolts at you even before you start to bounce. What's more, a Fiend awaits you at the top of the stairs. Blast away with the Rocket Launcher. Use any other weapon and you'll just waste a lot ammo. Remember, close only counts in horseshoes, hand grenades (or rockets, in this case), and atom bombs. When the Death Knights from above are down, dispatch the last Knight from the lip of the wind tunnel. The Fiends probably won't attack unless you battled the Knights from the floor.

The Thunderbolt's in the shadows to the right of the stairs, the Quad Damage rune is in Secret Area 5 (accessible from a hole in the floor at 4), and the Rockets (above and to the left of the stairs) are easily attainable by stepping off 5 and navigating the ledge that runs the room's perimeter.

4. Only the flashing disco lights makes killing the Fiends in this hallway difficult. Trigger them and backpedal with guns blazing. The fun begins when you mount the stairs and peek around the first right corner. Move just far enough up the stairs to trigger a single Fiend into action; go any deeper and you'll have a pair of frothing monsters to deal with. Exterminate the second Fiend and gain easy access to the mission's first Secret Area. Run past the pair of Health boxes (where the second Fiend was crouching) and angle toward the far right corner.

5. **Secret Area.** Approaching the hole in 4 triggers a Fiend from the left. Leave him alone for now, and drop into the hole. He can't follow you down. Dive through the Slipgate and, lo—the Quad Damage rune. Read ahead to 6, then grab the rune, drop down, and run through 4, killing Fiends as you go!

6. Once you slay the rest of the Fiends at 4, you should emerge at 6 with bulging eyes. A Death Knight attacks from the front, an Ogre from your left, and a pair of Scrags from above. Your Quad Damage should be burned out by the time you blow your foes to bite-sized chunks.

Hit the Quake switch to open the grate covering the tunnel entrance atop the stairs. Don't forget to go back for any supplies you may have missed. When you're ready, grab the Biosuit if you want, climb the stairs, and drop down the hole, ready for a close-quarters fight. (Ignore the water next to the Biosuit).

A Fiend leaps to attack the moment you hit the bottom, and a pair of Scrags emerges from the far end of the sewer as you approach. Nail them and swim down the tube to the grate. Follow the arrows up and angle for the light. Welcome back to 2.

7. The switch in 6 also opened the red tube in 2 (the one with the Flechette). Get out your favorite close-quarters Scrag- and Fiend-killer, and jump.

The fight here is as frantic as it gets. Your legs get Fiend-slashed while Scrags pound your head. What's more, all the excitement usually draws an Ogre from 8 into the fray.

We found it's best to cut down the flying foe population while bouncing. Then when you hang up on the tube's lip, drop down and toe-to-toe it with the leftovers. You'll take damage from the Fiend even if you stand on the edge of the tube to kill him from above. It's not fair, but there it is. If you sustain less than 50 damage points in this melee, you've done very well, indeed.

Also, try not escape by falling into the water. The monsters will gang-tackle you the moment you emerge. If you do fall in, you can only get back onto the deck in 8.

The large barred tube in wall is area 10. You must tube-jump to get there. Note also that the Rockets in 7 are under the platform. Claim those after you bag all the baddies.

8. Rocket the remaining Ogre to death from 7 and go in for your swag. The tube cover drops as you approach. But before you jump, dive into the drink to claim yet another Secret Area.

9. **Secret Area.** Face the far wall (past the tube) and drop into the water. Swim under the arch and up toward the light. Easy, eh? Don't forget to nab the Rockets in the water in 7 before you leave.

After you load up with supplies, return to the tube in 8, get out your favorite anti-Scrag device, stand so area 7 is to your left and area 9 is to your right, and jump.

10. You fly over 8 and 7 and land smack-dab in the middle of a Scrag gathering. Chunkify them and go toward the hole ahead. That's area 6 below. A pair of Scrags materializes when you hit the water. The wind tunnel to 11 and 12 also opens. So what are you waiting for?

11. Step under the tube in 6, face the pool, save your game, and get ready to leap into the mission's biggest battle. Your goal is to ride the currents to land on a ledge above 12, at least for a moment, and grab a Quad Damage rune in the process. Face the direction you're flying in while holding down your [↑] key and add a tiny tap on your jump key just before you enter the room to land on the far ledge—exactly where you want to be. It's a very tricky move that by no means works every time. Practice makes perfect.

If you land on the ledge, battle the Ogres and down the Knights from these rafters. These weenies aren't worth any precious Quad Damage time. Position yourself next to the Quad Damage rune, grab it, and fall toward the Quake switch. If you can't seem to do any more than grab the Quad Damage rune before you fall, that's fine. All you've done is shortcut through 11. You can go back for the Ogres once you clean out 13.

12. Hitting the ground triggers a vicious nail turret trap. There's a safe corridor in–line with with the Quake switch. Hit the Quake switch to both drop a panel in the right side of the hallway toward 13 (revealing a Health box, Green Armor, and a Fiend) and release a set of steel doors that would otherwise keep you out of 13.

Endure the nail trap as you grab the goods and blast the Fiend as you get the hell out of this room. As you exit the room itself, the nail turrets stop. Turn left and a set of floor-mounted nailguns erupt and Ogres attack. Quad Damage these losers, and press on. A pair of Shamblers awaits your wrath.

13. As you enter, Shamblers attack from the left and right. Quad them both from the hall. Your Quad power should be out by now, so go back and collect any prizes you may have forgotten in 12. Back in 13, watch for a pair of nasty Scrags who do great damage to the unwary. It's also very easy to slip down onto the lower ledge. If that happens, you can't get to Secret Area 14.

Take out the Fiends below as you work your way around the upper ledge. Note that the Fiends and Scrags sometimes drop into the water. You'll have to kill them en route to 15. Stop when you're opposite the Shambler bodies. Look up at the beams; see the Quake switch? Shoot it and another Secret Area is yours to keep.

14. Secret Area. Shooting the switch drops a panel left of the entrance to 13. Go in for your swag. Drop to the ledge below for any items you need, then hurry into the drink—that Biosuit time's a-wastin'.

Watch for Fiends and Scrags as you swim. This tunnel is the mirror opposite of the one you swam in 6. The Quake switch in 12 also lowered the grate in this tunnel, giving you free access back to 2. Watch out for any loose Scrags as you approach the silver-plated tube.

15. Get ready for a battle royal after you jump into the sliver-plated tube in 2. Face the tunnel that takes you to 3 before you leap. You'll land hard in 15, but it won't take long to execute a pair each of Scrags and Ogres. These are the last bad guys in this mission.

Once you've settled the score, you can simply walk through the Slipgate before you—or you can grab some goods in this mission's final Secret Area.

16. Secret Area. In 15, shoot the off-colored floor panel in front of the exit Slipgate. The panel slides away, revealing copious amounts of nails and Health. Angle off to the side to avoid falling into the Slipgate below. Easy enough to do. Stock up, jump into the Slipgate, and you'll find yourself back in 2. Return to 15 via the familiar silver-plated tunnel to end this way-cool mission.

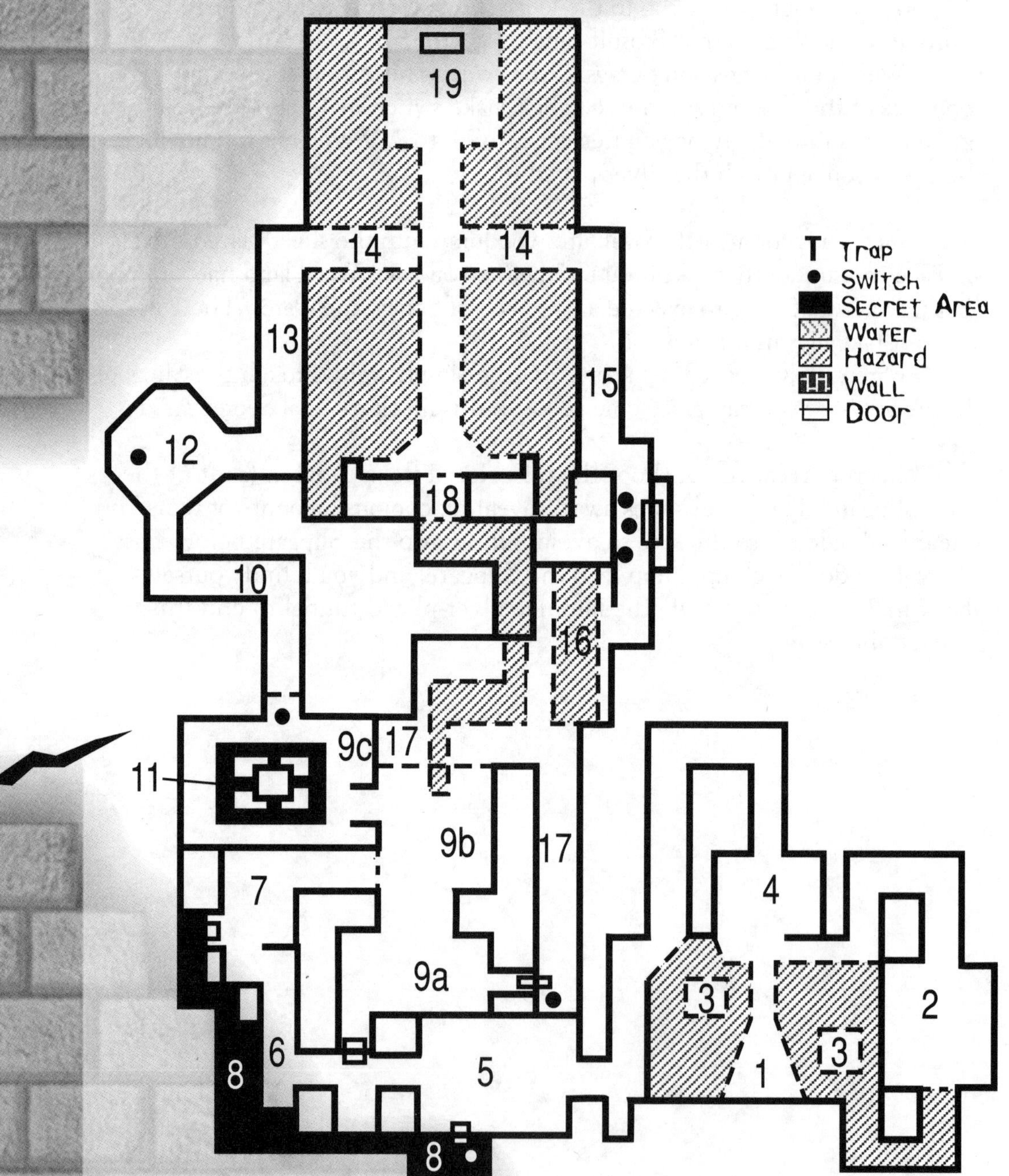

19
14
14
13
15
12
18
10
16
9c
17
11
9b
17
7
4
9a
3
2
6
3
8
5
1
8
T Trap
Switch
Secret Area
Water
Hazard
Wall
Door

Mission 6: The Chambers of Torment

This is the final mission of Episode 3, and make no mistake, this is a big one. Your ultimate quest is to capture the third Rune Key, and getting there is all the fun.

You'll get more than your fill of Vore killin' and skirt a fiery lava death many times as you work your way through the same few passages and rooms toward the Big Payoff. But with one well-placed Quad Damage Rune, a generous complement of Health, Rockets, and Shotgun Shells, all the hassle seems worthwhile. A more existential hero may wonder if all this killing is worth one measly Rune Key. A dyed-in-blood hero knows it is.

Mission 6: The Chambers of Torment At-a-Glance (E3M6)

1. Health, Flechette, Shotgun Shells
2. Cells, Rockets, Health, Shotgun Shells
3. Rockets, Health, Red Armor
4. Ring of Shadows, Health, Shotgun Shells
5. Green Armor, Health, Flechette, Silver Key Door
6. Shotgun Shells
7. Flechettes, Health, Silver Key, Quake Switch
8. **Secret Area.** Yellow Armor, Health, Flechette, Quad Damage Rune

9a. Shotgun Shells, Cell

9b. Shotgun Shells

9c. Rockets, Flechette, Health

10. Flechettes, Shotgun Shells, Health
11. **Secret Area.** Rockets, Shells, Health
12. Green Armor
13. Rockets, Health, Flechettes, Shotgun Shells
14. Rockets, Cell, Health, Flechette
15. Health, Shotgun Shells, Flechette
16. Shotgun Shells
17. Gold Key, Rockets, Flechettes, Health, Shotgun Shells
18. Health, Flechette, Shotgun Shells
19. Rune Key, Exit

Highlights:

- The Third Rune
- Two Big Money, Easy-to-Find Secret Areas
- Vore Blasting by the Ton

Torment Never Hurt So Good

1. Dash across the plank that spans the lava (the lava pool is 3), snatching goods as you go. Creep up the stairs in 4 and rocket the Knight down the hallway. Backpedal down the plank to finish the job.

You can knock out the Ogres on either side of the steps with a few rocket shots each. Leave the Ring of Shadows alone for now, and instead go down the right ledge toward the Shotgun Shells.

An Ogre rushes you as you turn the corner, and the Death Knight, who was probably taking pot shots at you from 2, will hopefully clatter down the stairs to confront you. Wait a moment and they might get a chance to fight each other before you join the fray. The stairway that leads into 4 is a great place to duck and cover.

If you want to avoid any Ogre damage, try going back to where you started and launching a rocket attack on the hapless villain from there. His grenades have no hope of reaching you. While you're at it, unload a few rockets through the Death Knight's window (area 2). If you're lucky you'll hit a waiting Ogre and raise all kinds of hell in there.

2. If you didn't pick them off from 1, a pair of Ogres lurk in the shadows to your left. This means you can opt for a very cool first strike initiative. A definite win-win situation. Once you dispatch these cannibals and sweep up the swag, go to the far end of the room and peer over the ledge, your favorite Scrag killing device to the ready.

3. There are two Scrags. The first rushes to embrace you when you step over the ledge; the second swoops down from above after you land. We suggest you jump past the lift to stir up the Scrag, backpedal onto the lift, and keep backing up as you fill the Scrag full of lead. So, what are you waiting for? You might as well jump.

Island hop to collect your booty. (You can also drop onto the islands from the ledges above, but it's hard to stick those landings. Unless you're really good, you'll take lava damage no matter which route you take.)

Once you grab the Red Armor, a pair of Scrags and a Vore materialize above you. Nail the Scrags from that island and then hop back to the lift and take up a defensive position in 2. If you didn't get the Scrags already, let the Scrags and Vore complete their dance of death and polish off the survivors from 2. The Vore is especially easy to kill—hide behind the wall and strafe with rockets. You shouldn't take any damage from his numerous spikeballs.

4. Grab the Ring of Shadows after you've gotten everything else you can carry, then dash down the hallway. Unleash an unholy rocket attack on anything else that's blind to your presence, namely Scrags, Ogres, a Fiend—who leaps out of a hidden room that also contains Green Armor—and a Vore in 5. Ducking into the Green Armor room seems to foil the otherwise impeccable guidance system in the Vore's spikeball.

After the invisibility wears off (about the time you slay the Vore), backtrack to sweep up any Shotgun Shells, Health, and Armor you may need.

5. Just past the devil-head panels at the far end of 5, a pair of Ogres leaps out, chainsaws swinging. Take them down, note the Silver Key door to your right, then carefully enter the next room. Be prepared to backpedal, Rocket Launcher blazing.

6. You can't get the Yellow Armor from here (it's Secret Area 8), but you can kill the two Ogres in the cage next to it. Watch out for a Dark Knight attack from the right! The best way to kill him is to backpedal down 5 and mercilessly rocket-attack from afar. The arrow-straight hallway was designed for rocket work, and the distance gives you all the time you need to dodge any attacks.

7. From the archway to this room you should be able to see a Vore and the shadowy outline of a Death Knight sword on your right. Lob a grenade just on the right side of the blue band on the wall and it should bounce back to land at the Knight's feet. Of course, you should run away as soon as you fire because both the Vore and the fair Knight are going to come out swinging. Slay them from afar, then go in to claim your ammo prizes.

Get ready for a real fight over the Silver Key. (FYI: The window behind the key looks into 9b.) Back into the key, then flee into 5—a few moments after you grab it a ceiling panel slides open and a pair of Ogres leaps down, grenades flying.

Nail the Ogres, then look up at the ceiling from where they attacked. Shoot the Quake Switch for access into the first Secret Area of this mission.

8. **Secret Area.** Shooting the ceiling-mounted Quake switch lowers the blue panel in the wall to the right of the archway at 7. Go inside for a whole heap of swag. Don't worry if you don't need the Yellow Armor yet—you can come back for it later.

Select your best close-range killing tool, step on the Quake switch at the end of the hallway, and only then snatch the Quad Damage Rune. Burst into the hallway, turn left, and run like hell through the Silver Key door.

9a. Nail the Death Knights and rush down the stairs to 9b.

9b. Note the Gold Key door and the Gold Key dangling on the ledge above it (that's area 17). Don't worry about the Ogre who guards it for now. Instead, concentrate your fire on the enemies in 9c.

9c. Slaughter the Death Knights (but ignore the Ogres on the beams above you for now). While the Quad Damage lasts leap into the lift at the right side of the room. Some more Death Knights need uncanning.

10. Your Quad Damage power will most likely be burned out by the time you finish pickling the three Death Knights here. Once all's quiet in the hallway, face 9 from the edge of the lift and look up. Hmmm. Another Quake switch…

11. **Secret Area.** Shooting the Quake switch lowers a section of wall past the lift. You now have access to the crossbeams above 9c. Help the Ogres to an early grave and then leap down for your supplies. Go back into 9a or 9b to carry out a death sentence on the Ogre who protects the Gold Key in 17. Get out your favorite close-range gun and return to 10. Some Scrags need a man-beating.

12. Besides the floating Scrag menace, you've got a nasty nail trap to contend with. You trigger the nail trap into action as soon as you near the ledge. Quickly look down at the floor on the left side of the towering column. You want to land on that Quake switch. Activating that switch opens the gate on the other side of the room, providing access to 13. You can grab the Green Armor on your way out..

13. The nail trap ceases firing the moment you careen into this hallway. But the fun doesn't stop yet—an Ogre picks up where the nail trap left off. Once he's down, heft your Rocket Launcher and get ready to rip a Fiend and some Vores to shreds.

14. A pair of Vores begin heaving spikeballs at your face the moment you poke the barrel of your Rocket Launcher through the doorway of 13. As a bonus, a Fiend comes leaping down the catwalk at the same time. Once the Fiend is down, stay tucked into 13 while you snipe the Vores. This prevents them from getting a good fix on you, which means their spikeballs tend to slam harmlessly into the walls (that is, if you duck back into the hall).

When the dust settles, note the promised third Rune Key on the platform above the walkway to your left (area 19). As you near the Flechette at the end of the walkway, a Fiend leaps out, fangs first. Backpedal, unleashing a barrage of deadly fire, to cut him quickly down to size.

15. A Death Knight comes out swinging the moment you enter this hallway. Beware of Scrags hovering just out of sight around the corner, past the aptly named dead Death Knight.

Completing the sequence of floor switches does two things: It drops the bars that block your entrance into 16, and it unleashes a pair of bloodthirsty Ogres from a pen embedded in the left wall of the passage.

To defuse this trap, step on the switches in the reverse order you encounter them. In fact, you can down most, if not all, of the monsters in 16—and maybe the Death Knight from 17—from your side of the barred doorway. Then when you're ready, step on the last switch and backpedal toward 14, banking grenades around corners as you bravely turn tail and flee.

16. The moving platforms are ridiculously easy to navigate. So easy in fact that even a Death Knight and Ogre can do it. If you didn't waste all the bad guys when the doorway was barred, you get your chance now. Sometimes an Ogre, Death Knight, or even a Vore will fall into the lava. So, if you think you murdered all the monsters in the mission but come up one or two kills short you now know where to look.

Cross the lava and get ready to battle another Death Knight (if you didn't kill him already) for the ownership of the Gold Key.

17. Once you dispatch the Death Knight to a realm that's grimmer than this hallway (and an Ogre if you didn't kill him when you were in 9a–c), get out your Rocket Launcher, dash over the Gold Key, and dive into 9b. In fact, go up the stairs to 9a. Why? You've just stirred yet another pair of Vores into action. The trusty long-distance rocket attack is your best bet for keeping your hide alive. When you've buckled their little bug legs, you have a choice: You can enter the Gold Key doors in 9b, or retrace your steps to the Gold Key ledge. Doing so grants you access to a whole cache of items and one really pissed-off Fiend who leaps out at you from the far end of the hallway. The Quake switch opens the door to your right, granting you access back to 9a. It also triggers a Death Knight attack on your backside. Yeouch! A few nails later and he'll know who's boss.

Either way, don't forget to grab the Green Armor in 5 or the Yellow Armor in 8—if you haven't already. You'll need it where you're going.

18. Open the Gold Key door and battle your way down the hallway, nailing a Scrag every few steps. Before you go up the lift, break out the Rocket Launcher and get ready to battle two more Vores—one on either side of the catwalk below you. Even though you have no room to maneuver in the tiny alcove atop the lift, the ledge in front of you is even worse—not only are you a sitting duck, but one misstep puts you neck-deep in lava. So, instead of rushing forward, stand at the lift's edge and peg each Vore from this niche. If a fireball comes screamin' at your face, fall back down the lift shaft. The fireball should miss you.

But wait! There's more!

When the Vores are history, get out your favorite Fiend-killing implement (we suggest a Supernailgun) and creep down the catwalk toward the Rune Key. Did we say Fiend? How about two Fiends? Just as you crest the hump in the bridge one Fiend materializes in your face and another one attacks your back. Simply drop off the catwalk onto 14 and run, pumping your adversaries full of nails. Easy.

19. Exit. Pluck the Rune of Hell Magic then exit the Netherworld once and for all. Don't forget to congratulate yourself before you go, you've earned it.

Episode 4

The Elder World

This is what you've been training for. The flagship of *Quake's* episodes, The Elder World sports a huge complement of dastardly traps, awesome hordes of mixed monsters, sprawling mission maps, and seemingly counter-intuitive puzzles. If you enjoy spending hours unraveling a single mission or doing battle with large parties of Deathmatch players, look no more. This episode was built with you in mind.

You begin this quest for the fourth, and final, Rune Key in *Quake's* sewers. Pain and agony ensue as you weave your way through the missions, defiling unholy altars, swimming with Zombies, electrifying Shamblers, and uncovering the veritable motherlode of Secret Areas. But the fun doesn't stop once you get your bloody hands on the Rune Key at the end of this episode—Shub-Niggurath patiently awaits an audience with you, should you prove yourself worthy…

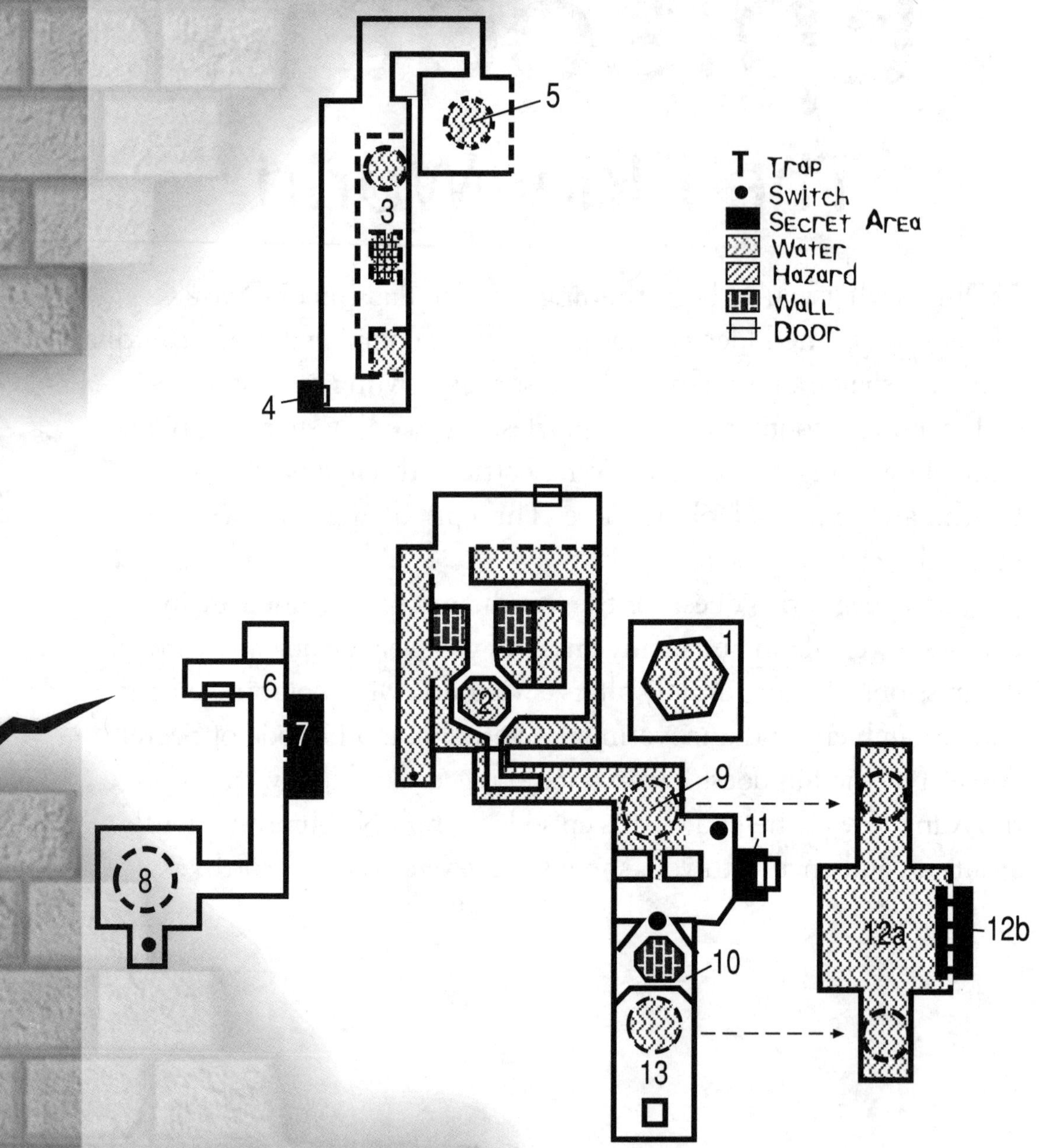
5
3
4
T Trap
Switch
Secret Area
Water
Hazard
Wall
Door
1
6
7
2
9
11
8
12a
12b
10
13

Mission 1: The Sewage System

Welcome to Episode 4, and let's hope you brought your lung capacity. In Mission 1 our hero seldom dries out, as the layout is full of underwater tunnels ready to befuddle the unwary. Fortunately, the only things in the way of opposition are Grunts and Enforcers, and you'll find plenty of shells to be had with them in mind.

Mission 1: The Sewage System At-a-Glance (E4M1)

1. Shotgun Shells
2. Shotgun Shells, Health
3. Health, Shotgun Shells, Flechettes
4. **Secret Area.** Quad Damage Rune, Yellow Armor
5. Gold Key, Nailgun, Health, Flechettes, Shotgun Shells
6. Health, Flechettes
7. **Secret Area.** Quad Damage Rune, Megahealth
8. Shotgun Shells, Health, Flechettes
9. Health, Flechettes
10. Health, Flechettes, Biosuit, switch
11. **Secret Area.** Flechettes

12a. Health

12b. **Secret Area.** Shotgun Shells, Health

13. Flechettes, Slipgate

Highlights:

- Four Secret Areas
- Multiple Exploding Boxes
- Underwater Enforcer Dueling

Ripe for Destruction

1. Grab the Shotgun Shells and jump down to the room below. Alternatively, you can try to peg the Grunts from up here, but they're too far away for you to do a lot of damage, even if you're supernaturally accurate.

2. Drop into the water, and surface in one of the room's corners to dispose of the Grunts and Enforcers. Shotgun Shells and Health wait in abundance above and below the surface, and you'll note some open underwater avenues while you dive. Play cat-and-mouse with the Grunts and Enforcers, and take advantage of the explodable box on the landing near the Gold Key door.

3. From the room where the ramp leads up to the Gold Key door, stand near the yellow-lit pad and drop into the water, follow the markers and you'll be lifted into a room of Grunts and Enforcers. When the lift reaches the top, step into the hallway (behind you, if you turned to face the large room) and deal with the Grunts and Enforcers here first. Note the Health on the walkway, where you'll be fodder for a nasty blaster trap. When you've cleared the upper area, blow the boxes below and hop down to dispose of any survivors. You'll net more Health and Shotgun Shells in the process, as well as a big box of Flechettes.

Note

In the long hallway that extends from the top of the lift, near the Secret Area (4), you battle an initial wave of Enforcers, and then usually another follows afterward. When you kill that final Enforcer, another will teleport into the hallway near the door to room 4, telefragging the unwary.

4. **Secret Area.** Ride the lift back up to the walkway, and notice the irregular wall panel where the walk makes a right turn. Shoot the wall to reveal a small room with a Quad Damage rune and Yellow Armor. Suit up and sprint down the walk to claim the Gold Key.

5. Traverse the walkway and then the hall, blasting a Rottweiler and several Enforcers en route to the prize. In the room with the Gold Key, you'll also lay claim to the Nailgun, Health, and Flechettes, and you should have spotted more Health and Shotgun Shells on the way there.

6. Through the Gold Key door, slay the Grunts and fight out of that corner of the hall, near the Health boxes. When enemies stop coming to try their luck, step out of the corner and deal with the Enforcer on the ledge overhead. When you round the corner, be ready to leap back. You can usually peg the Grunt on the ledge, near the Quad Damage rune, but about that time a wall slides on your left, unleashing Rottweilers. More Enforcers teleport in outside the Gold Key door about the same time. In the pups' room wait Health and Flechettes.

7. **Secret Area.** To access the ledge you can see from the walkway, and claim the Quad Damage rune and Megahealth dose, you have to bonk your

head on an overhead lighting fixture. Use the rise of the walkway as a ramp, and take a running jump at the fixture above. A door opens in the hallway, and invokes the wrath of the Grunt and Enforcer inside. If you sail the jump, you'll also get the attention of the two Enforcers up ahead, which would be unfortunate until you have the rune in your possession.

8. Up the ramp, dispose of Enforcers aplenty and lay hands on Shotgun Shells, Health, and Flechettes. Expect a Grunt to crawl out of the boxes on your left when you push the switch that lowers the floodgates.

9. Slay the newly arrived Grunt and take a look in the hallway leading from room 2, where you grabbed up Shotgun Shells. You'll see that the floodgate is, indeed, open. Jump in the pool there and sink until you see an entrance in front of you. Swim forward, turn 90 degrees to the right and surface up the steps. Slay the Grunt and the two Enforcers and claim Health and Flechettes. The switch opens an underwater avenue, but you should acquire the nearby Biosuit before exploring below.

10. Draw out the Grunts, then circle the obstruction to surprise an Enforcer. You'll find Health and Flechettes, and the aforementioned Biosuit. You can see the end-of-the-mission Slipgate below, and might even consider thinning the crowd from this vantage point. Also, if you look above the doorway inside the room, you'll spy a switch.

11. **Secret Area.** Shoot the switch above the door in room 10, and then check the hallway outside. Note the box of Flechettes and a Teleporter; the gate leaves you outside the Gold Key door.

12a. Biosuit up, drop into the water in room 9, and submerge rapidly. The floor will have opened to allow you to sink to new depths, and enter a large room down a tunnel where Enforcers try their hand at synchronized shooting. When you've scored their routine, surface on that side of the room to discover their secret stash.

12b. **Secret Area.** If you surface in the area above the two sunken Enforcers, you'll enter a small narrow room complete with Shotgun Shells and Health. Continue in the direction you were headed when the bums rushed you.

13. Surface and slay the Grunts and Enforcer, if you didn't peg them from room 10. The Slipgate awaits. Scoop up some Flechettes before exiting to Mission 2.

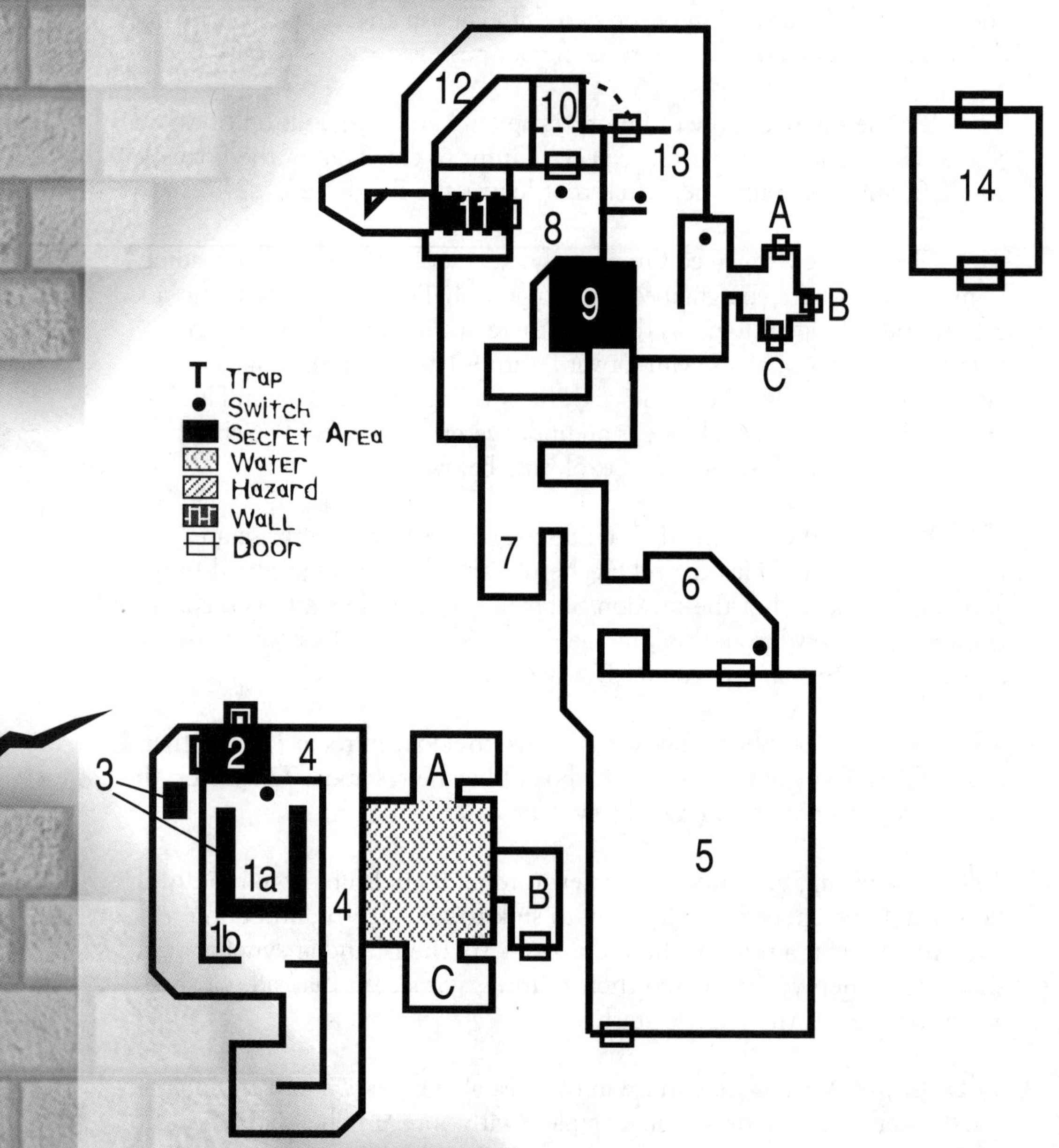
T Trap
Switch
Secret Area
Water
Hazard
Wall
Door
1a
1b
2
3
4
4
A
B
C
5
6
7
8
9
10
11
12
13
A
B
C
14

Mission 2: The Tower of Despair

After slogging through a high-tech sewer system, this second mission revives *Quake's* ever-popular Dungeon motif. If you can live with this inconsistency, then this mission shouldn't leave you in a state of despair—especially when you get your hands on some well-placed artifacts in lifesaving Secret Areas.

The action begins with Knight-to-Shotgun combat and quickly escalates into an armed conflict with a Shambler and a party of Vores. If you got bored with pegging these three-legged freaks at long range in Episode 3, you get your chance now to rip them to shreds up close and personal.

In all, you must endure a fair amount of backtracking en route to the exit. However, certain key walls and obstacles open up during your quest that provide both excellent shortcuts and tactically intriguing Deathmatch possibilities. Play here against your friends and see for yourself.

Mission 2: The Tower of Despair At-a-Glance (E4M2)

1a. Start: Megahealth, Shotgun Shells

1b. **Secret Area.** Double-barreled Shotgun, Shotgun Shells

2. **Secret Area.** Flechette, Ring of Shadows

3. **Secret Area.** Green Armor, Flechette

4. Health, Shotgun Shells

5. Health, Shotgun Shells, Double-barreled Shotgun, Pentagram of Protection, Flechette

6. Health, Shotgun Shells, Switch giving access to Pentagram in 5

7. Quad Damage Rune, Health, Flechette

8. Health, Flechette, Shotgun Shells

9. **Secret Area.** Megahealth, Health, Flechette, Quad Damage Rune, Yellow Armor, Silver Key, Megahealth

10. Health, Flechette

11. **Secret Area.** Health, Shotgun Shells

12. Health, Shotgun Shells

13. Flechette

14. End

Highlights:

- Five Secret Areas that Will Save Your Life
- Rippin' Vores Limb from Limb, Quadruple-Time
- Olympic "Caliber" Balance Beam Competition

Despair No More in this Tower of Power

1a. A Megahealth rests below the beams. Do not take it yet. Save it for when you assault area 5. The item-laden beams above you are in Secret Area 3. Your doubled-barreled buddy and some ammo wait behind bars in the corners of the room below; you'll need them to eradicate the Knights who rush in.

Creep up to the hole in the floor. Shoot the red disk below you. Drop down, run up to the wall, and press the sword switch. You now have free access to a Double-barreled Shotgun in 1b.

1b. **Secret Area.** Snatch any weapon and kiss those Knights goodnight with your newest toy. Don't let any sneaky Knights (to your left) turn you into the meat in a Knight sandwich as head to the right, down the hallway.

2. **Secret Area.** Shoot the wall at the end of what would otherwise be a dead-end hallway to gain access to this room. Don't take the Ring of Shadows yet. You'll need it when you attack area 5. Do you see the pattern?

Let the door seal you in, then go into the niche to the right of the doorway. Pressing the sword switch temporarily opens a pit in the hallway outside this Secret Area. Shoot the door to escape and go drop into the pit.

3. **Secret Area.** Scoop up the goods from the beams above 1a, exit the room and turn left.

4. Watch for an Ogre and more Knights as you battle down the hallway. Watch out for the Vore and his Ogre buddies on the right across what looks like a pond. You can't swim to them, and you don't have enough firepower to kill them and survive area 5. Don't worry, you will punish them, because you can attack, quadruple-time, from 9 ...

Kill the Ogre in the hallway past the Vore/Ogre ledges, grab the ammo and Health, then double back to 2. Get out your Nailgun, grab the Ring of

Shadows, pick up the Megahealth, then quickly jump into the drink before the Vore can heave a spikeball into your face.

5. Shambler attack! Your ring will probably be worn out by the time you flatten this furry abomination. Note that the Slipgate takes you back to 1a. Ride the lift to the left of the Slipgate up to the beams for yet another Double-barreled Shotgun and more ammo. You can get the Pentagram of Protection and Nailgun quite easily from 6—both of which you will definitely need in 7 and 8. Drop down and turn right in the hall. Approach the archway on the right, killing any fool Knights who get in front of your firestick of choice.

6. Watch out for a Death Knight sucker punch from the shadows to your right. Push the button at the end of the room to bring down a lift. Take it up to get a close look at the blessed Pentagram. Grab it and as many nails as you can carry, then barrel down the hallway to the intersection.

7. A Vore guards a Quad Damage rune. Combine your Nailgun and the Pentagram, and you've got a deadly mix indeed. Mercilessly work your way as far into 8 as you can get, focusing your eye-popping rage especially on the Vores and Ogres high above.

8. Shooting the red disk opens your way to 10, and the large off-colored wall panel left of the disk leads to 11 (which is opened by a switch in 10).

You can easily access the crazy lattice of beams by jumping from the area below the red disk. Once at the top of the beams (the same level as the Health box), turn right, away from the red disk, to get to the mission's next Secret Area.

9. **Secret Area.** Take out the Ogre in the cage below. Jump onto the Megahealth (its ledge is the Secret Area), then keep running to the left. Snatch the Quad Damage, take down the enemies that get in your way, hit the sword switch, then dash into the three-arched room.

Each arch corresponds to a ledge mentioned in 4. Go through the center one for the Silver Key and nail the Vore. Slaughter the Ogres while you're at it, then jump into the room's water-like center. Return to the three-arched room to claim the Yellow Armor. We recommend you save the Megahealth until you get to 12. Trust us, you'll be glad you did.

The Slipgate on the Vore's ledge takes you back to 8—onto the platform in front of the red disk. This is exactly where you need to be to get to 10.

10. From the Ogre's platform in 8, shoot the red disk to open it. Take a running leap into the tunnel and ride the lift up. Turn around at the top. Only a lowly Knight to the left of the sword switch stands between you and your destiny.

From the sword switch, turn right and shoot the far-wall. It slides away, revealing a pit that takes you to 11. Before you go, hit the sword switch and immediately jump back—you will ride the bars in the floor that slide away. If you don't jump back you'll be dropped onto the same Ogre's platform in 8—and spring a trap in 11. Read 11 to see how to best defuse this otherwise dastardly trap.

> **Note**
>
> **If the promised Vore isn't on his ledge, most likely he's stumbled through the Slipgate and waits for you on the platform in 8. If he's not where he ought to be, it's best to follow him through the Slipgate and vanquish him while your Quad Damage rune still works.**

11. **Secret Area.** With the pits to 8 and 11 open, go to the sword switch pit and look at the Death Knight and Ogres in 11. They won't jump into action until you either fall to 8 or shoot them…

Get out your Nailgun and stir both Ogres into action from the sword switch pit. Then meander to the other pit and finish off the Ogres free of charge. When they're dead, drop onto their platform and bring the Death Knight to his knees.

To defuse the spiked-wall trap, poke your nose between the spikes and leap back. The trap stays shut for a few moments, allowing you to jump between the bars. Watch out for an Ogre attack as soon as you leap through (the right niche provides good cover)! Also, don't bother trying to lure monsters into the spikes—they won't set off the trap.

12. A wall-mounted nail trap greets you as soon as you round the bend. Stop. Remember that Megahealth back on the Ogre's ledge above 5?

Go back and grab it, dash back to 12, dodge the nail trap as best you can, and stir up the Vore and Death Knights (who stand guard at the far end of the room) in the pit below. It's easy to fall through the lattice walkways—a nasty way to face the Death Knights and the Vore. They love to fight each other, and usually only one half-alive Death Knight is left standing after their spat. During their fight you'll take a few spikeballs to the face, but your Megahealth should more than compensate for it. Skip to 14 if you decide to pop through the Slipgate to finish this mission. Otherwise, drop to the floor next to the Vore and Death Knight bodies and creep through the archway to 13.

13. Chunkify the pair of Knights guarding the Flechette. The sword switch opens a panel of wall next to it—granting you direct access to the Ogre cage back in 9.

14. The Slipgate behind you takes you to the center platform in 8. The big archway before you is the Exit. Since you should have the Silver Key, the choice is yours.

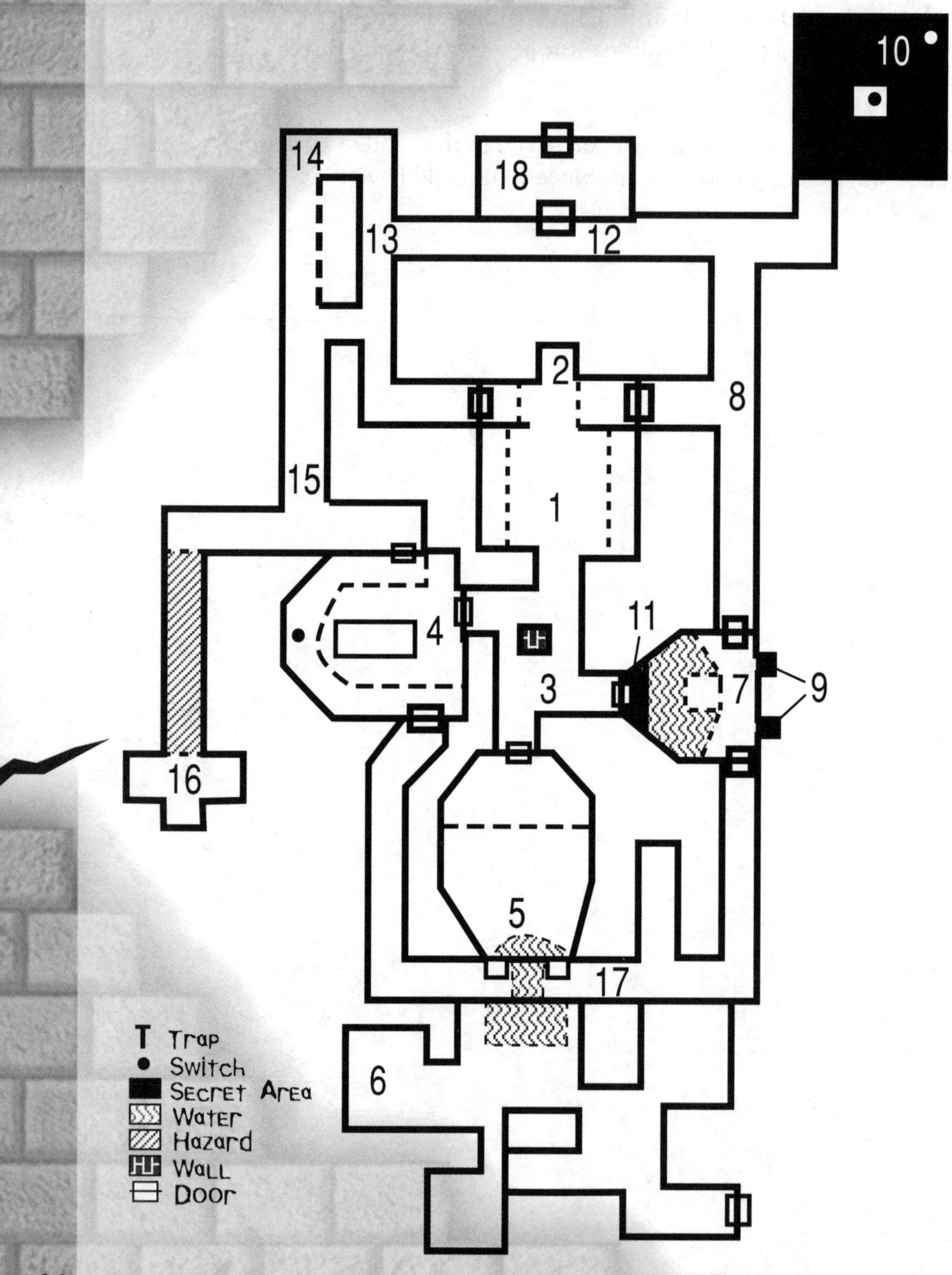

10
18
14
13
12
2
8
1
15
11
4
3
7
9
16
5
17
6
T Trap
Switch
Secret Area
Water
Hazard
Wall
Door

Mission 3: The Elder God Shrine

The Shrine of the Elder God could use a little defiling, and luckily you'll find plenty of goodies herein for just that purpose. Flechettes and Quad Damage runes appear in abundance, as do the monsters. What a combo.

Mission 3: The Elder God Shrine At-a-Glance (E4M3)

1. Health
2. Flechettes, Megahealth
3. Flechettes, Shotgun Shells, Quad Damage Rune
4. Health, Flechettes, Shotgun Shells, Green Armor
5. Health, Flechettes, Shotgun Shells
6. Grenade Launcher, Grenades, Megahealth, Guad Damage Rune
7. Flechettes, Health, Grenades, Quad Damage Rune
8. Grenades
9. **Secret Area.** Health
10. **Secret Area.** Green Armor, Shotgun Shells, Grenades, Double-barreled Shotgun, Quad Damage Rune
11. **Secret Area.** Red Armor, Grenades, Health
12. Grenades
13. Flechettes, Shotgun Shells, Megahealth
14. Grenades, Yellow Armor, Health, Ring of Shadows
15. Shotgun Shells
16. Lava Trap, Grenades, Health, Silver Key
17. Health, Gold Key, Quad Damage Rune
18. Exit

Highlights:

- Three Secret Areas
- Graveyard Zombie Battle
- Three Quad Damage Runes

Show No Mercy

1. Find Health on the stairs beside you as the mission gets underway, and those stairs can serve to confound the hyperactive offensive attempts of the Fiends in the next room. Back into a corner when they see you, and usually they won't be able to coordinate the stairs while you're dispensing death.

2. Grab up the Flechettes and Megahealth, and shoot the symbol on the wall to open the door in room 1.

3. Flechettes, Shotgun Shells, and a Quad Damage rune wait in this small hub-like juncture. Note the tip regarding the rune, and hang a right, passing through the lit portal.

4. Open the door and back off slightly, then charge forward and up the ramp. You want to fight from the ledge above, but there's a small gap between the ramp and the landing, so you have to jump to gain the vantage point. Slay the Ogres, then hop down and take care of the Knights. Gather Health, Flechettes, Shotgun Shells, and a suit of Green Armor, and look on the wall opposite the entrance for a large switch. Hitting the switch summons more Knights and a Fiend to the party, but also opens another door in room 3.

> **Note**
>
> **You can put the Quad Damage rune in room 3 to a variety of uses in the next few rooms. We advise that you preserve it until you decide, based on getting hammered a couple of times, when to activate the equalizer. When you're not rune-ing the day of the locals, dispense nails liberally. As you can see, plenty exists in the way of refills.**

5. Watch for a teleporting Fiend to your left as you approach the doorway. Another follows the first after about a minute. You should also expect Scrags to materialize in front of you when you set foot on the landing. Below await three angry Ogres, should you decide to take a swim. There's also Health, Flechettes, and Shotgun Shells. You may want to grab the Quad Damage rune from room 3 to deal with the horde of monsters, if you haven't burnt it already. There is another just up ahead, in room 6, if you want to jump directly in the water and then return to dispense justice.

6. Swim through the channel and hit the graveyard running. The object of your desire is the Grenade Launcher, placed atop a fresh grave site in the first area on your right as you surface. If you grab the Luancher and hurry back

to the water, you'll find the Zombies will gather at pool side for ease of disposal. In the section of graves adjacent to where you picked up the Grenade Launcher waits a Quad Damage rune—very helpful in cleaning out the rest of the graveyard, especially if you go and stir up the locals beforehand. There's also a Megahealth boost and two boxes of Grenades in the vicinity. Beware the Fiend that materializes when you approach the Teleporter.

7. Through the graveyard Teleporter, you arrive in room 7 at about the same time a couple of Scrags make their appearance. Make haste to the landing, as a whole pack of Scrags arrives. Luckily, there's a Quad Damage rune nearby, and another Health box. Deal with them harshly, and clean the small pool of Flechettes, Health, and Grenades. You may also notice that Fiends continue to arrive in room 3. Great.

8. Explore the nearby hallway while you still have a little Quad time, and inflict extreme discomfort on the Knights and slimy Spawn. You can duck through the door near where you detonate the Spawn and claim the Grenades off the ledge in room 2. That's also an excellent opportunity to backtrack and restock if you've left any goodies behind.

9. **Secret Area.** In 7, you can hop through either of the stained-glass windows on the ledge to claim a Health box. Whichever area you enter first, you'll receive the Secret Area message.

10. Follow the hallway from 7 and bear right at the intersection. Locate the switch on the wall and press it ready for action. The walls drop, and a Scrag and his Zombie pals attempt to keep you from Green Armor, a big box of Shotgun Shells, Grenades, a Double-barreled Shotgun, and even a Quad Damage rune. You'll want to save the Armor; you're about to strap on a suit of the red variety. Also set aside the rune until you need it. Climb the small stairs leading to the wooden lift in the center of the room, but when it starts to rise, quickly step back off. Hop through the Teleporter now revealed in the floor.

11. **Secret Area.** You arrive on the ledge you can see from 7; Red Armor, Grenades, and Health wait in easy reach. Clean house and hit the hall again, this time making the left turn where it branches.

12. As you approach the Grenades in the hallway, a pair of Ogres ambushes you through the window on your right. Put your back to the far wall and strafe them into submission, taking care not to go further down the passage, lest you attract unwanted attention.

13. Near where the hallway splits again, at a big box of Flechettes, you encounter a pair of Fiends and a Spawn. Fortunately, you have plenty of space behind you to fall back on, appreciating your enemies' fiendish exuberance while you unload some ammo. Angle left at that intersection, toward the box of Shotgun Shells; you can claim more Flechettes en route to the door you'll find farther down on the left. That's the access to the other ledge in 2, and a juicy serving of Megahealth.

14. From the ledge where you load up on Megahealth, it's probably most prudent to double back and work your way around, picking up Grenades and then rounding a corner to your left to spy a suit of Yellow Armor. If you come at the Armor from the other direction, it's easier to fall into a cross fire. When you grab the new suit, a wall drops on your left to unleash a Fiend and an impressive pack of Zombies. Hammer them into submission, and check their area for Health and a Ring of Shadows, which you might consider saving for when you open the Silver Door.

15. Proceed down the hall, ready for a Spawn ambush at the intersection where you face the window, with a door visible on your left. That door opens onto the upper tier of 4. Grab up the Shotgun Shells and continue down the hall where you find them, but stop when you round the corner to your left, facing down the long hallway.

16. A short way down the long hall the floor starts moving beneath your feet, leaving you no place to stand but the huge pool of lava below. Very bad. As soon as the floor starts to move, back up, and let it retract into the wall. The instant it starts to extend again, run out onto it and sprint down the hall. When you claim the Grenade Launcher you find at the other end of the passage, three rooms open nearby to emit a Fiend and some Knights. You should, however, have enough time to grab the weapon and hightail it back down the hall, narrowly avoiding a lava bath—perhaps with a tremendous leap—as the floor opens once more. With any luck, the Fiend won't be quite so fortunate. Though the lava won't kill him, you'll find he's somewhat akin to fish in a barrel, milling around below you. Those three rooms hold Grenades, Health, and the Silver Key.

17. Through the Silver Key door, grab the Quad Damage rune from near the Spawn (easily accomplished if you brought the Ring from room 14) and use the power to mop up the blobs and Knights. Health and the Gold Key wait nearby. Be wary of a lurking Scrag when you double back to apply the key.

18. Through the Gold Key door, you'll find renewed Ogre resistance, and nothing else between you and the end-of-the-mission portal.

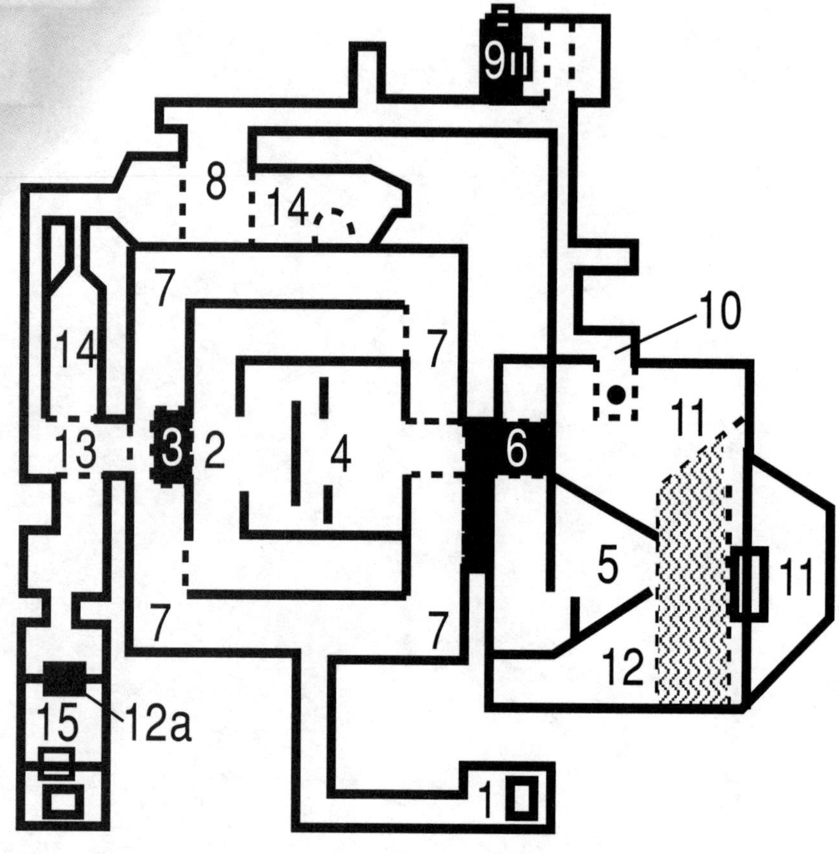
9
8
14
7
7
14
13
3
2
4
6
10
11
11
5
11
7
7
12
12a
15
1

T Trap
Switch
Secret Area
Water
Hazard
Wall
Door

Mission 4: The Palace of Hate

Mission 4: The Palace of Hate At-a-Glance (E4M4)

1. Megahealth, Double-barreled Shotgun, Shotgun Shells
2. Health, Shotgun Shells, Flechettes
3. **Secret Area.** Pentagram of Protection, Flechette
4. **Secret Area.** Grenade Launcher, Healing Pool, Shotgun Shells, Flechettes, Rockets, Heath
5. Shotgun Shells, Flechette, Health, (you can acquire the Supernailgun in 11 from here)
6. **Secret Area.** Red Armor
7. Flechettes, Health, Shotgun Shells, Green Armor
8. Shotgun shells, Health, Nailgun, Flechettes
9. **Secret Area.** Quad Damage Rune
10. Grenade Launcher, Ring of Shadows
11. Rockets, Megahealth, Health, Flechettes, Supernailgun
12. Silver Key, Pentagram of Protection, Health, Shotgun Shells

12a. **Secret Area.** Ring of Shadows, Health

13. Flechette, Rockets, Health, Shotgun Shells
14. Green Armor, Health, Flechettes, Shotgun Shells, Rockets
15. End, Flechette, Green Armor

Highlights:

- Five Healthful Secret Areas
- One Explosive Slipgate Shortcut
- Five Shamblers vs. Two Pentagrams of Protection

If you've spent any time at all in this palace, you'll quickly realize that there are many, many routes through. The path we chose isn't the most efficient one; rather it maximizes the time you spend under the influence of magical power-ups, and lets you see all the sights while efficiently managing your armor and ammo resources.

The lay of the land dictates your tactics big time here. In essence you must use your enemies' chief innate weakness (attacking you in a blind rage on sight) against them. Expect to stir up bad guys while you turn tail and flee, guns blazing as you backpedal.

This tactic has only one drawback—because there are no true barriers in the mission, the monsters won't stay put. It's our experience that, for example, we may kill one Fiend in a group of three only to have the other two escape. So, if the monsters aren't where we say they ought to be, don't think we've made a mistake. Trust us, the bad guys are in the palace somewhere, roaming the halls, alone or in ad–hoc goon squads, looking for you. Just be a good *Quake* scout and always be prepared.

In the Hard setting, a total of five Shamblers beg to be toppled. More than any other monster in this mission, they love to run wild. If you reach the end of the mission and your Shambler body count is fewer than five... well, get out your Supernailgun and enjoy the hunt.

A Palace You'll Love to Hate

1. Get out your Nailgun, run over the Megahealth, and perforate the Fiend lurking in the hallway before you. Without pausing to rest, snatch the Double-barreled Shotgun and dash up the ramp into 2.

2. Use the rest of your Megahealth to take down the Scrags and chunkify the Knights (one hides in the shadows on either side of the red disk). The tunnel between the stairways is area 6; the arch in the center structure leads to area 4. The red disk conceals the first Secret Area of this mission.

While the Megahealth is still working, dash into 4, grab the Grenade Launcher, and leap back out. Doing so energizes the shadow-lurking Knights, allowing you to chunkify them from a safe distance. You'll also find two more Knights behind the center wall, and one in each corner deep in the shadows beside the stairs. Don't go up the stairs yet!

Once you've wasted all the bad guys in 1, 2, and most of 4, tuck yourself into the shadows next to the red disk, and take aim at the sunny sword-switch symbol at the top of the arch. Get ready for a Fiend to leap out from behind the red disk as soon as you shoot it...

3. **Secret Area.** Don't use the Pentagram yet! You'll need it and the Flechettes when you charge into areas 5 and 11. Trust us on this one.

4. **Secret Area.** Dawdle around in the Grenade Launcher pool to receive a fabulous Health boost. The pool is loaded with 25-point Health boxes.

Atop the stairs a pair of Fiends awaits the business end of your Nailgun. They seem to have a problem going all the way down the stairs, especially if you're off to the side near where the Knights were hanging out.

Once you've put them to sleep, creep to the end of this hallway. Prepare for a Fiend attack from the right! The Shotgun Shells and Health box to your left are yours to keep. See the Red Armor between the stair slats? That's 6, your second Secret Area. We'll go there after we flatten a Shambler in 5.

5. Maximizing your Pentagram time means doing three things:

- Take the Flechette and Pentagram in 3.
- Run into 5 and let the Shambler feel your wrath.
- While the Pentagram is still working, go past the Shambler corpse to the pond (area 11), leap onto the left plank, grab the Supernailgun, dive off the ledge and swim back to 5. Your goal is to get the Supernailgun, and escape with your life.

Not only have you now maximized your Pentagram time, but you've got yourself the most effective Shambler killin' device in the whole game. You can fish for Fiends and Rotfish with Grenades at this point if you like, but we suggest you wait until you've gone to 9, the third Secret Area, and have a Quad Damage rune coursing through your veins supplemented with a Ring of Shadows. It's more fun that way.

6. **Secret Area.** In the dark passage where the Fiends lurked on the walkway in 4, note the lighted rectangle to your right. It's a lift that takes you to 7. But before you go, step on the edge of the lift and quickly jump off. Dash under the platform, immediately turn around and slay the Knight, then follow the passage to the Red Armor. Stepping on the floor switch slides part of the stairway back, providing you an easy escape.

7. Once in the hallway atop the lift you'll battle Death Knights and Fiends aplenty. Lucky you. We suggest you rely on your Grenades and Shotgun. You'll want to save your nails for killing Shamblers. Don't get yourself pinned into a corner when all the baddies are still kicking—not unless you like being the absolute center of everyone's attention all at once.

To that end, we suggest you clear out the halls until you get to a corner. Then stop; assess your ammo and Health situation; jump out to lure the enemy toward you, then backpedal like crazy. As you fight the lesser monsters, be careful not to trigger the Shamblers on the bridges that lead to 8 and 13—at least not yet. They'll see you as soon as you stumble past the entrance to their bridges. If you don't kill the Shambler in 13 and 8 from here, they'll fall from their respective perches and roam the mission map looking for you, usually assembling a posse of other free-range baddies.

8. Once you've secured 7, stand near the opening to take out the Shambler if he's there. If you see a box of Shotgun Shells on the bridge, you'll know you're at the correct place. If the Shambler falls off the ledge (he almost always does), don't worry. You can blast him from the bridge while he occupies himself fighting Fiends and Death Knights.

Grab the second box of shells and immediately leap back—a Fiend jumps out from the left, claws first.

As you battle your way down the hall toward the T intersection, prepare for Scrags and Fiends—especially when you come to the left niche in the hallway (where the Nailgun rests) and the T intersection itself. Killing the Fiend who guards the Nailgun teleports in a Scrag over the Health box in the hall.

> **Note**
>
> **You may find a Scrag or two guarding the bridges to 8 and 13; a Shambler may actually barge into 7 from his bridge; or Death Knights may attack as you try to snipe Shamblers from the bridges… in other words, prepare for anything.**

Snatch the Flechettes in the middle of the T and jump back to evade yet another leaping Fiend. Ignore the Flechettes on the left side of the T for now, and battle your way down the right side of the T (watch for another Fiend attack from the left niche!) until you get to the guillotine. It's off with your head, unless you defuse the trap. How? Simply stick you neck out and snap it back before the blade falls. Once it's down, all you have to do is crowd up next to it and dash through when it raises.

Listen for the tell-tale teleport sound behind you once the guillotine falls. That's the sound of incoming Fiends back from whence you came.

Backtrack to the Flechettes you should have ignored, using the long hallways to help you murder Fiends that stand between you and the next Secret Area.

9. **Secret Area.** The Flechettes waiting left of the T are bait for a nasty Knight trap and Fiend trap! Get near the box and a horde ambushes you from the left and right. Once you chunkify them, ride the left platform up. This lift is tricky to open—keep moving and touching the walls until it drops. Drop down into the pit for a Quad Damage rune. The Teleporter takes you past the guillotine directly to 10. Grab the stuff and jump into the Slipgate as fast as you can.

10. Welcome to the telepad pad past the guillotine. Juiced up, run up the steps, grab the Ring, plant your foot on the switch to get the far plank moving, and unleash an unholy sortie on your flying and swimming foes. Remember the Fiends who attacked you when you grabbed the Supernailgun at 5? They're in the water now. While you're powered up, dive beneath the waves with your Supernailgun blazing. Killing the Fiends and Rotfish gives you unmolested access to the huge amount of goods underwater.

11. Once on terra firma, leap to the closest plank to access the second one (that you activated with the switch in 10). Break up the Scrag party in 12; if you need more ammo or health, plenty awaits you in the briny deep. Walk to the end of the plank and make a heroic leap toward the Silver Key.

12. Watch for a sneak Fiend attack from the left! Nothing attacks you when you grab either artifact—which means you must take matters into your own hands.

Since we like to use the Pentagram power on Shamblers, our favorite place to go (when we've got this power-up) is to 13. Besides using the Slipgate to 12a, here's the fastest way to get there from here: Jump in the water and go through 5, run up the stairs to 4; ride up the lift to (7); turn left, dash down the hallway until the first archway/bridge on the left. But instead of doing all that, why not try to "Explode" into 12a?

12a. **Secret Area.** The Slipgate hanging around above the Pentagram is the gateway to this secret shortcut. There's no penalty for skipping this teleport, but if you're fast you'll have loads of Pentagram time to spend on your dungeon buddies. Making this secret work for you can also be a fine way of escaping the final showdown. What you do when you get there depends on how healthy or yella you are...

Even your manly muscles aren't mighty enough to let you jump through this Slipgate. You need a little help from your Grenade Launcher. Here's what to do:

- Save your game
- Grab the Pentagram of Protection
- Stand back just past the edge of the Slipgate and aim your Grenade Launcher at the tiny hole in the floor. Your goal is to lob a single grenade into that hole. It's tough to do. Keep trying and you'll eventually get the angle.
  If that oblique angle doesn't work for you, try standing a single small step from the wall where the Fiend was hiding, such that you have a straight line view of the grenade hole. (Use the bricks on the floor to keep you line-of-sight true.) Launch a grenade on a straight, flat-trajectory, and it will either sink or fall close to the hole.
- Once you've planted a grenade, look down at your feet and step on it.
- Hit your jump key at the moment the grenade detonates. Viola! You're there! The area below you is 15. Since you can get invisible and have the Silver Key, there's nothing to stop you from dropping to the floor and exiting this mission. But if your Pentagram hasn't burned off yet, why not pause a few moments to give those Death Knights and their Shambler pal some hell?

If, for whatever reason, you simply can't make this grenade jump work for you, you may be ill-fated to completing the mission through honest work. Load your game, grab the Pentagram, and run into harm's way.

If, on the other hand, you're dying to make this jump (without flying) and don't care what it takes, try this:

- Save your game
- Cheat your way into a Rocket Launcher
- Grab the Pentagram
- Stand under the Slipgate
- Point the muzzle of the weapon at your feet
- Simultaneously pull the trigger and jump

If you made the leap and want to finish up, skip to 15. If not, read 13 and either Rocket Jump or run there.

13. Leap off the left side of the bridge and go into the first part of 15. If you're fast, and don't get held up by a gang of lesser losers, you'll have just enough Pentagram time to take down one Shambler free of charge. With any luck, the Pentagram won't go completely to waste.

Once you've bagged a Shambler, you can go to the exit in 15 or go under the bridge toward the T intersection.

14. Your reason for going to 14 is two-fold: killing of any the remaining monsters (so they don't attack your back while you battle the fifth Shambler), and suiting up with a nice Green Armor vest.

Watch for a Fiend attack from the left the moment you step into the T. Also watch for any roaming Knights, Scrags, Death Knights, Fiends, or Shamblers you haven't already killed.

Go down the stairs next to the armor, but stop just before the rectangle of light. You're about to become the lunchmeat in a Fiend sandwich. Trigger the trap by crossing over the second strip of shadow (closest to the box of nails). Backpedal through the light-rectangle, Grenades flying. Once the Fiends skid to a halt, grab the goodies in their respective pens, then head toward 15 and the final showdown.

15. Unless you're under the influence of The Ring of Shadows, stepping past the juicy Flechettes sends two Death Knights into a frothy tizzy. The last Shambler of this mission teleports in behind you when you stir up the Death Knights. We suggest you poke your nose in to energize them, then run away as fast and far as you can. If you're lucky, the Death Knights and Shambler will fight to the death. Slay any survivors and head for the exit.

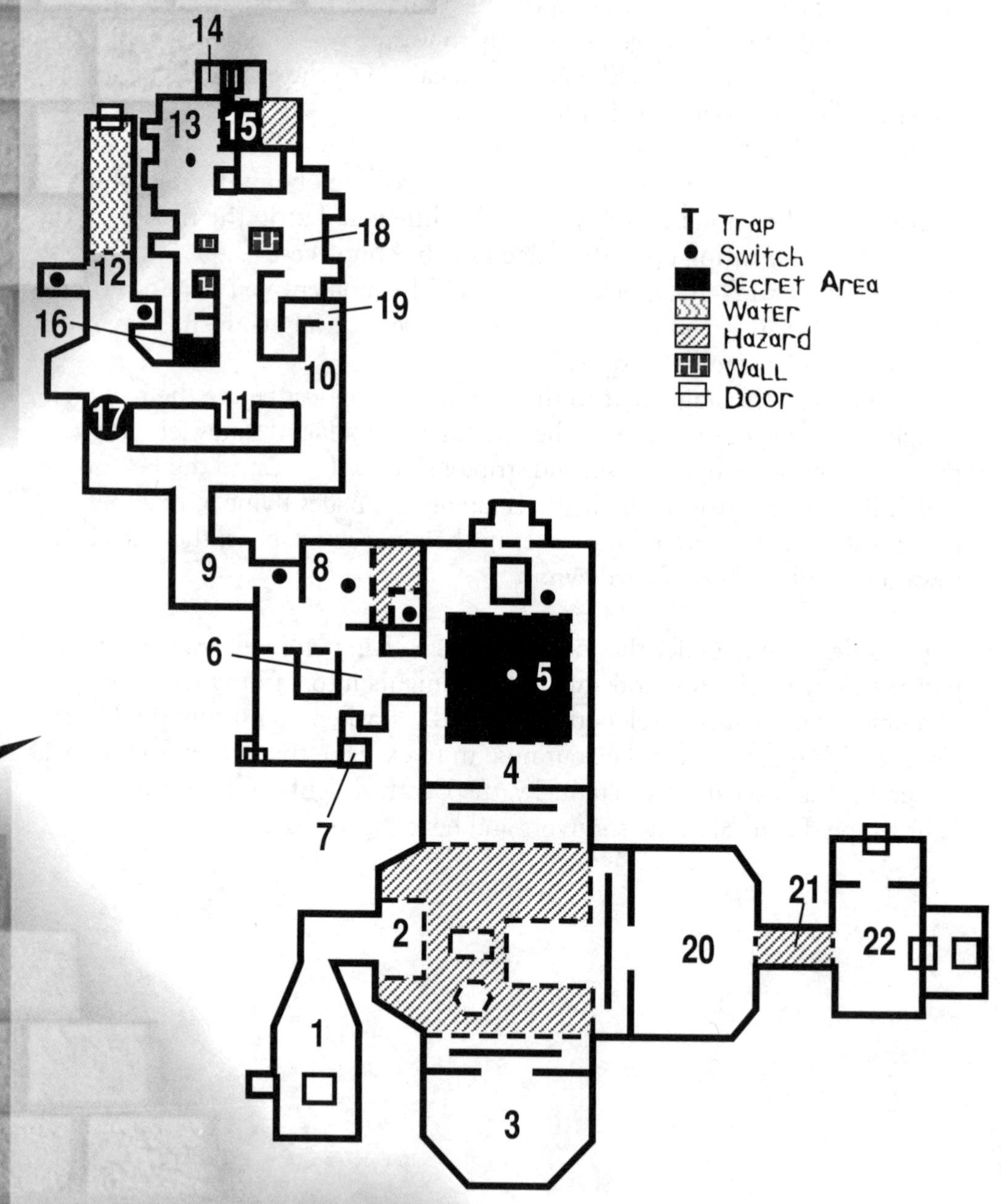

14
13
15
18
12
19
16
10
17
11
9
8
6
5
4
7
2
20
21
22
1
3
T Trap
Switch
Secret Area
Water
Hazard
Wall
Door

Mission 5: Hell's Atrium

The sprawling environs of "Hell's Atrium," and the merciless combat you'll experience on your visit, let you know that *Quake* is hurtling toward its climax. As a bonus, this mission contains one of the trickiest tricks in the whole game. Even when you know it's coming, it's still tricky. And if you don't know, you'll inadvertently seal the entrance to Episode 4's Secret Mission, and never be the wiser…

Mission 5: Hell's Atrium At-a-Glance (E4M5)

1. Megahealth, Flechettes
2. Flechettes, Grenades
3. Gold Key, Flechettes, Grenades, Health
4. Health, Shotgun Shells
5. **Secret Area.** Health, Megahealth, Cells, Flechettes, Quad Damage Rune
6. Supernailgun, Grenades, Flechettes, Health
7. Megahealth, Grenades, Ring of Shadows
8. Pentagram of Protection
9. Ring of Shadows, Quad Damage Rune, Grenades, Health
10. Health, Flechettes
11. Health, Flechettes, Grenades, Shotgun Shells, Thunderbolt
12. Grenades, Flechettes, Green Armor, Cells, Quad Damage Rune
13. Flechettes, Grenades, Quad Damage Rune
14. Lift
15. **Secret Area.** Cells, Yellow Armor, Pentagram of Protection
16. **Secret Area.** Cells, Health
17. **Secret Area.** Cells
18. Flechettes, Health, Grenades
19. Cells, Health, Silver Key
20. Health, Ring of Shadows, Grenades, Green Armor, Quad Damage Rune
21. Flechettes, Lava Leap
22. Silver Key door; Entrance to Secret Mission: The Nameless City

Highlights:

- Four Secret Areas
- Big Bunches of Bad Guys
- Entrance to Secret Mission

Hot House

1. Hammer the Zombie before he has a chance to leave, and dine on Megahealth if you're so inclined. When you pass the two large torch fixtures, turn around and aim toward the one on the right. An alcove opens to eject a pair of Death Knights, keeping company with Flechettes.

2. Proceed to the large courtyard wary of lurking Spawns. If you hug the wall on either side of the hall approaching the courtyard, you can quickly get the attention of both the blobs. By taking up a position beneath one of the large wooden beams, the monsters will be momentarily frustrated in their attacks, and leap crazily in front of you. Angle a Grenade downward and back quickly away, and a little luck will have to do the rest. You'll find Flechettes nearby, but note that if you grab the Grenades you must take a dip in the slime to regain access to the area you wish to explore first. That's the area on the opposite side of the courtyard, to your right.

3. Through the entrance, be prepared to dismember some Zombies, and deal harshly with the Death Knight who follows. Inside, the Gold Key waits—and you'll be Spawned excessively when you acquire the prize. Let the Spawns get a good look at you, then run outside and activate the octagonal lift. Usually, the Spawns get stuck in the hall, and you can Grenade them from atop the lift. Along with the Gold Key, Flechettes, Grenades, and Health are available.

4. Health waits in the vicinity of the Gold Key door, across the acid pool from where you acquire the Gold Key. Beyond the door, move left to dispose of a Spawn hiding behind one of the far pillars before gathering Health and Shotgun Shells. You'll probably attract the attention of the Zombies in the room where you can see the Supernailgun in the doorway, and, should you kill the entire horde, a Fiend will follow. Step on the switch in the center of the room, and ride the lift up. Shoot the switch you see on the wall from the elevated ledge, and in you stride to the obvious Secret Area.

5. **Secret Area.** Plenty more Zombies and a Death Knight await. Inside the small area find major goodies—Health, Megahealth, Cells, Flechettes, and even a Quad Damage rune. Unfortunately a Vore will show up when you enter either of the reddish rooms, which also feature crushing ceilings.

6. Heist the Supernailgun and clean out any straggler Zombies—a Fiend arrives when you've reduced a goodly number of flesh-flingers to chunks. You'll find Grenades, Flechettes, and Health nearby.

7. When you enter area 6, bear left and then turn around when you enter the small room. You should see a window encircled in light. Shooting the window slides the wall behind you, releasing a Vore on your backside. In the Vore's lair waits Flechettes and a Ring of Shadows. Once the Vore is unleased, rush to the next area and claim the Pentagram.

8. Stepping on the switch gives access to the Pentagram of Protection, which you should use while disposing of the Zombies and Death Knights that come a-runnin' to investigate. Dispense Grenades liberally, and don't forget about the Vore from room 7.

9. Taking the Ring of Shadows from the Vore's room (8). drop through the trap door and acquire the Quad Damage rune. This area of hallways is filled to the hilt with Zombies, Fiends and Spawns, so you'd better put that Quad time to good use. Where the hallway intersects down the ramp from the rune, lob Grenades liberally in each direction to start the cleaning process. You'll want to wait for most of the Fiends to come looking for you, and peg them coming up the stairs. Afterwards, approach each intersection cautious for Spawns or Zombies.

10. Down the ramp to the right, dispatch the Zombies and the Spawn, and gather more Health and also Flechettes. Through the window at the end of the hall, you can see the Silver Key, guarded by a Death Knight.

11. Make a left where you can see the Silver Key, and clear out more Zombies, Spawns, and perhaps the occasional Fiend. Health, Flechettes, Grenades, and Shotgun Shells lie scattered about, and is that… could it be?… Yes, Virginia, that's the Thunderbolt. More Fiends teleport into the area when you claim the prize.

12. Finish the circuit, collecting more Grenades and Flechettes, and even a suit of Green Armor. Watch for the Death Knight above you. When you approach the Teleporter, a pool opens, as do two alcoves on either side of you, complete with Fiends. Pressing the switches in the Fiends' halls extends a ramp across the water, wherein waits the standard school of Rotfish, guarding a big box of Cells and a Quad Damage rune.

13. Up the ramp, use the Quad Damage rune from 12 to slay the Spawn and then the Death Knights on the overhead ledge, in the same room where there's a switch on the floor. Stepping on the floorplate opens most of the stained glass windows in the vicinity, releasing another horde of Zombies in your direction. Once things calm down, check those newly revealed alcoves for Flechettes, Grenades, and another Quad Damage rune. Also, note that two of the niches now grant access to the room next door.

14. If you step into the room adjacent to the switch room that released the Zombies, you'll find it's larger than the others. Shoot the wall to your right as you enter, and ride the lift to the upper tier.

15. **Secret Area.** Flip a couple of Grenades into the acid bath to clean out the Spawn, then hop in to claim a large box of Cells, Yellow Armor and a Pentagram of Protection, not necessarily in that order. If you're already reasonably buff, you might want to save the stash for rooms 18 and 19. Hop along the upper ledges to find more Cells, and another Secret Area.

16. **Secret Area.** Near where you came in on ground level, you'll spy an upper portal off one of the upper ledges. Inside more Cells await you, as well as a pair of Death Knights and access to a nearby wooden beam, where you can claim a box of Health.

17. **Secret Area.** From the beam where you claim the Health, hop along the beam peaks to the intersection. From that last beam, let yourself slide down to the left, slowly, and you can leap to the beam at the corner, where you can see the Cells. Cresting that beam gives the Secret Area message, and from there you can leap to claim another Cell box.

18. In the room adjacent to 13, be ready for the old Zombie-behind-the-glass trick when you lay hands on the Cells. A couple of Spawns are thrown in for good measure. Once you restore order, you can collect Health and Grenades from the Zombie niches.

19. Up the wooden ramp dispose of the Death Knights quickly, and gather Cells and Health. At the end of the walkway the Silver Key awaits. Use the Teleporter in area 12 to exit back to 6.

20. Through the final unexplored avenue off the large central courtyard, watch those nails, then grab up the Ring of Shadows and Quad Damage rune before testing out the Thunderbolt on the resident Vore and Death Knights. There's also Health and Grenades nearby, and a new suit of Green Armor. Expect Spawn trouble when you go to suit up, and notice a lonely Vore has appeared outside. Whatever you do in the next room, don't press the Silver Lock until you read the next area description, or you absolutely will lose access to Episode 4's Secret Mission.

21. A Fiend greets you when you round the partition in the room's center, keeping company with Flechettes, and a Vore waits across the lava. If you use the Silver Key on the lock, a bridge drops, allowing you to cross the lava—and sealing the entrance to Episode 4's Secret Mission. The entrance to the Secret Mission lies through a huge doorway to the left of the standard end-of-the-mission portal you can see from across the lava; you must have the Silver Key to open it. Notice that you have only one Silver Key… Instead of using the Silver Key on the lock in this room, hop across the wooden beams sticking straight out of the lava to make your way across. Yes, it is very tricky. Yes, it can be done. Jump to one of the closest pilings first, correcting as you land so that you don't slide forward—you want to arrest your forward momentum the instant you touch the top of the beam. If you look down at your "feet" once you're atop the piling, you'll see that you actually seem to be standing on a much larger area than the end of the stick. Back up as far as you can—tap, tap—and jump for the second piling, springboarding off of it when you hit the top, thus achieving the ledge across the lava.

22. Dispatch the Vore and give yourself a pat on the back. Through the large Silver Door lies this Episode's Secret Mission: "The Nameless City."

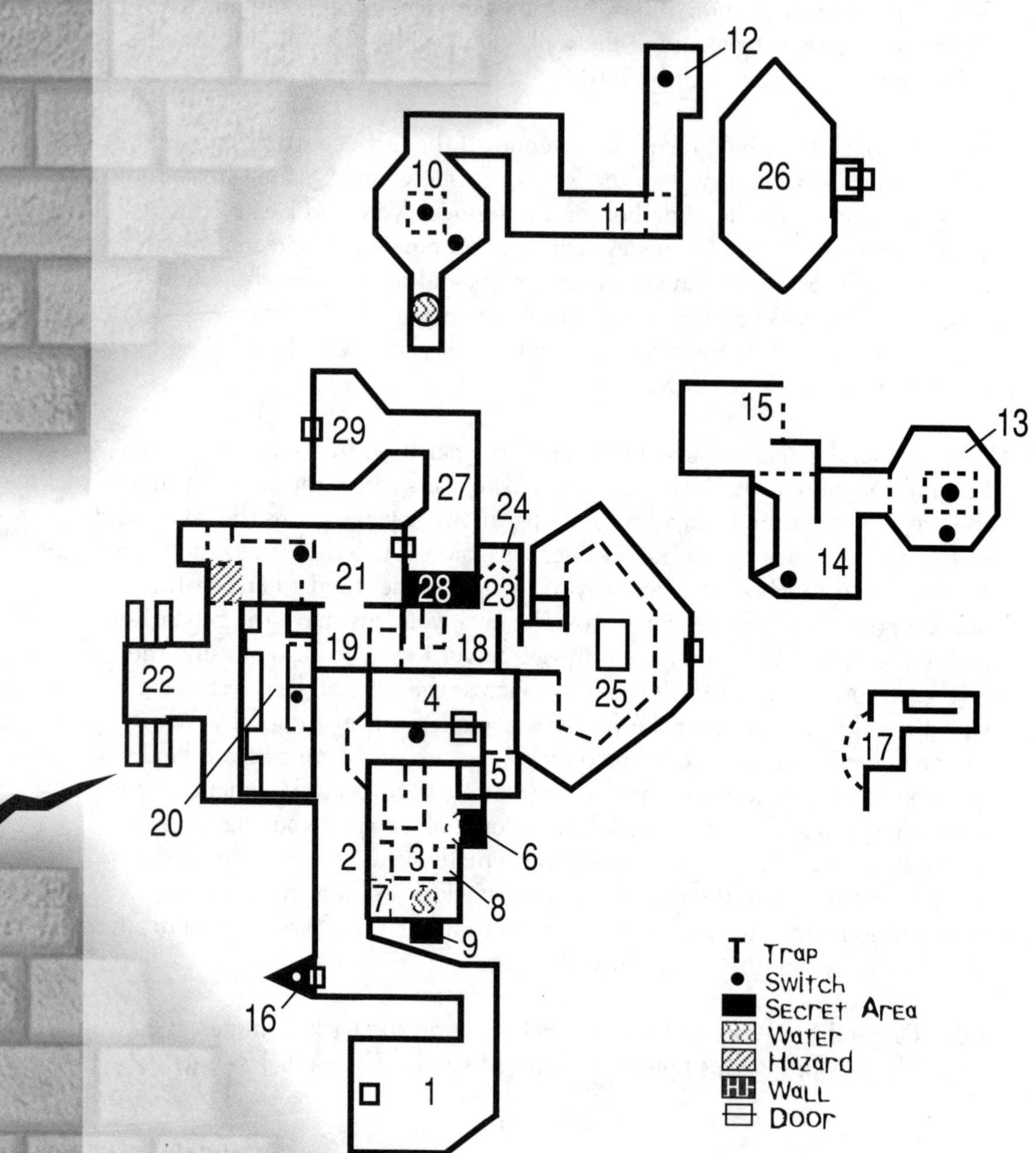
12
26
10
11
15
13
29
27
24
14
21
28
23
22
19
18
25
4
17
5
20
6
2
3
8
7
9
16
1
T Trap
Switch
Secret Area
Water
Hazard
Wall
Door

Secret Mission: The Nameless City

You'll think up plenty of appropriate monikers for the Nameless City—few of which would be suitable for publication—while you trudge its gloomy halls. Play it conservative with the ammo, or there's just no way you'll get through the end of the mission without cheating your brains out. You'll find a Quad Damage rune and a Pentagram of Protection just about right where you need them, but if you burn them for anything but the intended purpose, life gets ugly in a big hurry.

Secret Mission: The Nameless City At-a-Glance (E4M8)

1. Health, Megahealth, Shotgun Shells, Cells
2. Health, Flechettes
3. Shotgun Shells, Health
4. Health, Grenades
5. Health
6. **Secret Area.** Red Armor
7. Health, Shotgun Shells
8. Health, Flechettes, Cells, Shotgun Shells
9. **Secret Area.** Health, Cells, Quad Damage Rune
10. Green Armor, Shotgun Shells
11. Shotgun Shells, Cells
12. Flechettes, Health, Grenades
13. Health
14. Health, Grenades
15. Gold Key
16. **Secret Area.** Flechettes, Health
17. Shotgun Shells, Health
18. Ogre's Ledge
19. Vore Ambush
20. Shotgun Shells, Grenades, Flechettes, Pentagram of Protection
21. Silver Door, Health
22. Green Armor, Shotgun Shells, Health, Flechettes, Grenades, Thunderbolt
23. Health
24. Fiend Ambush
25. Health, Shotgun Shells, Flechettes, Cells, Quad Damage rune
26. Silver Key, Health, Shotgun Shells, Flechettes, Grenades
27. Flechettes, Shotgun Shells
28. **Secret Area.** Megahealth
29. Grenades, Mission Exit

Highlights:

- Four Secret Areas
- The Thunderbolt
- Sealed Room of Death

City Limits

1. Bomb the Zombies and welcome to the Nameless City. Health, Megahealth, Cells, and Shotgun Shells also are on hand to greet your arrival.

2. Slay the Ogre at the top of the ramp and be ready for a vicious Fiend attack. There are three, and they're in a foul mood. Health and Flechettes wait upstairs, and an Ogre arrives to pepper you from the ledge near the Gold Key. Get beneath the ledge, and he's easy pickings. Expect Fiend trouble when you claim the nails, though you can usually Grenade him into submission before he traverses the long hallway.

Note

If you'd like to lay hands on the Thunderbolt right now, you can see it from room 2 floating at the bottom of the ramp. But explore in the other direction, through the passage beneath the Gold Key platform.

3. Enter the hallway and turn down the short, dark passage on the right. At the end, turn to your right again and claim the Shotgun Shells. At the top of the ramp wait a pair of Ogres; try to peek out of the hall below and nail them, but rush up if they start dropping Grenades into the small area. Gather Health, and before you deal with the Zombies in the well, and at the bottom of the short stairs, leap out the ledge and push the switch high on the wall.

4. Pushing the switch high on the wall opens a passage in the hallway nearby. Dismember the local Zombie populace, and collect Health and Grenades. Hop on the lift.

5. Ride the lift up and proceed with caution. A Shambler guards the room ahead, where you'll find naught but a Health box… and a hole in the floor.

6. **Secret Area.** Drop down from the Shambler's abode to the ledge you saw from 3, and claim the Red Armor. Now it's time for those nearby Zombies.

7. At the bottom of the short dead-end stairs, a lone Zombie desperately defends Health and Shotgun Shells. The two at the rim of the well go to pieces near a box of Health—and another short hallway full of Zombies. To reach the lip of the well—and thus the nearby hidden chamber—run into the pit along one of the opening's diagonals, holding down the Forward button as you fall.

8. To the right of the short hallway where that last pack of Zombies cringed, shoot the wall; it slides to reveal a small room with Health, Flechettes, Cells, and Shotgun Shells.

9. **Secret Area.** Stand with your back to the wall between the aforementioned short hall of Zombies and the hidden chamber, and look into the well. You should see a Health box and other goodies on a ledge in the opposite wall of the well. Bomb the ledge to dispose of the Ogre, then walk straight forward, and keep walking forward as you fall. You'll catch on the ledge, claiming the Health, Cells, and a Quad Damage rune. Jump down to the area below to put the rest of your Quad time to proper use.

10. Dispose of the Zombies, and duck into the next room for more mayhem if you still have some rune power left. Push the switch on the wall, and one of the beams surrounding the central structure reveals itself as a lift. On the beams above, claim Green Armor and Shotgun Shells, but don't drop into the cage until you've explored the nearby area completely.

11. Follow the hallway full of lifts, disposing of Death Knights and Zombies while collecting Shotgun Shells. After you make the right turn, and ride up the lift, do an about-face and take out the Ogre on the ledge behind you. You can leap to his ledge for Cells, and the next lift in the sequence features the same trap. To reach that ledge, you must first hop to the top of the wall fixture.

12. Claim the Flechettes and ride the large lift up, pivoting to your left to lob a few Grenades through the upper entryway. At the top, complete the process of cleaning out the Zombies, then follow the hall to the end for Health and Grenades. Step on the switch you find there to lower the large box in the outside area, but don't linger near the window! Now make your way back to that cage in room 10.

13. The cage lowers you to a room full of Zombies, where you'll quickly find you're a sitting duck. Shoot the red switch on the wall to escape the trap, and exact your revenge. There's Health nearby.

14. Dispatch the Death Knight and lay claim to more Health, as well as a big box of Grenades. Push the switch and a large lift descends (watch your head!); ride up. Two more Death Knights wait when you leap to the nearby ledge, which also holds more Grenades.

15. From the previous area, one more long jump nets you the Gold Key. Hop down from the ledge to put it to use.

16. **Secret Area.** The Gold Key door, at the end of room 2, opens onto a Secret Area. Inside wait Cells and Health, and a switch that lowers a lift in the adjacent outside area, allowing you to climb back onto the ledge.

17. Follow the hallway behind the Gold Key ledge, collecting Shotgun Shells and then Health. A Death Knight hides in the dark just beyond the Health box. Slay the nearby Ogre and jump to his ledge.

18. Flip a few Grenades below the ledge to deal with the lurking Death Knight and Fiend, the hop down to the floor. You want the passage where you can see the demon's head nail trap.

19. Through the passage with the nail trap, get the attention of the Fiend and lure him to his doom. When you exit into the outside area, stick to the left wall and look up above the doorway you just came through. On a ledge waits a Vore and a pack of Zombies. If you let him, the Vore will put on quite a display at the Zombies' expense, after which you should apply the Thunderbolt liberally.

20. Hop over the bar on the floor of this hallway, or the nasty spiked thing overhead turns you into a medieval waffle. Slay the Fiend leaping in your direction, and, as you explore, be ready for Zombie trouble. Collect Cells and Grenades, and save that Pentagram of Protection until you really need it. Specifically, save it for room 26. Trust us. The switch in one of the Zombie rooms works the lighting.

21. Backtrack through the spike trap and hang a left—carefully. Another Vore waits inside, near the Silver Key door. Check the lower alcoves for Health—the switch activates a lift—before crossing the lava and heading down the hall.

22. Gosh, does that look like a trap centered around the Green Armor? If you'd like to preserve the suit in its pristine condition, just step to that end of the area to open the nearby alcoves. As you advance toward the Armor, then back away again, the alcoves on your left open first, releasing Zombies. The alcoves on your right will open a couple of seconds later. Once you've chunkified the Z-men, collect Shotgun Shells, Health, Flechettes, and Grenades. And don't forget the Thunderbolt at the end of the hall, adjacent to 2, if you didn't nab it earlier. Head back to room 18, and take that hall where you can see the box of Shotgun Shells.

23. Gather Health. Depending on whether you stirred up the crowd in the large room when you stepped on that switch at 12, there may be monsters lurking in the hall.

24. When you round the corner past the health, a nail trap activates in front of you at the same time that a wall drops to the rear. Inside the newly revealed alcove reside a pair of Fiends, and you should dispatch them quickly.

25. Blast the Vore and any Fiends or Ogres remaining in this large area, and collect Health, Cells, Shotgun Shells, and Flechettes. There's also a Quad Damage rune close by. Note the location of the window above, where you stepped on the switch earlier in 12. If you caused a commotion, most of the bad guys ended up through the Teleporter below the window, and that's where you're headed next. Go back and acquire the Pentagram from room 20, then grab the Quad Damage rune from the ledge, and beat feet through the Teleporter. When you arrive in the next area, be ready to dispense justice.

26. A huge hoard of Fiends welcomes you on the other side of the portal. Hopefully, you brought the Pentagram of Protection and the Quad Damage rune along to the party. Dispense Grenades liberally. More Fiends and a Shambler 'gate into the center of the room just about the time you think things have calmed down, so target the central podium when they start to appear. When you've introduced the entire throng to the afterlife, a door opens in the wall nearby. Inside is a Teleporter (that drops you back at 25), and also the Silver Key. You may collect the Health, Shotgun Shells, Flechettes, Cells, and Grenades scattered around the room.

27. Through the Silver Door, hammer the Zombies and the Death Knight. Claim the big box of Cells from the area to the right. Drop through the darkened triangle in the platform's top, near those Cells, to reach the Secret Area below.

28. **Secret Area.** Suck down the Megahealth and push the button to exit the area.

29. Up the ramp on the opposite side of 27, gather Grenades and then tackle the Vore upstairs. That's all that stands between you and the end of the mission.

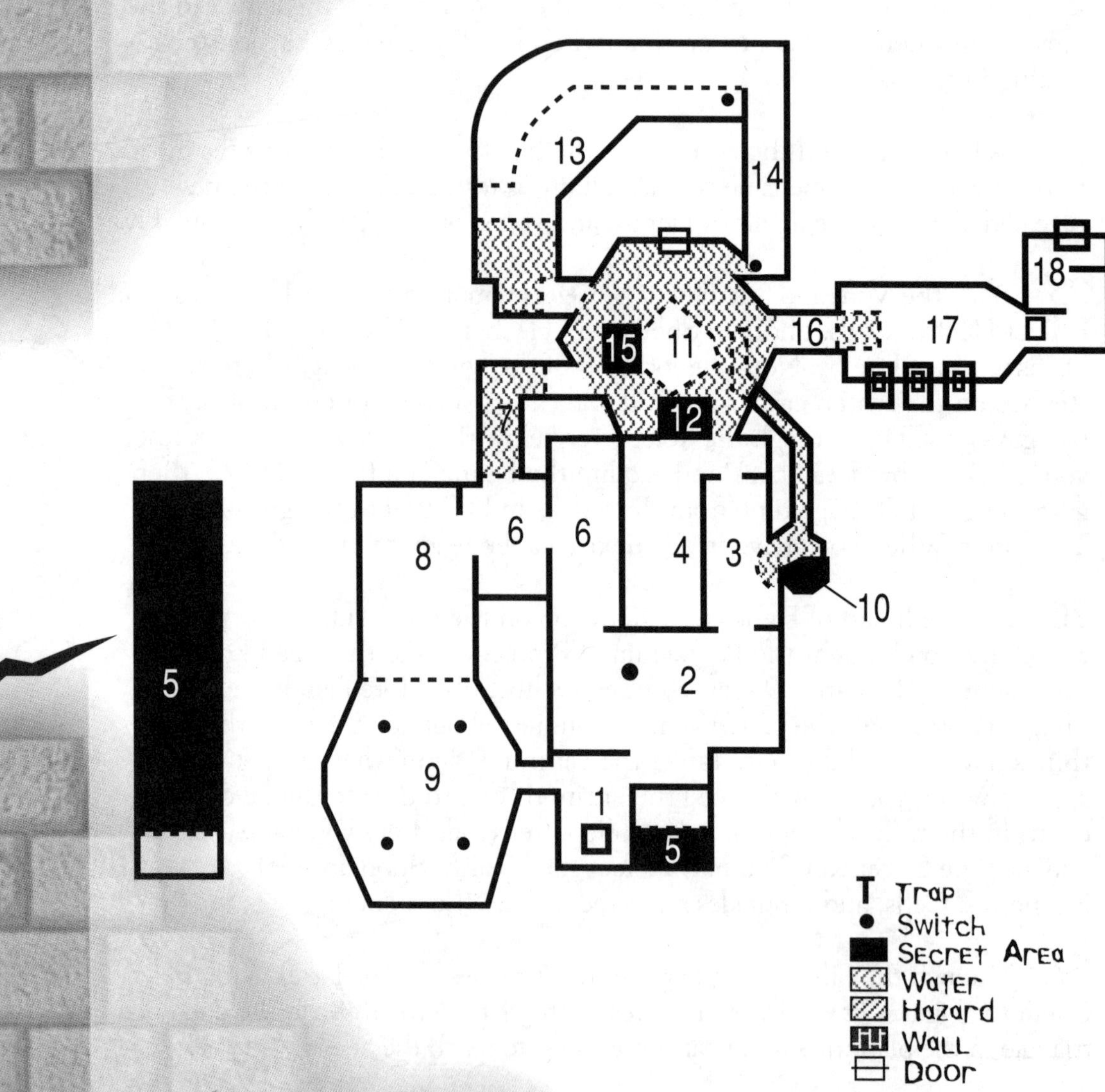
13
14
18
17
16
15
11
12
7
6
6
8
4
3
10
5
2
9
1
5
T Trap
Switch
Secret Area
Water
Hazard
Wall
Door

Mission 6: The Pain Maze

You start out with a Megahealth and a Quad Damage rune, and things only get better from there—that is, if you like pain. During your adventure in this maze you'll defile two demonic alters and waste a load of Vores, Death Knights, and Spawns—more than once. No, no. The monsters don't respawn: They repopulate. This happens in three areas (called out as 2, 3, and 11 in this walkthrough), and the second time you pass through these areas, new, tougher monsters appear near the bodies of their fallen comrades-in-arms.

Last, but not least, the item you've all been waiting for, the Rocket Launcher, makes its glorious appearance in Episode 4. Unfortunately, you can only get your grubby hands on it late in the mission. There is an upside, however: You get the opportunity to show it off to a pair of Vores and a gang of Spawns—with the help of a Pentagram of Protection, and a Quad Damage rune. Proof once again that the best things in life are truly worth waiting for.

Mission 6: The Pain Maze At-a-Glance (E4M6)

1. Quad Damage Rune, Megahealth
2. Shotgun Shells, Health, Cells
3. Water pool, Fiend/Spawn trap
4. Health, Flechettes, Shotgun Shells, Cells, Unholy Altar, Silver Key
5. **Secret Area.** Flechette, Cell Rockets
6. Green Armor, Cell; Flechette, Rockets
7. Health, Flechette
8. Trap; Shotgun Shells, Rockets, Health, Cell, 4-Switch Sequence
9. Gold Key
10. **Secret Area.** Thunderbolt, Health, Biosuit, Rockets
11. (Below Water) Flechette, Biosuit, Ring of Shadows, Shotgun Shells, Health, Cells; (Above Water) Rockets, Flechettes, Shotgun Shells, Quad Damage Rune; Rocket Launcher (acquired from 14)
12. **Secret Area.** Red Armor, Cell
13. Shotgun Shells, Flechette, Health, Yellow Armor; Rockets, Ring of Shadows
14. Rockets, Biosuit
15. **Secret Area.** Pentagram of Protection, Rockets, Cells
16. Flechette, Rockets
17. Quad Damage Rune, Flechette, Health, Shotgun Shells, Cell, Unholy Altar, Megahealth
18. End

Highlights:

- An Awesome Foursome of Secret Areas
- Re-"Spawn"ing Monsters
- Completing Your Arsenal with the Famed Rocket Launcher

Shoot It Repeatedly!

1. You begin this adventure with two great things that go great together—a Megahealth sitting in front of you and a Quad Damage rune dangling in the shadows to your left. Prepare to dish up a generous helping of gangland justice.

But before you get out your Supernailgun, power-up and go, please read the descriptions and look at the map for 2, 3, and 4. That's where we recommend you go while the power-ups last. What's more, if you stick with us you'll also Quad-Damage-kill the guys in Secret Area 5. Are you ready to rumble? We'll see you at 5.

2. A trio of Fiends leaps out to say hello. Once you've said good-bye, hustle into 3 for another quick round of Fiend sparring.

3. A complement of Fiends teleport in when you dash past the pool. As soon as you kill the Fiends, a troop of Spawn commandos plops down from the ceiling. Run away toward 4 (they're easier and safer to kill from there). Turn left as you ride the lift up.

4. Defile the alter and nail the Vore—and the Vores that fall down from the ceiling! While you're at it, take down the Death Knights and Fiend in the shadows behind the altar—they're in Secret Area 5. Snuggle up to the wall behind the alter for protection. Your Quad Damage rune's power should be used up by now, so take your time vanquishing the Death Knight on the ledge next to the lift. Defiling the altar also grants you access to the Silver Key. Stand on the lift with your back to the altar and look into the niche—the blessed key should be dangling before your very eyes.

Note that if the Fiend from 5 comes down to play, simply stay in the Silver Key niche and let the him fall into the pit. He won't go far, and it's ridiculously easy to peg him from either side of the lift.

Run into 3, stir up the Spawns, then dash back to lift. From the top of the lift, take potshots at those fool enough to follow. To rid the world of the Spawns that refuse to follow, lob a few grenades into 3. An extra-big explosion means you've hit pay dirt. If you still hear Fiends or Spawns, check the pool for any sunken scum. Backtrack to 2.

5. **Secret Place.** Hit the obviously protruding switch on the pillar in room 2—it's on the side opposite the door where you first entered.

Look in front of you to the left. A blue window next to the entrance to 1 should have slid open, revealing a passageway. Jump in and ride the lift up. If you didn't kill the Fiend or Death Knights when you were in 4, you get another chance to strut your stuff.

6. Now's your chance to prove your virility by fighting a Vore sans power-ups. He's hidden in the Shadows in the far left corner. Use the hallway leading to 5 to your advantage by making him follow you. Leave a Grenade present for him each time you backpedal around a corner.

7. Dive into the small cesspool to the right, swim down the passage, and ride the lift up to claim some valuable prizes. Use your Silver Key on this set of bars—also opens another barrier preventing access to 13. Go back to 6, stand in front of the bars, and save your game.

8. This room is a trap reminiscent of a midway arcade game—specifically, the one where a metal broom non-stop pushes an oh-so-precarious pile of quarters toward a ledge. Except here the quarters are you; and instead of a big payoff, you get the booby prize. As soon as you step onto the darkened floor (away from the low bloody-skull wall), the wall grinds toward you. Since you can't stop it or leap on top of it, you get shoved off the ledge into a waiting mob of Spawns. Nasty.

To defuse the trap, stand at the edge of the circle of light and lob Grenade after Grenade over the far ledge. Since you can't check your work and try again (unless you quicksave), you'll have to trust your own judgment. Then get out your favorite Spawn killer and run to the ledge. Waste as many remaining Spawns as you can before you get shoved into their pit. After that? There's lots of health boxes to help you live to fight another room.

9. Complete the four-switch sequence and the Gold Key comes down to you. Grab it and ride the lift up to 1 facing straight ahead, favorite Spawn

killer to the ready. Watch out for one that materializes in the far right corner. Also watch out when you drop down into 2: Where there were Fiends, there are now plenty of Spawns. Go to 3 and dive into the fetid pool.

10. **Secret Area.** Once the underwater coast is clear, look up before you start any serious swimming. Do a 180-degree turn before you break the surface. Only two Spawns cower between you and a sporting cache of goods. Before they see you, lob a genade or two into 10 from underwater. The Spawns won't know what hit them.

11. Welcome to a huge room that you'll return to again and again. Note the Red Armor perch (Secret Area 12), and the Slipgate and Rocket Launcher pad high in the wall opposite it. Note also the off-colored wall directly beneath the Gold Key floor switch on the side of the submerged center structure: Shooting the wall reveals Secret Area 15. Save the Ring of Shadows for when you mount an attack on 17.

We found it easiest to pick off the perched Death Knights from the water. They have a terrible time targeting you when you keep dipping below the surface. Be aware of your ammo levels at all times! When you're playing submarine, nothing's worse than running out of nails and automatically switching to the Thunderbolt!

> **Note**
>
> Area 11 sports two waves of bad guys. The second team comes out to play as soon as you grab the rockets in 14. But doing business in 11 from 14 is surprisingly easy, thanks in large part to a distinct height advantage.

Once the fuss dies down, step on the Gold Key switch and ride the lift up to scour the beams for lifesaving items. Don't grab the Quad Damage rune yet!

Check out the location of the higher, formerly barred Silver Key hallway. (Near the beam where one of the Flechette rests.) Once you note it, work your way toward the Red Armor, stand against the wall, and look up.

12. **Secret Area.** Shoot the dome in the center of the ceiling. The beam you (hopefully) stand on lifts up past the Red Armor platform. Drop off the beam to claim your prizes and save your game. It's Quad Damage time for Fiends, Vores, and Spawns alike.

Leap onto the Quad Damage rune, fall into the water, splash onto the Gold Key lift, dash through the Silver Key gate, dive in, turn right, and swim.

13. Splash up the ramp and nail the Fiend in front of you. A section of wall to your right immediately drops, revealing a host of items you can use, and a row of compressed Spawns. Setting off a Spawn chain reaction has never been easier. Relentlessly press on with the attack.

Round the corner and wipe out the Fiend and his Spawn buddies in quadruple time. Watch out for the Vore that teleports in from the ceiling! When all's clear, hit the switch at the far end of the room to lower a huge section of wall next to you. You now have access to 14. Grab the Ring of Shadows beneath the stairs and then ascend, ready for a fight with a Death Knight and Vore. If you're lucky you can get them to fight each other, at least until you step in and throw in the towel. To dodge the Vore's parting volley, run back into the water and swim up toward the Silver Key gate. His Spikeball seems to have a hard time following you up this vertical passage.

14. As soon as you collect the Rockets, a pair of Death Knights and a Vore materialize in 11. Step on the switch to lower the platform next to the Rocket Launcher and Slipgate. One of the Death Knights is on this platform (he stays down at the water level), the Vore likes to hide behind the closest section of beams on the Gold Key switch platform. The second Death Knight hangs out on what was the Red Armor platform.

Flatten the closest Death Knight and crumple the Vore from here. Then dive into the water, ride the lift up to the Rocket Launcher, and show the distant Death Knight what a Rocket Launcher can do in the hands of an expert.

You can go through the Slipgate to 16 right now if you want. Or you can drop into the water and pick up the Pentagram of Protection and Ring of Shadows beforehand. The choice is yours.

15. **Secret Area.** In the water, face the center structure directly below the Gold Key switch and shoot the wall. It slides away to reveal an ever-popular Pentagram of Protection and other valuable ammo. But before you greedily snap up the artifact, read ahead through 17. The following information may just save your life.

Grab the Pentagram, swim into the ring and hop onto the platform below the Slipgate. Get out your heavy artillery as you ascend, leap through the Slipgate, dash along the beam and dismount into the opening, 16.

16. Drop off the ledge and dive as fast as you can: The exit—and 17—are dead ahead.

17. The trick to surviving this room is never to stop running toward the exit. Leap out of the water, grab the Quad Damage rune immediately to your right, and run toward the Vores and Unholy Altar spewing death as you go. Shoot the Unholy Altar to open the brown doors at the far end of the room; grab the Megahealth just past the altar, breech the entrance, and make the Death Knight live up to his name. By now a huge gang of Spawns will have plopped into the room behind you (they came from behind the stained-glass windows on the right). Only a few of them seem to have the presence of mind to immediately follow you down the hall, which is just as well—two more cleverly placed Death Knights lie in wait near the maze's exit. Once you've felled Death Knights in battle, what's stopping you from going back to the hallway's entrance and blowing the Spawns to bits from afar? A sudden pity for lesser beings and sense of fair play? Yeah, right.

If you don't have the Pentagram going, or it runs out prematurely, it's best to cower in the turgid water and lob grenades into the room to thin out the Spawn population though you'll have to abandon that tactic if too many blobs wind up in the pool. Shooting Rockets into the Stained-glass windows is also a wise use of ammo.

18. Get out your Supernailgun before you exit—it's the first thing you need where you're going next.

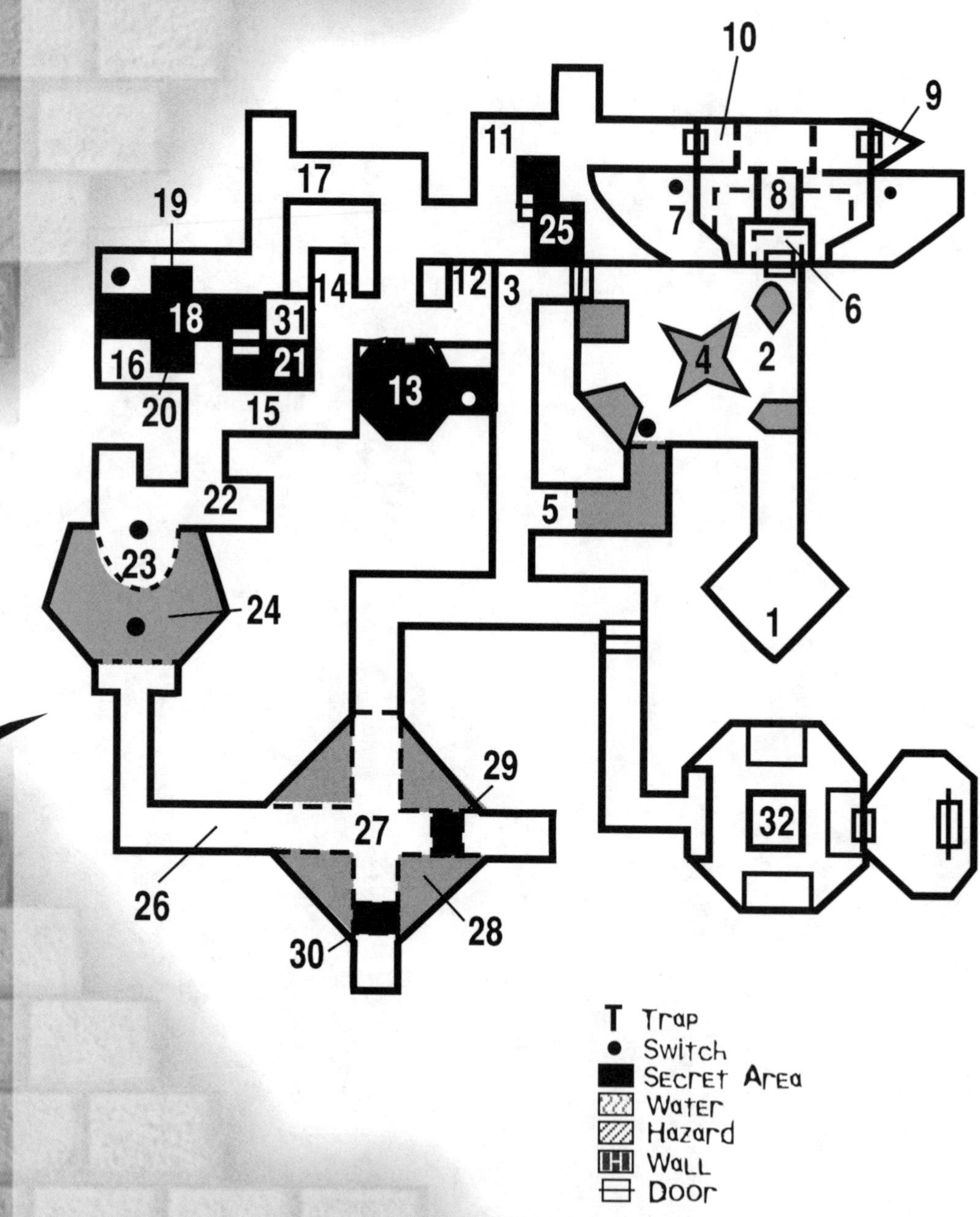

1
2
3
4
5
6
7
8
9
10
11
12
13
14
15
16
17
18
19
20
21
22
23
24
25
26
27
28
29
30
31
32
T Trap
Switch
Secret Area
Water
Hazard
Wall
Door

Mission 7: Azure Agony

One last mission to go before the big showdown, and it's a doozy. "Azure Agony" pretty much pulls out all the stops, as Vores, Shamblers and Death Knights become almost commonplace, and anytime a Spawn isn't bouncing in your direction, you feel like you should pause and give thanks. Fortunately, with all the Secret Areas disclosed, you'll also have plenty of goodies on hand to turn the tide. The final Rune Key awaits.

Mission 7: Azure Agony At-a-Glance (E4M7)

1. Megahealth
2. Health
3. Flechettes
4. Grenades, Flechettes, Health, Cells, Yellow Armor
5. Flechettes
6. Grenades
7. Flechettes, Cells
8. Quad Damage Rune, Health
9. Shotgun Shells, Flechettes, Health, Ring of Shadows, Cells
10. Green Armor
11. Flechettes, Grenades, Shotgun Shells, Health, Biosuit
12. Health, Quad Damage Rune
13. **Secret Area.** Red Armor, Grenades, Cells, Flechettes
14. Flechettes
15. Flechettes, Health
16. Health, Shotgun Shells, Flechettes, Switch
17. Flechettes
18. **Secret Area.** Health, Grenades, Cells, Flechettes, Shotgun Shells, Ring of Shadows
19. **Secret Area.** Grenades
20. **Secret Area.** Grenades
21. **Secret Area.** Cells, Health, Quad Damage Rune
22. Shotgun Shells
23. Ceiling Switch
24. Health, Quad Damage Rune, Switch
25. **Secret Area.** Cells, Grenades
26. Vore
27. Silver Key, Pentagram of Protection, Quad Damage Rune
28. Flechettes, Health, Grenades
29. **Secret Area.** Grenades
30. **Secret Area.** Teleporter
31. **Secret Area.** Megahealth
32. Megahealth, Quad Dameage Rune, Cells, Rune Key

Highlights:

- Nine Secret Areas
- Plenty of Power-Ups
- End-of-the-Episode Mayhem

The Color of Pain

1. The agony starts early in the final mission of Episode 4, especially if you grab up that Megahealth and go charging off down the hallway. There's a Shambler above you, ready to drop down when you venture forth. If you step towards the hallway and jump back, however, the big freak hops down and marches off in front of you, oblivious to his impending demise.

2. In the large room with the star-shaped pool in the center, shortly after you detonate the Spawn, you'll hear the playful sounds of a Zombie horde below you. Collect the Health nearby, but go through the door across the room, in the far left corner as you enter, before dealing with the scum underfoot.

3. Through the doorway, dispose of the Death Knight goon squad and collect more Flechettes. Clear the hall of Spawns, beginning with the nook on your left about halfway down. When the hallway makes a T, stop short of the intersection and bounce a few Grenades in either direction to defuse still more Spawn trouble. Now double back to the star room.

4. Pepper the pool openings with Grenades; you'll know when you've dealt with the initial Zombie wave when more Zombies teleport into the room above, dropping into the water below. When the coast is finally clear, lay claim to Grenades, Cells, Flechettes, Health boxes, and a new suit of Yellow Armor. The floor switch opens the barred doorway.

5. If you surface beyond the portal you unbarred from the previous room, you're in the small nook in the adjacent hallway near more Flechettes. Hopefully you took our advice and dealt with the Spawns and Death Knights beforehand. Make your way back around to the previous pool room, and proceed through the other portal.

6. Through the doorway, you'll have to jump to one side of the room to gain the ledge with the Grenades, as a trap door in the center of the chamber prevents your pilfering otherwise. Drop through the hole in the floor.

7. Leaping from the ledge above, turn to your right and nail the Death Knight. Run into his area, and slay the second Death Knight bearing down on your backside. Finally, peak into that other side of the hallway and detonate the cluster of Spawns before they have a chance to mobilize. Gather the Flechettes and Cells, and push both switches to unbar the nearby portal and lower a lift.

8. When you approach the lift, the hall on either side of you opens for more Spawn and Death Knight adventures. If you stick to the left side of the hall as you head for the platform, the Spawns will usually stay inside their alcove if you back quickly into the hall behind you. The blobs' alcove holds a Quad Damage rune, while the Death Knight was hoarding Health.

9. Up the lift, one ledge holds Shotgun Shells, Flechettes, and Health, while the door there opens onto a small room with a Ring of Shadows and Cells protected by a nail trap.

10. The other ledge sports Green Armor, with a door that opens onto a passageway.

11. In the hallways beyond the Green Armor, watch your step as you descend the stairs. A nail trap whacks your knees from the right, though you can hop up onto the fixture to get past it. There are plenty of Fiends and Spawns about, unless you previously lured them to their doom. There are also Flechettes, Grenades, Shotgun Shells, and Health. Near the intersection where you spy the Biosuit, things get messy in a hurry. Either hallway from that point is going to the same place, but we'll start on the left, for reasons that will become obvious. Suit up and go.

Note

Notice how the nail trap in room 9 fires at the door on the opposite side of the chasm, across from where the lift rises... If you use the Ring of Shadows, you can venture a ways down the halls beyond the Green Armor ledge, and wait for the magic to wear off. When it does, the Fiend population will be so excited to see you, they'll follow you all the way back to the nail trap, and... See if you can figure out the rest for yourself.

12. Turn left at the top of the stairs, after perhaps confronting a Fiend, and discover a large box of Health and a Quad Damage rune. When you go to grab the rune, the floor parts, and you and the prize drop into the acid bath below. Grab the rune and turn around. You'll see a Teleporter, but it's not the one you want. That ride drops you back at the Green Armor in 10. Buttonhook around the corner to your right, however, and spy a Teleporter worthy of the trip.

13. **Secret Area.** From the correct Teleporter you find while slime diving, you arrive in the vicinity of the Red Armor. Push the switch on the wall, and hammer the arriving Death Knights. You'll also unveil Grenades, Cells, and Flechettes.

14. Hang a left when you jump down after acquiring the Red Armor, and look to your right as you approach the intersection. An alcove of Spawns and Flechettes begs for your gentle touch. Be ready for a contingent of Death Knights and Spawns to head in your direction from the stairway leading up, with the occasional Fiend thrown in for good measure.

15. Up the stairs and to your right, approach the big box of Flechettes with caution. You'll want to peek down the right-hand avenue until you spy the Vore on the raised ledge—and hopefully hammer him before he realizes what's going on. That accomplished, deal with the Death Knights coming from the other direction, gather the Health and head downstairs, passing the Vore ledge on your right.

16. Down the stairs, collect plenty more Health, Shotgun Shells, and Flechettes. Don't shoot the switch you spy beneath the stairs just yet. Instead, climb those stairs, hang a right, and dispose of more Spawns.

17. Follow that passage up, again passing the Vore ledge on your right, and you'll discover more Spawns, yet another Fiend, and more Flechettes. Now return and shoot the switch beneath the stairs.

18. **Secret Area.** When you shoot the switch below the stairway, the stairs above reconfigure, allowing you to reach the ledge where the Vore resided earlier. If you stand on the bottom step to shoot the switch, you won't have to loop around to access the new route. Ascend to the top stair keeping against the left wall. Back along the step until you can see a ledge at the far end of the Secret Area. There's a Shambler up there, and several Spawns. If you launch a Grenade onto the ledge, the Spawns detonate, and the

Shambler comes out to play. If you then retreat down the steps you just raised, the Shambler jumps down into that area. Now you can hop all the way up the stairs, and the Shambler remains trapped below you. Show him no mercy, then gather Health, Flechettes, Cells, Grenades, and Shotgun Shells. There's even a Ring of Shadows as reward for your tactical brilliance… but don't grab it until you've opened the other three nearby Secret Areas.

19. **Secret Area.** From that ledge, notice the two small pools of light in the darkened place on the walls. Shoot one, and the wall opens to bestow Grenades.

20. **Secret Area.** Shoot the other small circle of light, and garner another big box of Grenades.

21. **Secret Area.** Stand and face the ledge where the Shambler lived, and shoot the wall on your right. It slides to unleash another Vore from a room holding Cells, Health, and a Quad Damage rune.

22. Facing the Shambler's ledge, grab the Ring of Shadows from the Secret Area and make a right turn, ascending the stairs. At the top, you'll find Shotgun Shells to your left, then more stairs guarded by a Death Knight, Spawns, lurking in an alcove to your right.

23. Having dealt harshly with the Spawns and Death Knight, climb the steps and blast the Death Knight waiting across the water. Shoot the overhead symbol to produce a platform across the water, within jumping distance from the top of the stairs. If you hop in the water and swim straight forward, through the teleporter, the Rotfish will attempt to follow. When you reappear on the stairs up top, won't they feel silly?

24. Beneath the water, grab up some Health and a Quad Damage rune, then hit the switch beneath the steps and hop in the Teleporter.

25. **Secret Area.** Double back to near where you entered this network of tunnels. As you approach the Biosuit juncture, turn to your right and you'll see that the wall has dropped at the end of the passage. You'll also see a couple of Fiends leaping in your direction, followed shortly by a swarm of Spawns. Quad the scum, then gather Cells and Grenades, before heading back to 23 and crossing the water.

26. Hop over the pool of water (to the ledge you raised by shooting the ceiling) and be ready for Vore trouble as you round the corner to the left. When the first one succumbs, you'll be able to see another in a distant alcove, across

the room where you're headed. If you take that one out with the Rocket Launcher, from near the corner of the hallway, you'll be too far away for the scum to target you.

27. Approaching the entrance to the large chamber where you can see the Silver Key, creep to the threshold and look to your right. Another Vore waits in an alcove, and you now have the drop on him. Once you've dealt with him, charge across the room and nab the Silver Key en route to the Pentagram of Protection you can see ahead. When you grab the Pentagram, a Shambler drops from an upper alcove. Ignore him for now, and run to the niche where you can see the Quad Damage rune. *Now* it's party time. Hammer Shaggy, then blast the Zombies and Rotfish beneath the water.

28. Below the water, in addition to far too many Zombies, an abundance of Flechettes, Health, and Grenades await. You'll also find a pair of Secret Areas.

29. **Secret Area.** Shoot the wall, relatively underneath the upper area where you picked up the Pentagram of Protection a moment ago, and you'll reveal a room full of Grenades.

30. **Secret Area.** Shoot the wall beneath the relative position of the niche with the Quad Damage rune, and a Teleporter appears.

31. **Secret Area.** The Teleporter from 30 drops you on the Shambler's ledge above 18, with Megahealth nearby. Kinda like two Secret Areas in one…

Note

To raise the bars across the hallway from room 27, shoot both of the large red emblems—one underwater and one on the ceiling. Since completing the sequence ushers in a Vore, it's advisable to shoot the ceiling emblem last, preferably from the hallway through which you first entered. Afterward, pass through the unbarred portal, and turn right to locate the Silver Key door.

32. Through the Silver Key door, traverse the hallway and greet four last Vores. On the ledges above you, bouncing crazily, they make difficult targets, but there's four kills between you and the final Rune Key. Don't spare the ammo. There's Megahealth, a Quad Damage rune, and Cells on the ledges. When the final Vore crumples, you'll be able to claim the ultimate prize. In the room beyond, the Teleporter you face as you drop to the floor ends the Episode, while the one behind you returns you to the adjacent room.

End

Shub-Niggurath's Pit

Cutthroat and to the point, Shub-Niggurath's Pit will humble you—unless you take your time and make the quirks of the Pit work for you, or accept the fact that 100% kills with your weaponry isn't what this mission is all about. However you approach the combat here, your objectives are simple: Annihilate Shub-Niggurath at all costs and save the earth.

Once you've acquired the fourth and final Rune Key, you'll find yourself standing in the select-a-mission room. You know the one. Except now an imposing downward flight of stairs beckons. The time is now. Your destiny awaits.

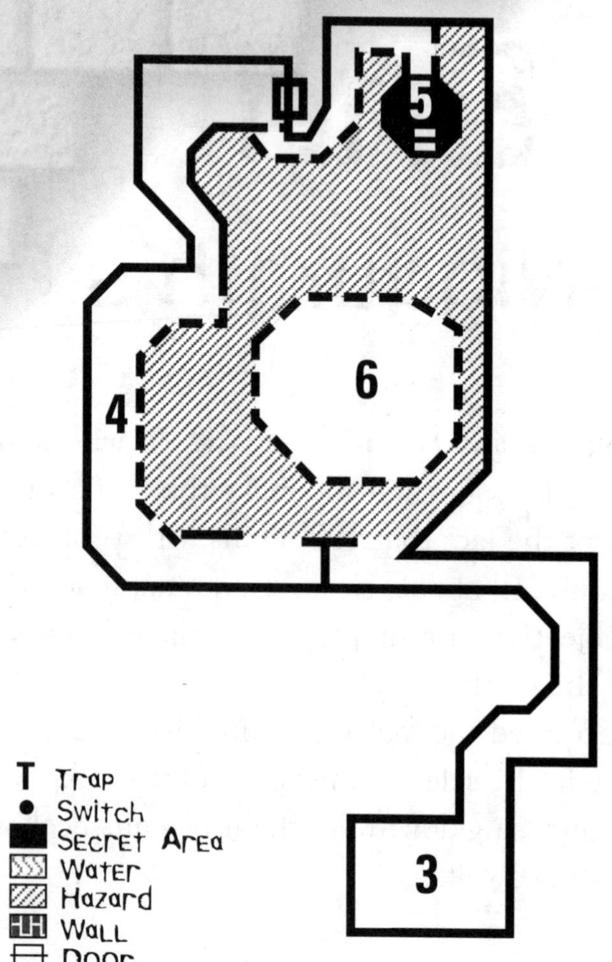
5
6
4
3
T Trap
Switch
Secret Area
Water
Hazard
Wall
Door

2
1

End: Shub-Niggurath's Pit

Like a true crime boss, Shub-Niggurath herself doesn't soil her delicate tentacles with killing. Her minions do the dirty work for her. This has led her to fall prey to the deadly sin of Sloth. She can't run, she can't fight back.

The trick here isn't in killing Shubbie herself, rather it's surviving the gauntlet of fire en route to your date with destiny. If you don't kill all of her minions along the way, don't worry. When you kill Shubbie, all of her followers die of natural causes—sometimes monsters just explode. Even so, we've devised a method to pick off all of her protectors a pair at a time. It takes patience and a fair amount of environment savvy; but if it worked for us it should work for you, too.

So, how exactly do you kill Shub-Niggurath? The same way we all hate to die—telefragging. It's an ill-fitting, an inglorious way to go, we know. But there it is.

When it's all over you may find yourself sitting behind your large desk. You may ask yourself: Where do I go from here? The answer, my friend, is clear. Say it loud, say it proud: Deathmatch, Deathmatch, Deathmatch!

Shub-Niggurath's Pit At-a-Glance

1. Shotgun Shells, Thunderbolt
2. Rockets, Shotgun Shells, Health, Double-barreled Shotgun, Flechette, Cells
3. Health, Rockets, Rocket Launcher, Supernailgun, Nailgun, Grenade Launcher, Flechette, Spiketrap
4. Flechettes, Cells, Health, Nailgun trap, Rockets
5. **Secret Area.** Quad Damage Rune
6. End

Highlights:

- Spikeball Telefragging
- One Powerful-Strong Secret Area
- Nasty Traps, Shamblers, and Vores

Death Becomes Her

1. The moment you drop into the water, a school of Rotfish start gnawing on your hide. This is the only time in *Quake* where the Rotfish are truly worthy adversaries, thanks in large part to your lack of armor and real weaponry.

We found it was best to surface as soon as possible—the Rotfish don't seem to notice or really attack you until you sink beneath the surface. Use that to your advantage: go under (alerting them to your presence), surface, then shoot the dorsal fins. Beware the flying Rotfish, however. With a little practice, you could very well enter room 2 with a high 80's health rating.

Be careful not to swim around the center structure while you evade the Rotfish—that's where the Thunderbolt lies. (The bars above the Thunderbolt keep you out of 2, for now.) If you grab this weapon during the melee you'll no doubt accidentally pull the trigger and become the butt of this sick practical joke. It's reloading time.

Once you're done fishing, dive into the tiny hole near where you dropped in, and swim as fast as you can. Hang a right and kill the Rotfish. Going up toward the bars lowers them, and the bars at the water's surface retract as well.

2. One lowly Scrag floats between you and the Slipgate to 3, Shub-Niggurath's Pit proper. If you choose to battle the slug while in the water, be careful not to run down your shell supply, thereby automatically switching to the Thunderbolt. Grab the loot and head out. Her Nastiness awaits.

3. The Spikeball that floats away from you is your portal into the belly of the beast. Don't shoot it, just let if fly. We'll tell you how it works when you get to the Slipgate at the end of the long path. Until then, let's murder some monsters.

As soon as you ascend the steps past the Grenade Launcher, a Shambler roars into action from Shubbie's platform to you right. Beware the hidden wallspike in the left wall—it flashes out to skewer you when you get near the wall past the Flechette.

Once you've toasted Shubbie's Shambler pal, the wall before you drops and that's when the real fighting begins. Or should we say the real running?...

4. You've got six more Shamblers and six Vores to battle before the day's through. Between your limited ammo supply, the lava pit, nail traps, and wall-spike trap, even the Quad Damage rune doesn't give you much of a fighting chance, and it's a long ways awat. You can, however, use your brains and the Pit's environment to your advantage. As you may know by now, nail traps make excellent Shambler killers.

Take out the first wave of bad guys from the relative saftey of 3 and 4. Then creep up to each nailtrap and Rocket the Vores (before they get you). Attacking a Vore usually sets a Shamber into action. Snuggle up against a nail-trap once the furry freak gets close to you, and the Shambler will spasm in a hail of nails until he dies. Repeat the process until you're either out of nailtraps or out of monsters.

If that doesn't suit your style, try immediately dashing past the all the enemies you see (and don't see) after you kill the first Shambler. The longer you stand your ground and do battle, the more bad guys that show up. If you opt for this tactic, your aim is to kill the dark princess of evil, not to get side-tracked slaughtering Shamblers and Vores. When she dies, so do will her minions, and by default you'll get your 100% kills.

Run up to the Slipgate and stop. If you thirst for battle, read 5. If you want to get this game over with and spend some time with your family or loved ones, read 6 and end it all.

5. **Secret Area.** After you've run around (or through) the gauntlet, stop just before the Slipgate and peer over the edge of the passage. See that thin ledge? Drop onto it and follow it to a small room. The Quad Damage is yours. The Slipgate deposits you right in front of the Slipgate in 4. Lay waste to as many of the baddies as you can, then…

6. End. There's only way to slay this bad mamma-jamma, and here's how:

- Standing in front of the Slipgate at the top of 4, watch the spikeball. Where-ever that spikeball happens to be is where the teleporter will take you. If it's over the lava, you fall into the lava. If it's over a ledge, you materialize over a ledge. If it's in Shub-Niggurath herself… Did we say *in* Shub-Niggurath?
- Wait for the spikeball to float around 5, the Quad Damage room. You should be keeping one eye on Shubbie, one on the spikeball, and one on the Slipgate…
- When the spikeball passes through the crowned princess of vile, hop on into the Slipgate. As you'll see, she can't believe she ate the whole thing.

And that's it. Or is it? Go ahead, take some time and finish that Masters thesis you've been putting off for the last 10 years. Or perhaps you could do some volunteer work. Then again, maybe you should think about going on-line and playing a little Deathmatch. Heck, if you've gotten all the way through the game you must be good. But just how good are you? The maps in the next chapter are bound to help your cause. Just watch your back if you go on-line and happen to encounter Fragboy and Sirloin… they know this game inside and out.

Deathmatch, Quake Style

It's obvious id's designers lovingly crafted each *Quake* mission with Deathmatch in mind. Further, remember that *Quake's* game engine treats a single-player game as if it's a multiplayer game with only one player. No, it isn't some weird philosophical conundrum. It's actually the best thing that's ever happened to Deathmatch.

The Buddy System

One of the most innovative aspects of *Quake* Deathmatch concerns team play, and the ability that *Quake* gives players to gain advantages by being "team members."

If you wear the same color pants as other team members, you have the option of not being harmed by friendly fire. This can be a huge advantage, allowing you, in effect, to use members of your team as bait. Of course, the "bait" has to survive being the center of attention long enough for that kind of trap to be effective.

Alternately, of course, the pointman for your team can be the ace, able to draw out trouble and survive long enough for other team members to gain an advantage.

Multiplayer *Quake* also offers players the ability to set Time or Frag limits, join a game already in progress, and advance with other players between missions.

For details on how to configure a multiplayer battlezone, check out the documentation that comes with the game. There are also numerous Usenet newsgroups devoted to the subject, most notably:

- rec.games.computer.quake.servers
- rec.games.computer.quake.playing
- rec.games.computer.quake.misc

If you have the time and patience to wade through the cross-posts and nonsense, you'll find all things great and small related to *Quake* (and Deathmatch) at these sites.

The Lay of the Land

Online multiplayer software and hardware considerations aside, pay special attention to the structure of the missions themselves. Very circular in general, and the Deathmatch-specific missions are downright claustrophobic... which is almost a segue...

There are numerous ways to access each encounter area, and several sneaky routes to get you from point A to B. You'll notice—probably right before some pain or death—that new avenues and teleporters appear when the game is in Multiplayer mode, further enhancing the circular nature of the standard Episode missions. Take the time to check out the missions in Multiplayer mode by yourself, just so you won't be completely surprised with the alterations.

You'll find that the inclusion of niches and hidey-holes that seem irrelevant in single-player action makes perfect sense once you step into Deathmatch. Suddenly treasure populates those insignificant places, making an already out-of-this-world slaying ground truly stellar.

For Deathmatch Only

Included with the full game are six dungeons accessible only in Multiplayer mode, and each of them are worth a look. Maps and legends for those missions, as well as a few pertinent notes, are included later in this section.

Of the six, four of the arenas are slanted towards one-on-one play, featuring tiny layouts loaded to the brim with goodies. The two larger missions—DM2; Claustrophobopolis, and DM3; The Abandoned Base—could support virtually any number of players.

Tactically Speaking

We could blather on and on about the greatness of the mission design... and the coolness of crowded combat... and how much fun it is to play "Axes Only"... But there are some universal Deathmatch tactics that probably need mentioning.

One caveat: We don't know many people who prefer cooperative play over the down-and-dirty, chunkify-yer-buddies Deathmatch. We wager that you feel the same, and so most of these tactics apply best in head-to-head play. *Quake* threatens to broaden the generally accepted notion of Deathmatch as a homicidal free-for-all, with the added ability to form cooperative teams. Most of these single-player tactics still apply, you just have the added security of someone watching your back.

It boils down to this: The better your single-player skills, the more deadly you'll be in Deathmatch.

Specifically:

- Run, don't walk. If you don't run, you're dead. The first thing you'll notice is that your human opponents move much faster than their monster counterparts. The hero in *Quake* doesn't move as fast as *Doom's* Space Marine or *Duke Nukem*, but he's quick for his size.

  Because you all move at the same speed, all things are essentially equal. That is to say, the best player usually wins. If your movement and battle strategies aren't sharp, precise, and almost second nature, you'll be dead before you know it. If you don't know the lay of the land, and use it to your advantage, you're also at a tremendous disadvantage.
- Be unpredictable and opportunistic (especially if you play against the same opponents a lot).
- Hide out in darkened corners, niches, and alcoves. Don't forget where the monsters hang in the most difficult modes of single-player games: Chances are you can stage an even better ambush than the average Ogre.
- Listen for gunfire and try to anticipate where your enemy or enemies are coming from, or where they're going.
- Knowing that adversaries are also listening for clues, create distractions. Waste a few rounds to make others think something's going on. When they come to investigate, they'll walk right into your ambush. Hopefully.
- Get an elevated vantage point, and use it.
- Speaking of elevation, don't forget to practice your Rocket Jumping, the better to gain those otherwise inaccessible ledges. If you're good enough to complete the jump on the first or second try, the detonation of the leap may even draw a crowd you'll be delightfully well-prepared for…
- Let the number of players help determine which mission you fight on. Simply put, the fewer players you have, the smaller the area you'll want to use as your venue. Otherwise you'll waste a lot of time just trying to find each other.
- Consult the game documentation for some basic strategies, as well as hardware/software technical information, to optimize or modify your gameplay.

An Encouraging Word

Every professional hit man knows there are countless ways to kill. Your only limit is your creativity. And while there must be weirder aspirations than to be the Leonardo da Vinci of *Quake* hit men, we can't think of any off the top of our collective heads. But surely there must be…

Be bold. Be brave. Set the standard.

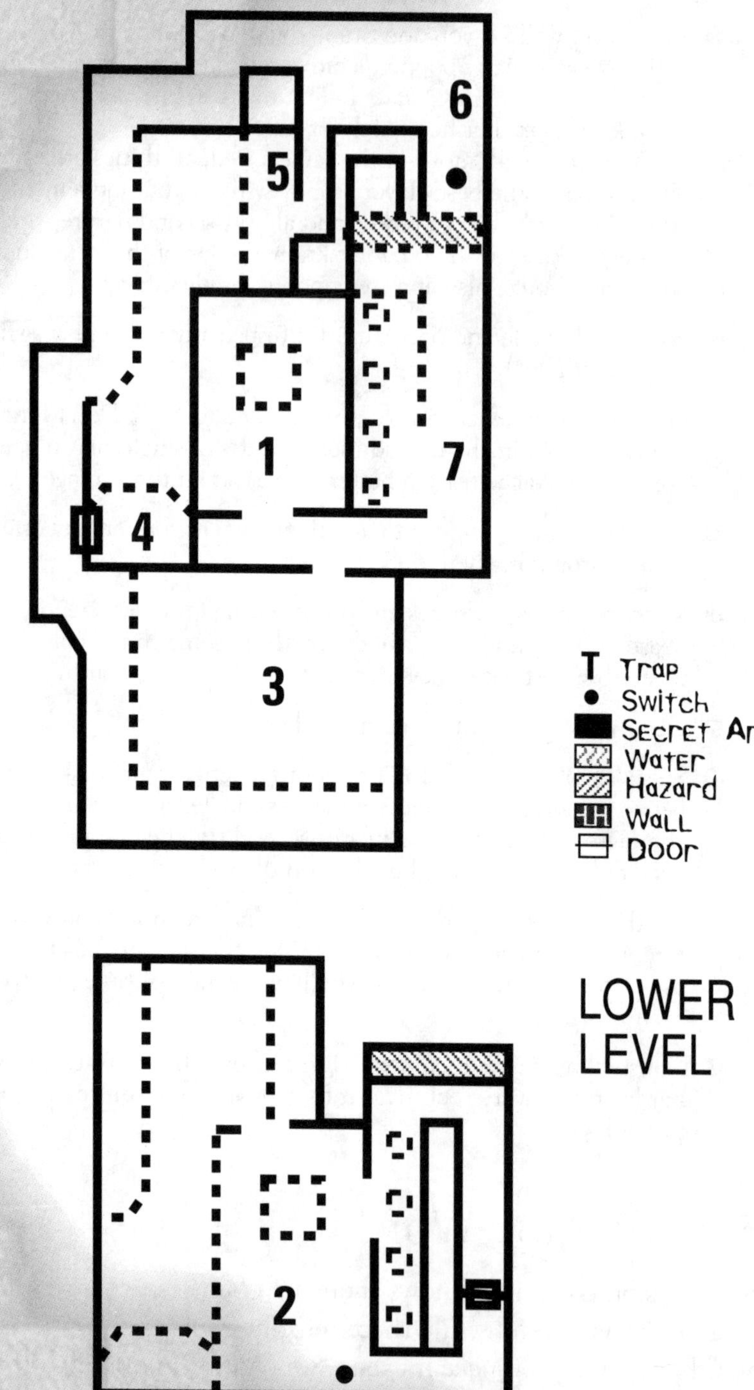
6
5
1
7
4
3
T Trap
Switch
Secret Area
Water
Hazard
Wall
Door
LOWER
LEVEL
2

Deathmatch 1: Place of Two Deaths

The first Deathmatch arena is an intriguing battleground obviously designed with one-on-one combat in mind. Even the larger rooms are somewhat cramped, with relatively few prime vantage points, and the Nailgun and Grenade Launcher are the top end of the weaponry. Notice that the teleporter near room 2 takes you right back upstairs—not a bad device for turning the tables in a hurry. You'll also have to be careful not to extend the ramp to the Yellow Armor when someone else is in a position to beat you to it.

Deathmatch 1: Place of Two Deaths At-a-Glance (DM1)

1. Double-barreled Shotgun, Shotgun Shells, Health
2. Green Armor, Flechettes, Switch, Shotgun Shells, Health, Teleporter to 1.
3. Nailgun, Grenades, Shotgun Shells, Health
4. Megahealth (Secret Door)
5. Grenade Launcher
6. Nailgun, Flechettes, Shotgun Shells, Switch for Yellow Armor in 7.
7. Yellow Armor

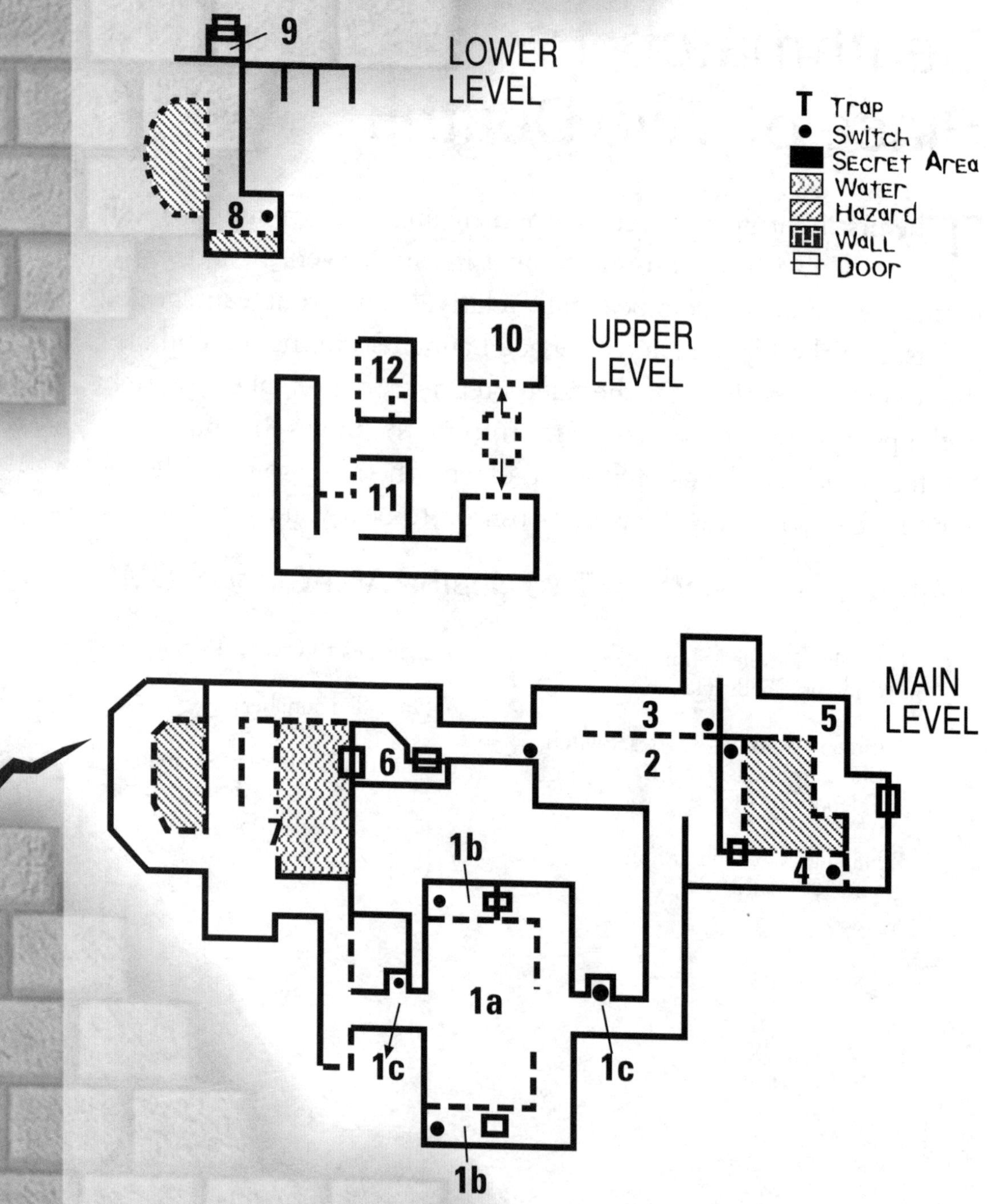
9
LOWER
LEVEL
8
T Trap
• Switch
Secret Area
Water
Hazard
Wall
Door
10
UPPER
LEVEL
12
11
MAIN
LEVEL
3
5
6
2
7
1b
4
1a
1c
1c
1b

Deathmatch 2: Claustrophobopolis

This is a frantic and furious battlezone for perhaps two to four players, with some large rooms and heavy artillery, as well as tight corridors and hazardous terrain that demand a certain skill with the controls. The switch at (8) is definitely noteworthy, as it leads to the upper platform in the large room, as well as granting access to Yellow Armor, a Rocket Launcher and ammo, and a Quad Damage rune. Look out below!

Deathmatch 2: Claustrophobopolis At-a-Glance (DM2)

1a. Lava Pool Room

1b. Yellow Armor, Switches to open Lava Pool

1c. Switches to Crushers in Yellow Armor rooms

2. Rocket Launcher, Flechettes, Health

3. First/Third Switch in Red Armor Sequence

4. Second Switch in Red Armor Sequence

5. Double-barreled Shotgun, Red Armor, Megahealth, Grenades, Teleporter to 1.

6. Red Armor (Turn and shoot Switch after riding lift up; door opens. Press against wall for exit to 7.)

7. Nailgun, Flechettes, Health

8. Grenades, Switch opens 9.

9. Yellow Armor, Teleporter to Moving Platform

10. Grenade Launcher, Grenades, Megahealth

11. Rocket Launcher, Grenades (Accessed through 9)

12. Quad Damage Rune, Health (Accessed from 9)

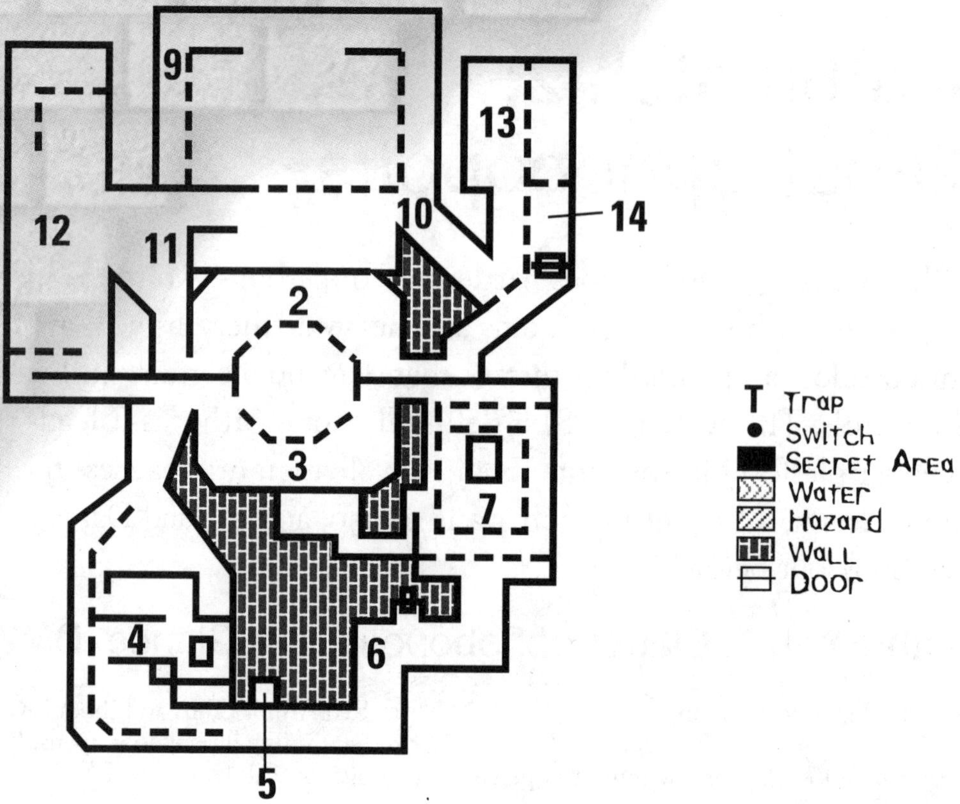

9
13
12
11
10
14
2
3
7
4
6
5
T Trap
Switch
Secret Area
Water
Hazard
Wall
Door

8
8
12
1
LOWER LEVEL

8
UNDERWATER

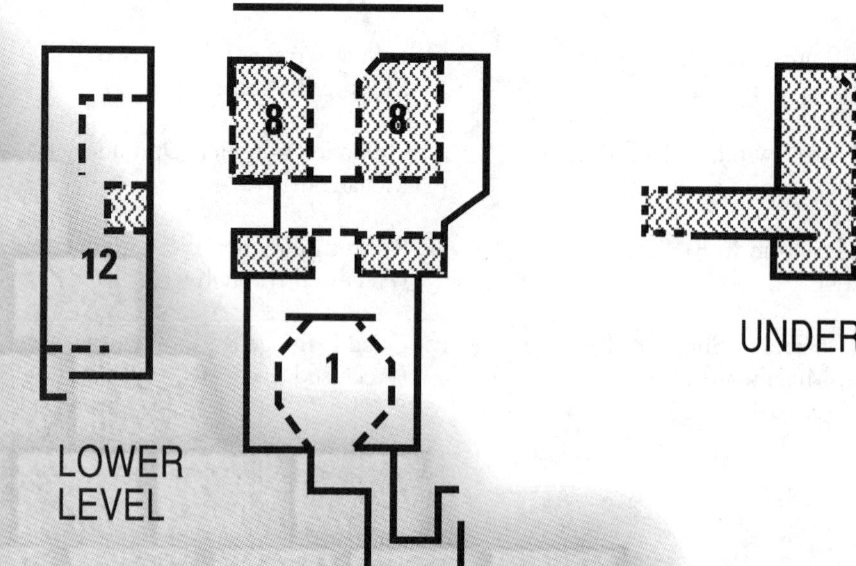

Deathmatch 3: The Abandoned Base

Whovever abandoned the base left plenty of goodies behind to Deathmatch with, including all the baddest weapons and power-ups. With one properly executed pass, through rooms 14, 11, 8, 12 and 3, you can grab up Yellow Armor, the Thunderbolt and Cells, a Pentagram of Protection, Megahealth and a Ring of Shadows. That takes maybe 25 seconds. Your opponents' death will be even quicker. Get used to the layout of this mission; it's sure to be a crowd pleaser. With the load of supplies, the Base functions as a frantic frag-fest for any number of combatants.

Deathmatch 3: The Abandoned Base At-a-Glance (DM3)

1. Megahealth
2. Quad Damage Rune, Grenades, Shotgun Shells, Flechettes
3. Ring of Shadows, Grenades, Shotgun Shells, Flechettes
4. Supernailgun, Flechettes, Grenades, Shotgun Shells, Cells, Health
5. Megahealth
6. Health, Flechettes, Teleporter to 3
7. Grenades, Nailgun, Shotgun Shells, Flechettes, Red Armor, Access to 3 and 1.
8. Thunderbolt, Cells, Flechettes, Grenades, Underwater Tunnel to 11.
9. Rocket Launcher, Flechettes
10. Shotgun Shells
11. Arrive from 14
12. Pentagram of Protection, Megahealth, Underwater Tunnel to 8, Lifts to 3
13. Double-barreled Shotgun, Health, Grenades
14. Yellow Armor, Teleporter to 11, Access to 2

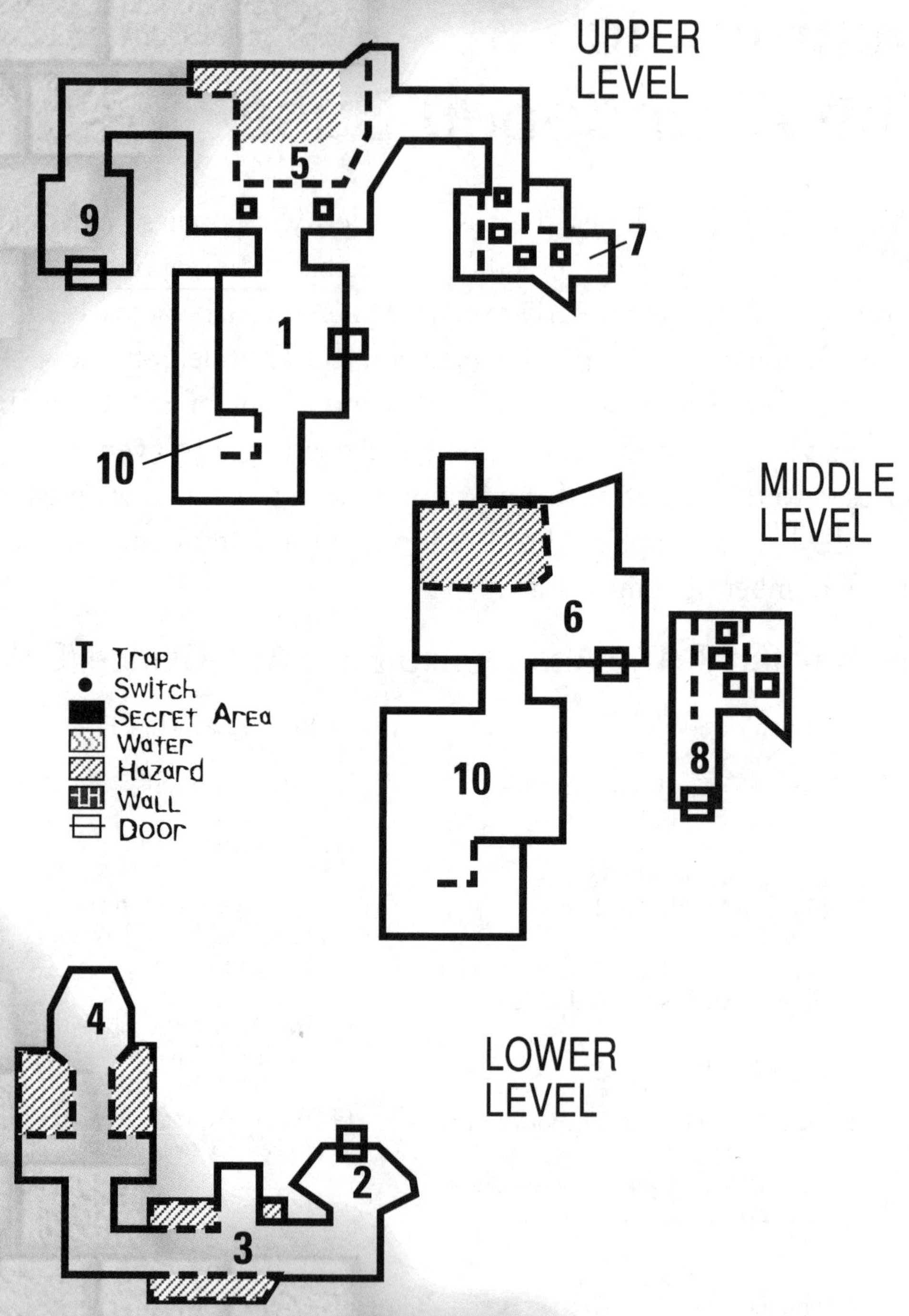
UPPER
LEVEL
9
5
7
1
10
MIDDLE
LEVEL
6
10
8
T Trap
Switch
Secret Area
Water
Hazard
Wall
Door
4
LOWER
LEVEL
2
3

Deathmatch 4: The Bad Place

Small and filled to the hilt with weaponry, The Bad Place makes an excellent one-on-one arena. There's a grand total of one magical power-up: a Quad Damage Rune on a precarious ledge. Expect everyone to hear when it gets grabbed, and, since the mission is downright tiny and complete with several teleporters, you can count on a lot of company in short order. There's no finesse here; just large weapons waiting to be gratuitously unloaded.

Deathmatch 4: The Bad Place At-a-Glance (DM4)

1. Flechettes, Cells, Teleporter to 2
2. Green Armor, Health, Teleporter to 1
3. Nailgun, Shotgun Shells
4. Rocket Launcher, Grenades, Megahealth
5. Cells, Supernailgun, Quad Damage Rune
6. Thunderbolt, Cells, Grenade Launcher, Green Armor, Teleporter to 2.
7. Cells, Shotgun Shells, Yellow Armor, Drop to 8
8. Cells, Flechettes, Red Armor, Rocket Launcher, Shotgun Shells, Teleporter to 3
9. Flechettes, Health, Teleporter to 7
10. Double-barreled Shotgun, Grenades, Health, Shotgun Shells, Flechettes, Access to 6

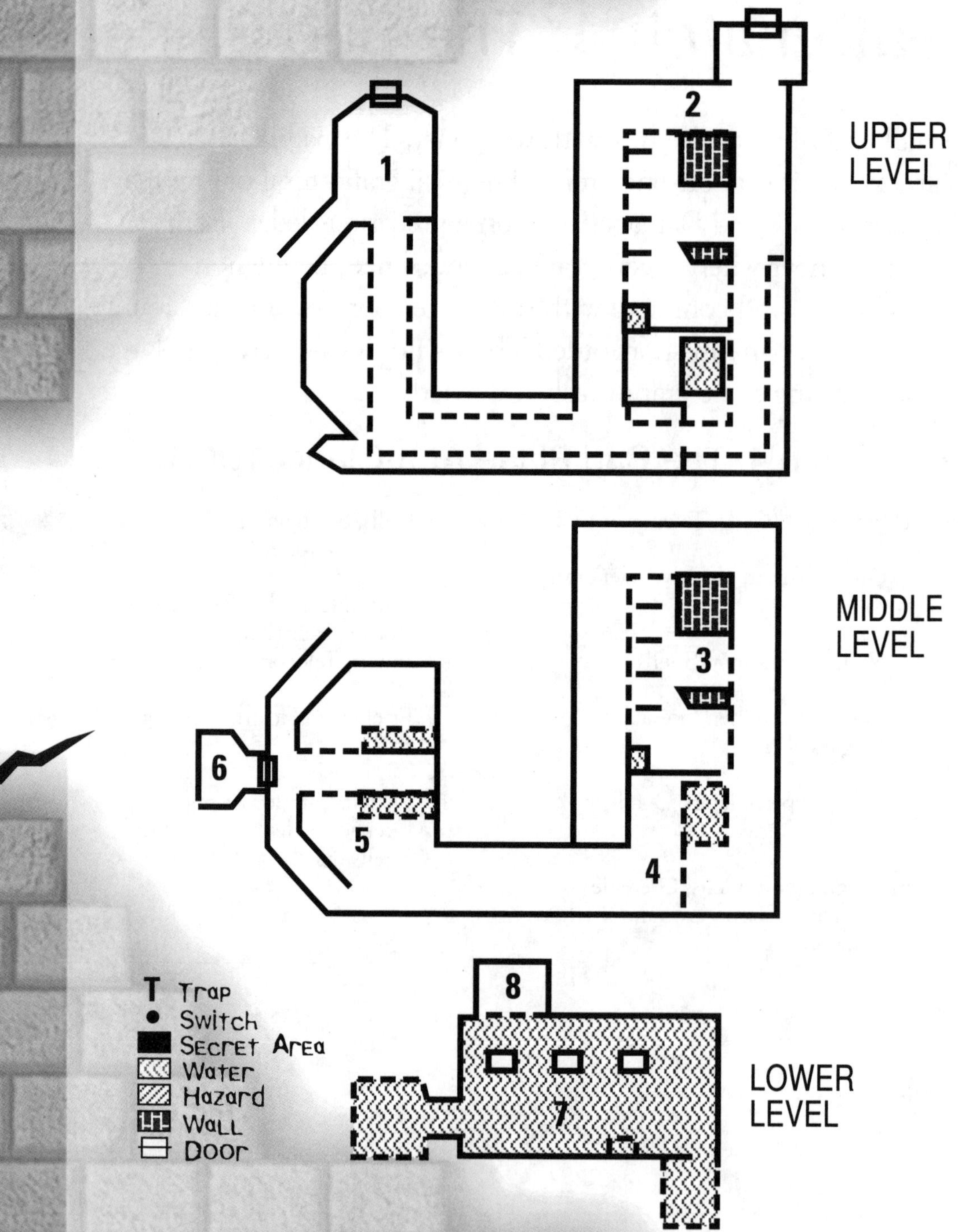

1
2
UPPER LEVEL
3
4
5
6
MIDDLE LEVEL
8
7
LOWER LEVEL
T Trap
Switch
Secret Area
Water
Hazard
Wall
Door

Deathmatch 5: The Cistern

A compact little arena is The Cistern, just right for a couple of combatants who don't mind reaching their frag limit in a big hurry. Whatever you do, don't be the second person to go for the Rocket Launcher…

Deathmatch 5: The Cistern At-a-Glance (DM5)

1. Health, Grenades, Shotgun Shells, Teleporter to 2
2. Shotgun Shells, Flechettes, Supernailgun, Teleporter to 1
3. Yellow Armor, Flechettes, Grenades, Drop to 7
4. Cells, Health, Grenade Launcher, Access to 7
5. Shotgun Shells, Flechettes, Nailgun, Access to 7, Switch to 6
6. Rocket Launcher, Megahealth
7. Shotgun Shells, Health, Grenades
8. Pentagram of Protection, Thunderbolt, Cells

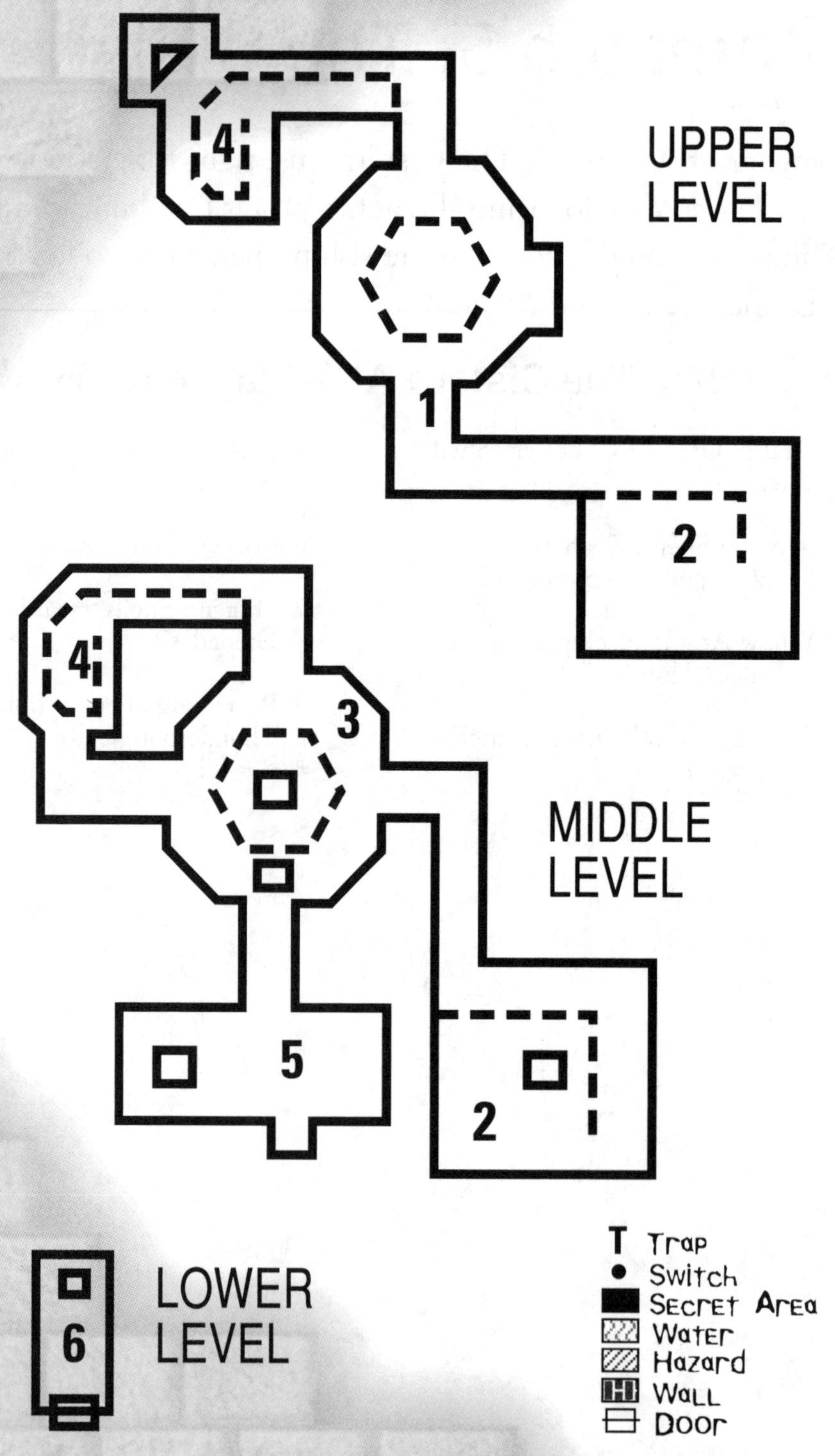
4
UPPER
LEVEL
1
2
4
3
MIDDLE
LEVEL
5
2
6
LOWER
LEVEL
T Trap
Switch
Secret Area
Water
Hazard
Wall
Door

Deathmatch 6: The Dark Zone

One last fast and furious Deathmatch arena, and this one comes complete with a spoiler. Grab some Armor and maybe a Megahealth, then beat feet to room 3. Notice the irregular floor piece in front of the tunnel leading to room 5. Shoot it, and drop down into room 6. The rest, as they say, is history.

Deathmatch 6: The Dark Zone At-a-Glance (DM6)

1. Grenade Launcher, Health, Cells
2. Supernailgun, Green Armor, Grenades, Health, Shotgun Shells, Teleporter to 5
3. Shotgun Shells, Health, Nailgun, Teleporter to 2
4. Rocket Launcher, Health, Flechettes, Red Armor, Access to 1
5. Rocket Launcher, Megahealth, Teleporter to 2
6. Thunderbolt, Cells, Ring of Shadows, Teleporter to 3

Cheat Codes

You want 'em, we got 'em. This is by no means the definitive list of every *Quake* cheat code in existence. It is, however, a complete listing of all known game-play relevant codes. If you thirst for the obscure, hit the myriad *Quake* Web pages and Usenet boards.

Unlike other DOS-based, *Doom*-style games, you don't type in a cheat code during gameplay. To activate your cheats in *Quake*, hit the ~ (tilde) key to bring down the Running Events log. This pauses your game (thankfully). Then type in your cheat; hit ←Return; then hit Esc or ~ to resume play. To deactivate your cheat, repeat the same procedure.

Once you get used to this new way of doing business, it's a piece of (death) cake.

Note

Quake doesn't recognize capitalization, which means you can safely leave your school-trained writing conventions at the Slipgate. However, *Quake* does recognize the spaces between individual components of a cheat command. In other words, enter the cheat codes exactly as they appear in these tables, spaces and all.

Cheat Code	What It Does/How It Works
GOD	Invincibility
FLY	(while flying use: D to ascend; C to descend)
KILL	Suicide (ends game and reloads at beginning of current mission)
MAP ExMy	Warp between levels * x = episode; y = mission number
SKILL x	Change skill level between missions ** x = skill level (0–3)
NOTARGET	Makes you invisible to all monsters, until you attack them
NOCLIP	Walk through walls, ceilings, floors, and more!

* The parenthetical code in the "At-a-Glance" headline cooresponds to the appropriate episode and mission number. When you warp between levels, you lose all weapons and bonuses. In other words, you start with 100 Health points, no armor, an Axe and your trusty Single-barreled Shotgun. Note that the code for the very last mission is "END"

** 0–3 is Easy through Nightmare skill. The skill level itself only changes between missions and before new games.

The "GIVE x" cheat provides you with your weapon of choice, but without ammo.

Cheat Code	Weapon (w/o ammo)
GIVE 1	Axe
GIVE 2	Shotgun
GIVE 3	Double-barreled Shotgun
GIVE 4	Nailgun
GIVE 5	Supernailgun
GIVE 6	Grenade Launcher
GIVE 7	Rocket Launcher
GIVE 8	Thunderbolt

The "GIVE x 255" cheat supplies you with full ammo. The letter selects the ammo type. The number after the letter selects the total amount of ammo (255 is the maximum you can carry). So, to give yourself a total of 20 Shotgun shells, you'd type: GIVE S 20 and then hit Return. If, for some strange reason you want to get rid of all your ammo, type GIVE x 256.

Health works a little differently. You can have a maximum of 1,000 Health points. Unlike a Megahealth boost, these points don't bleed out of your body over time. However, you go back to 100 Health when you start a new mission.

Cheat Code	Item
GIVE S 255	Shotgun Shells
GIVE N 255	Nails
GIVE R 255	Rockets/Grenades
GIVE C 255	Charges (for Thunderbolt)
GIVE H x	Health (x = 1-1000)

Act on Impulse

The "IMPULSE" cheat provides you with everything else that makes this world worth killin' for.

Cheat Code	What It Does
IMPULSE 9	All Weapons; Full Ammo
IMPULSE 11	Gives you a Rune*
IMPULSE 255	Gives you Quad Damage

* You need four runes to complete the game. Check the top right side of the status bar each time you activate this cheat to see a new rune "light up."

Computer Game Books

1942: The Pacific Air War—The Official Strategy Guide $19.95
The 11th Hour: The Official Strategy Guide $19.95
The 7th Guest: The Official Strategy Guide $19.95
Aces Over Europe: The Official Strategy Guide $19.95
Across the Rhine: The Official Strategy Guide $19.95
Alone in the Dark 3: The Official Strategy Guide $19.95
Armored Fist: The Official Strategy Guide $19.95
Ascendancy: The Official Strategy Guide $19.95
Buried in Time: The Journeyman Project 2—The Official Strategy Guide $19.95
CD-ROM Games Secrets, Volume 1 ....$19.95
Caesar II: The Official Strategy Guide...$19.95
Celtic Tales: Balor of the Evil Eye—The Official Strategy Guide $19.95
Cyberia: The Official Strategy Guide...$19.95
Computer Adventure Games Secrets $19.95
Dark Seed II: The Official Strategy Guide...$19.95
Descent: The Official Strategy Guide $19.95
DOOM Battlebook $19.95
DOOM II: The Official Strategy Guide..$19.95
Dracula Unleashed: The Official Strategy Guide & Novel $19.95
Dragon Lore: The Official Strategy Guide $19.95
Dungeon Master II: The Legend of Skullkeep—The Official Strategy Guide......$19.95
Fleet Defender: The Official Strategy Guide $19.95
Frankenstein: Through the Eyes of the Monster—The Official Strategy Guide ..$19.95
Front Page Sports Football Pro '95: The Official Playbook $19.95
Fury3: The Official Strategy Guide $19.95
Hell: A Cyberpunk Thriller—The Official Strategy Guide $19.95
Heretic: The Official Strategy Guide $19.95
I Have No Mouth, and I Must Scream: The Official Strategy Guide...................$19.95
In The 1st Degree: The Official Strategy Guide $19.95
Kingdom: The Far Reaches—The Official Strategy Guide...................................$14.95
King's Quest VII: The Unauthorized Strategy Guide $19.95
The Legend of Kyrandia: The Official Strategy Guide $19.95
Lords of Midnight: The Official Strategy Guide $19.95
Machiavelli the Prince: Official Secrets & Solutions $12.95
Marathon: The Official Strategy Guide $19.95
Master of Orion: The Official Strategy Guide $19.95
Master of Magic: The Official Strategy Guide $19.95
Microsoft Arcade: The Official Strategy Guide $12.95
Microsoft Flight Simulator 5.1: The Official Strategy Guide $19.95
Microsoft Golf: The Official Strategy Guide $19.95

Microsoft Space Simulator: The Official Strategy Guide....................................$19.95
Might and Magic Compendium: The Authorized Strategy
Guide for Games I, II, III, and IV $19.95
Myst: The Official Strategy Guide $19.95
Online Games: In-Depth Strategies and Secrets $19.95
Oregon Trail II: The Official Strategy Guide..$19.95
The Pagemaster: Official CD-ROM Strategy Guide $14.95
Panzer General: The Official Strategy Guide $19.95
Perfect General II: The Official Strategy Guide..$19.95
Prince of Persia: The Official Strategy Guide $19.95
Prisoner of Ice: The Official Strategy Guide $19.95
Rebel Assault: The Official Insider's Guide..$19.95
The Residents: Bad Day on the Midway— The Official Strategy Guide $19.95
Return to Zork Adventurer's Guide $14.95
Romance of the Three Kingdoms IV: Wall of Fire—The Official Strategy Guide$19.95
Shadow of the Comet: The Official Strategy Guide $19.95
Shannara: The Official Strategy Guide $19.95
Sid Meier's Civilization, or Rome on 640K a Day..$19.95
Sid Meier's Colonization: The Official Strategy Guide $19.95
SimCity 2000: Power, Politics, and Planning..$19.95
SimEarth: The Official Strategy Guide $19.95
SimFarm Almanac: The Official Guide to SimFarm $19.95
SimLife: The Official Strategy Guide $19.95
SimTower: The Official Strategy Guide $19.95
Stonekeep: The Official Strategy Guide $19.95
SubWar 2050: The Official Strategy Guide..$19.95
Terry Pratchett's Discworld: The Official Strategy Guide $19.95
TIE Fighter: The Official Strategy Guide $19.95
TIE Fighter: Defender of the Empire—Official Secrets & Solutions $12.95
Thunderscape: The Official Strategy Guide $19.95
Ultima: The Avatar Adventures $19.95
Ultima VII and Underworld: More Avatar Adventures $19.95
Under a Killing Moon: The Official Strategy Guide..$19.95
WarCraft: Orcs & Humans Official Secrets & Solutions $9.95
Warlords II Deluxe: The Official Strategy Guide $19.95
Werewolf Vs. Commanche: The Official Strategy Guide......................................$19.95
Wing Commander I, II, and III: The Ultimate Strategy Guide $19.95
X-COM Terror From The Deep: The Official Strategy Guide $19.95
X-COM UFO Defense: The Official Strategy Guide $19.95
X-Wing: Collector's CD-ROM—The Official Strategy Guide................................$19.95

How to Order:

For information on quantity discounts contact the publisher: Prima Publishing, P.O. Box 1260BK, Rocklin, CA 95677-1260; (916) 632-4400. On your letterhead include information concerning the intended use of the books and the number of books you wish to purchase. For individual orders, turn to the back of the book for more information.

To Order Books

Please send me the following items:

Quantity	Title	Unit Price	Total
______	______________________________	$ ______	$ ______
______	______________________________	$ ______	$ ______
______	______________________________	$ ______	$ ______
______	______________________________	$ ______	$ ______
______	______________________________	$ ______	$ ______

Shipping and Handling depend on Subtotal.

Subtotal	Shipping/Handling
$0.00–$14.99	$3.00
$15.00–$29.99	$4.00
$30.00–$49.99	$6.00
$50.00–$99.99	$10.00
$100.00–$199.99	$13.50
$200.00+	Call for Quote

Foreign and all Priority Request orders:
Call Order Entry department
for price quote at 916/632-4400

This chart represents the total retail price of books only (before applicable discounts are taken).

Subtotal $ ______

Deduct 10% when ordering 3-5 books $ ______

7.25% Sales Tax (CA only) $ ______

8.25% Sales Tax (TN only) $ ______

5.0% Sales Tax (MD and IN only) $ ______

Shipping and Handling* $ ______

Total Order $ ______

By Telephone: With MC or Visa, call 800-632-8676, 916-632-4400. Mon-Fri, 8:30-4:30.
WWW {http://www.primapublishing.com}

Orders Placed Via Internet E-mail {sales@primapub.com}

By Mail: Just fill out the information below and send with your remittance to:

Prima Publishing
P.O. Box 1260BK
Rocklin, CA 95677

My name is ______________________________

I live at ______________________________

City ______________________ State ______ Zip ______

MC/Visa# ______________________ Exp. ______

Check/Money Order enclosed for $ ______________ Payable to Prima Publishing

Daytime Telephone ______________________________

Signature ______________________________